DRUGS, THUGS, AND DIVAS

Drugs, Thugs, and Divas

TELENOVELAS AND NARCO-DRAMAS
IN LATIN AMERICA

By O. Hugo Benavides

 UNIVERSITY OF TEXAS PRESS
Austin

Requests for permission to reproduce material from this work
should be sent to Permissions, University of Texas Press, P.O. Box
7819, Austin, TX 78713-7819.
www.utpress.utexas.edu/index.php/rp-form

♾ The paper used in this book meets the minimum requirements
of ANSI/NISO z39.48–1992 (R1997) (Permanence of Paper).

LIBRARY OF CONGRESS CATALOGING-IN-PUBLICATION DATA
Benavides, O. Hugo (Oswald Hugo), 1968–
    Drugs, thugs, and divas : telenovelas and narco-dramas in Latin
America / by O. Hugo Benavides. — 1st ed.
        p.   cm.
    Includes bibliographical references and index.
    ISBN 978-0-292-71450-2 (cloth : alk. paper) —
    ISBN 978-0-292-71712-1 (pbk. : alk. paper)
    1. Soap operas—Latin America.   2. Drugs in motion pictures.
3. Motion pictures—Latin America.   I. Title.
    PN1992.8.S4B47   2008
    791.45'6—dc22

                                                        2007015807

To Beverlee Bruce and Pupi Avati, scholars and artists, who in their own way helped remind me to seriously engage my own vocation to life.

To Gregory Allen, for being there.

En cuanto a mí, ese último día ante mi botella de cerveza en La Ballena, Culiacán, escuchando canciones de la rockola entre parroquianos bigotudos y silenciosos, lamenté carecer de talento para resumirlo todo en tres minutos de música y palabras. El mío iba a ser, qué remedio, un corrido de papel impreso y más de quinientas páginas. Cada uno hace lo que puede.

—ARTURO PÉREZ-REVERTE, *LA REINA DEL SUR*

CONTENTS

Acknowledgments   ix

ONE   *Melodrama as Ambiguous Signifier: Latin American Telenovelas and Narco-Dramas*   1

Part One

TWO   *Seeing* Xica *and the Melodramatic Unveiling of Colonial Desire*   25

THREE   *Producing the Global West through Latin Tales of Seduction and Envy*   46

FOUR   *Karen's Seduction: The Racial Politics of Appropriate Dinner Guests*   67

FIVE   *A Mother's Wrath and the Complex Disjuncturing of Class*   88

Part Two

SIX   *Being Narco: The Evolution of a Continental Sensibility*   111

SEVEN   *Saintly Figures and Icons: The Migration of a Continental Dream*   132

EIGHT   La Reina del Sur: *Gender, Racial, and National Contestations of Regional Identity*   152

NINE   *Sex, Drugs, and* Cumbia: *The Hybrid Nature of Culture*   171

TEN   *Conclusion: The Postcolonial Politics of Melodrama*   191

POSTSCRIPT Ugly Betty 211

References 217

Index 229

ACKNOWLEDGMENTS

Sex was a form of departure, a passionate sacrifice of farewell,
and even his writing these days had the unanswerable finality
of a suicide note. Take that! he thought with grim pleasure.
He wanted to write everything down so there would be noth-
ing more to say and no more to remember, to burn out his self
so he could vanish.
—PAUL THEROUX, *BLINDING LIGHT*

Like James Scott (1998) I have acquired the addictive habit
of writing books. As an immigrant Ecuadorian child in New York City
I never thought that I would be able to do so, since writing was something other people did, and anybody in my family or immediate surroundings would simply have laughed at such an intellectual pursuit.
For that reason, it has taken me decades to come to terms with this
addiction and to realize that words are not mere tools of the powerful
but, rather, can be a democratic medium of political transformation. As
such, words have nourished and allowed me to survive what otherwise
would have been an unlivable reality. Therefore, it is with a faith similar
to Latin America's literary tradition that I now offer my own words.
My wish is that this analysis of Latin American melodrama will provide
a hope similar to the one that the continent's fiction, telenovelas, and
narco-dramas has offered to millions of us.

Once again I must thank a host of institutional and personal sup-
porters who have made this project a possibility. First of all, two Fordham University faculty grants allowed me to travel and carry out my
research plan during several summers. Many of my colleagues, particularly Jeanne Flavin; Jacqueline Johnson; Orlando Rodríguez and his
wife, Phyllis Rodríguez; Luz Lenis; Mark Naison; Angela Belsole; and
Greta Gilbertson (for being chair of the department with such grace and

competency) among many others, have made my stint at Fordham an intellectually productive one. It is with sorrow that I recognize the contribution of Father Gerry Blaszsak and Dr. Nina Tassi to the heart of this research. I say with sorrow because neither of them is still at Fordham, and that loss to me and the institution is immeasurable. Both of them embody to an enormous degree the scholarship committed to social justice that makes Fordham so different from the myriad of universities in New York City. And to Rosa Giglio and Paula Genova, who always provide a much-needed dose of humor and camaraderie in the department; many thanks for your work and effort.

Also to my friends and family who continue to provide a support system in New York City and throughout the Americas. I will not mention them by name because the list would be too long and they know who they are.

To Gregory Allen, G. Melissa García, and Elissa West for their love and support over many years, too many to count. And to Melissa as well for our endless discussions and her close reading of this manuscript.

Many thanks one more time to Kathy Bork for her expert editing as well. There is no doubt in my mind that this book has once again benefited enormously from her expertise. Her work contributed to making the ideas in the book clearer, stronger, and more coherent. Of course, all final shortcomings are only my own.

And special thanks to the journal *Social Text,* where an earlier version of Chapter 2 first appeared.

To Los Tigres del Norte and the many *norteño* groups that have provided continued life to this research. Of course, to the continent's ballad tradition of *boleros,* which also constantly refuels the melodramatic enterprise. And also to the memory of Celia Cruz, whose music and work captured the explosive mixture that characterizes the ever-elusive Latin American dream.

Finally, to the chance that this project offered me in terms of getting to know and experience two of the continent's most powerful countries, Brazil and Mexico. I have much gratitude toward the many Brazilians and Mexicans I met throughout my research who were more than willing to discuss and explore the power of melodrama in their daily lives. I have particularly heartfelt memories of Rio de Janeiro, without a doubt a "cidade maravilhosa," and to Mexico City and Puebla for taking me in almost as one of their own.

And of course to all those involved in the production of telenovelas and narco-dramas, for enriching our lives with mirrors and reflections that help us assess not only who we are but who we would really like to be.

DRUGS, THUGS, AND DIVAS

One

MELODRAMA AS
AMBIGUOUS SIGNIFIER
Latin American Telenovelas and Narco-Dramas

> Vine a Comala porque me dijeron que acá vivía mi
> padre. *Híjole. Los personajes de aquella historia estaban
> todos muertos, y no lo sabían.*
> —ARTURO PÉREZ-REVERTE, *LA REINA DEL SUR*

As a result of the postmodern turn, Latin America is more
than ever a crossroads of local and global interaction. Many times it is
difficult, or even impossible or irrelevant, to differentiate the local from
the global. Yet, within this cultural problematic, what García Canclini
(1992) refers to as a process of reconversion, incredibly vibrant and provocative identities are reworked and represented throughout the American continent. It is also within this postmodern framework of hybridity
and reconversion that multiple hegemonic constraints and ideologies of
resistance are being represented through popular media such as soap operas (telenovelas) and film. Therefore, one of my objectives in this book
is to assess the dynamic role of melodrama, particularly Mexican narco-
dramas and South American telenovelas, in the ongoing reconfiguration of social identities, hegemonic constraints, and popular culture in
Latin America today. My main concern is to place the contributions of
the melodrama within the historical events that determined many of
its cultural and political embodiments, both in terms of hegemonizing
constructs and resistance-filled agency.

Telenovelas have a very recent history in the Americas, yet from their
impact it would seem that they have been always part of Latin American
culture. Telenovelas did not make their appearance in South America
until the early 1960s, when television entered the Latin American market. This market explosion, however, was prefigured in *radio-novelas* (radio soap operas) and *folletines* (pamphletlike novels) from several decades
before. Thus telenovelas inherited the structure of the melodrama from

both of these visual and aural media and fused them into one incredibly powerful medium of Latin American popular cultural representation.

Since their development, telenovelas have had an important impact on people's daily life, as they dramatically portray such controversial issues as illegitimate children, misplaced identity, the burden of social conventions, amorous rejection, and the ever-productive notion of forbidden desires, sexual and otherwise. It is a testament to the telenovela's success that many of the plot lines are reused or that a telenovela will be rebroadcast in different countries after being adapted to their national language and cultural configuration. This transnational element is only heightened by the incredible export success of telenovelas throughout the Americas (including the United States) and all over the world. Latin American telenovelas have been exported, with extraordinary cultural implications, to Egypt, Russia, and China, as well as throughout Europe (Rowe and Schelling 1992). This global interaction has led some Latin American theorists (Martín-Barbero 1987) to argue that melodrama might be the most successful and culturally authentic revolution affecting the continent since the 1960s, and not only, or even mainly, the Marxist-inspired revolutions that have left thousands, if not millions, of people dead or committed to the struggle.

Similarly, the narco-drama is indebted to earlier radio and *folletín*-like melodramatic forms, perhaps more to the latter in content and the former in stylistic structure. Narco-dramas have also been enriched by almost two decades of telenovela production (approximately from the 1950s to the 1970s) that in many ways provided for a visual model of what a film-length version could look like. In many ways the narco-drama is a combination of the telenovela and films from Mexico's golden age (1930–1960), producing (or selling out to) what many consider to be a B-film market. However, and not coincidentally, this shift to more violent and drug-inspired content for Mexican films marks not only greater popular participation in film making but also more realistic interpretation of the country's *realidad nacional* (national reality), that is, a greater democratization of the media of sorts. It is quite interesting and telling that this broadening of melodramatic possibilities has been met with harsh judgment from academics, intellectuals, and film critics.

Narco-dramas today control Mexico's film market and are particularly influential along the border between the United States and Mexico, powerfully affecting a Latino cultural market created by Mexicans and other Latin Americans living in the United States. Narco-drama films originated in the 1970s, with their own style, their own set of producers, directors, actors, and screenwriters. Not unlike porn film crews, narco-drama artists have been significantly and consistently ostracized by their colleagues and intellectuals, who have criticized them for their populist appeal and their glorification of drug-related behavior and violence. To a degree, narco-dramas reflect a distinct regional, north Mexican culture, particularly of the border states, but including states as far away as Sinaloa, which further explains their dual border/hybrid appeal. It is this hybrid identification that largely explains their success among Latinos in the United States.

METHODOLOGICAL CONUNDRUMS

As are all works of cultural analysis, the assessment of the political role of the melodrama in contemporary Latin American culture is mammoth in scope. Because of the breadth of Latin American melodramatic production, I have limited this analysis to smaller regional and stylistic variants of the genre. More than an encyclopedic or even historical work, I envision this book as a long-overdue theoretical engagement with the postmodern tropes elaborated within melodrama over the last four decades. The book's contribution, I hope, will be an assessment of the ambiguous legacies and significations present in these melodramatic forms—the same ones that explain their popular success during a period that saw the decline of other state-led and elite intellectual projects.

This book is also intimately related to my research into the nature of Latin American hegemony and political domination. I strongly believe that melodrama is as important as all of Latin America's other political projects, state or otherwise, including the more explicit forms of historical production (Benavides 2004) and discourses of sentiment (Benavides 2006). Thus the book shares with my previous ones a desire to understand Latin America's form of political domination within the most subtle elements of cultural production and livelihood. Contrary to most academic analysts, I would maintain that the greatest political decisions are being made, every minute of every day, with little input from official or educational discourse, even without much conscious awareness, but, rather, with a sincere desire just to survive another day.

Thus this book is my own form of political survival, that is, my personal contribution to seeing another day, one in which I (and those around me) may imagine ourselves immersed in less-coercive political relationships (Foucault 1991) but also one in which I too must work out the conundrums of my daily life. It is this approach that enables me to connect my academic work to who I am or become every day: a Latin American in exile with dynamically productive cultural ideals and historical nostalgia.

This connection determined the methodological approach of this book in relation to my previous work. Although I carried out fieldwork for this endeavor, I have been working on this book and its themes my whole life. Just as were history and national sentiment, melodrama was a profoundly important part of my existence in New York City as an Ecuadorian child who did not see Ecuador before the age of twelve, and it helped me make sense of an otherwise nonsensical familial and globalized world.

More concretely, the research for this book took me to over fifteen cities in Mexico and Brazil during a sabbatical year. In all of these cities I decided against the traditional research methods of structured interviews, note taking, and analysis. Instead, I kept, almost religiously, a fierce participant observation and textual analysis. Paradoxically, these anthropological methods allow me to sustain a relatively objective assessment of the different melodramatic elements I wished to analyze, affording me also a greater sense of freedom to explore them at my leisure.

I spoke with both intellectuals and scholarly colleagues, as well as with other cultural practitioners such as artists, students, and service professionals, just to mention a few. I carried out archival research, seeking out reference material and other bibliographical work to balance my understanding of Latin American melodrama and the societies that produce it. I also watched innumerable telenovelas and narco-dramas besides those I was already familiar with from watching them almost daily for over two decades. My main concern was less cultural investigation, in the limited sense of definition and categorization, than understanding the cultural parameters in South America and Mexico that most enabled melodrama to take on these specific forms, to achieve national and international success, and, most of all, to provide a sense of belonging and hope to a continent that almost never has one.

LATIN AMERICAN TELENOVELAS: THE POLITICAL POWER OF MELODRAMATIC RESIGNIFICATION

The power of telenovelas in propagating meaningful cultural images is rapidly becoming a concern of scholarly debate. Rather than seeing Latin American soap operas as a lower form of cultural production, scholars are assessing their effect as demonstrated in ambiguously (and economically) meaningful images throughout the Americas, and even worldwide (see Kuhn 1987 and Santos 2001 for related analyses). The popularity of the Colombian soap opera *Betty la fea* (Ugly Betty) (adapted in 2006 for Mexico as *La fea más bella* [The prettiest ugly one] and in the United States as *Ugly Betty;* see Postscript) highlights the telenovela's role as a tool of local and global cultural resignification (see García-Canclini 1992). Telenovelas manage this resignification by using several power effects, the most obvious of them being entertainment.

The fact that telenovelas are able to provide emotional relief to a continent burdened by enormous socioeconomic and material hardships is not devoid of importance. Therefore, it is not surprising that millions of Latin Americans sit in front of their (and others') television sets to escape the conundrums of daily existence for at least a couple of hours each day.

We must not minimize the importance of entertainment, even if it only allows human beings to cope with what are, many times, insurmountable socioeconomic odds. This coping mechanism, coupled with the commodification of cultural images for export, has supported several delineations of the telenovela as a recent example of Marx's "opium of the people." However, it is clear from recent social theory and media studies, as well as from a less superficial reading of the telenovelas themselves, that such an analysis begs the question more than addresses it (Martín-Barbero 1987); that is, the power effects (see Foucault 1990) of telenovelas are taken for granted without really understanding why they have such wide continental and even international appeal. Moreover, the specific power effects that these telenovelas have on different groups of consumers are left unexamined, within both those groups' societies and those of their Latin American counterparts.

Just as melodrama's enormous ability to entertain should not be underemphasized, neither should its economic power. Along with tourism and remittances, the telenovela is the continent's most lucrative legal industry. The genre's ambiguous position in terms of its clever use of the world market through the articulation of cultural differences within that market is clearly a result of contemporary globalization (see Hall 1997a, 1997b). What allows oppressed national communities to herald a medium as economically successful as telenovela production is its "otherized" position in the modern global order. Telenovelas exoticize these communities to create a media image that is then reprocessed for export, making the people's marginality the key element in the telenovela's production.

This cultural reconfiguration allows Brazilian, Colombian, Mexican, and others' soap operas to become hot commodities in the United States and throughout the Americas. It is this same process of cultural resignification that makes U.S. soap operas similarly popular throughout the West Indies (see Miller 1990).

But if U.S. and other First World media images, particularly end-of-the-world and disaster films, hold such a central place in the daily consumption of the Americas, it makes sense that "other" American images would also be avidly consumed. It is within this continental reconfiguration of consumption that the process of cultural resignification takes place. The process of reconversion does not discount the colossal commodification that is taking place, but, rather, highlights its powerful effects beyond the realities of national media borders.

It is this powerful process of cultural commodification and reconfiguration that has made even the original national groups lose their economic monopoly on telenovela production. The traditional soap operas produced by mighty media empires in Venezuela, Argentina, and Mexico are now rivaled by similar enterprises in Colombia and Brazil. Even within national borders, competing media corporations have been able to destabilize others with the success or failure of one telenovela, as was the case for *El Globo,* which had to restructure its soap opera production because of the enormous success afforded by the telenovela *Xica* (see Chap. 2). A similar "democratic" process took place when Colombian and Peruvian media enterprises began producing their own soap operas for export, particularly after older programs such as *Escalona* and *Betty la fea* met with so much success.

Partly due to this regional competition, I have chosen to analyze *Betty la fea, Adrián está de visita* (Adrián is visiting), *Pasión de gavilanes* (The passion of the sparrow hawk) (all from Colombia) and *Xica* (Brazil) for this book. In many ways, all highlight the hegemonic power of democratic repositioning in Latin American cultural production and its productive tension within a globalized Western identity and/or a Western identification in general (see Chap. 3).

COLONIAL LEGACIES

Telenovelas provoke questions regarding two main historical elements: the colonial legacy of the continent; and, most interesting, the postcolonial transformation of the past (see Stoler 2002, 1996).

However, within both of these elements a smaller yet more central question arises: How are colonial desires constituted within the legacy of both colonialism and postcolonial transformation. In this regard it is important to note that by "colonial legacies" I am referring to a cultural and economic experience of colonialism that lasted several centuries in the Americas (in some nations until the twentieth century) and its paradigmatic role in the emergence of the Latin American nation-state: it was out of this colonial experience that most of South and Central America "liberated" itself. But it is the fact that this liberation seems to have occurred exclusively within the political sphere (and even that is questionable—see Galeano 1973) that allows (or demands) a contemporary interpretation of the colonial past, that is, the interpretation of the colonial legacy.

Perhaps Quijano (1993) is most accurate in his assessment of the colonial legacy as a coloniality of power, thus avoiding the political/cultural dichotomy that has limited most other analyses (e.g., Cueva 1988; Ribeiro 1988, 1972). I would add the need to talk about legacy and coloniality in the plural to avoid the limited descriptions of these discourses in the past and to provide a closer approximation to the ambiguity of "lived-in" reality (see Williams 1977). It is this same ambiguity that is highlighted by the constitution (and constitutive nature) of what may be called "colonial desire." The phrase "colonial desire" as I use it throughout this book expresses a particular kind of longing, even a nostalgia, that is defined both by its characteristic failure (i.e., not being as good as something else in racial and/or cultural terms) and by the constant comparisons to the "other" (i.e., that which is not me/us and that I/we would want to be). It is this political process, exemplified in the corrosive power of envy, that locks both the colonizer (secretly wanting what is projected onto the darker, enslaved bodies: lust, emotional freedom, less "civilizing" constraints, etc.) and the colonized (striving for political and economic freedom while being injected with markers of cultural inferiority) into a bitter struggle that, although initiated five centuries ago, continues to fuel the interaction of people locally and globally.

Furthermore, the first element, colonial memory, is defined specifically in terms of the second: the contemporary representation in both historical and popular discourse of the colonial period. How do we represent and remember the colonial past? And perhaps a better question is How is the colonial past embodied in its representation itself?

The second element links the colonial past and its cultural/social legacy. How "past" is the colonial past? What are the main elements that tie or connect us to this past and that form part of the colonial legacy? And, ultimately, what are those colonial elements that, albeit transformed, infuse our contemporary postcolonial identity? As we are reminded by Stuart Hall (1993: 448), there is never a simple return to or a recovery of the past but, rather, a reappropriation of it through our present. The past is always an approximation afforded by the "technologies and identities of the present" (Hall 1993: 448). These two elements—colonial legacies and their postcolonial transformations—are central to the telenovela's success and make this melodramatic historical representation, as are all successful historical representations, particularly significant.

AFRICAN AMERICAN REPRESENTATION, CONTINENTALLY SPEAKING

Within a larger theoretical context, telenovelas are also a good vehicle through which to discuss some of the current debates on popular culture as expressed by Stuart Hall in terms of ethnic cultural production and Jesús Martín-Barbero with respect to melodramatic representation and mass hegemonic media devices. One of the most successful elements in two telenovelas is the representation of the black experience in a more rounded manner than is typical in Latin American melodramatic and popular venues. Without a doubt, one of the most controversial aspects of the telenovela is its representation of the Afro-American (continentally speaking) subject and its refusal to present the black experience as perfect and nonproblematic.

In this regard, the telenovela refuses to represent what Hanif Kureishi refers to as "cheering fictions" in which the oppressed are described as "sexually stabilized, self-contained, and monolithic," in other words, not human (Kureishi in Hall 1993: 449). In this sense, all characters express a myriad of ambiguous positions without needing to define themselves as either good or bad. For example, in one telenovela Xica prefers her "white" lover to her long-suffering (and enslaved) mother, while in another Adrián is able to seduce a black go-go dancer and use her to obtain information about her rich white male lover (who happens to be Adrián's father). Linda Williams (2004, 2001) provides quite an insightful analysis of this phenomenon in her work on black images in U.S. melodrama. Her scholarship focuses on the complex political articulation that melodrama expresses, particularly when it comes to racial identity. I highlight her work because, along with Martín-Barbero's, she emphasizes the subtle contribution of melodrama to the racialized social context that produces them.

The problematic portrayal of black characters in the telenovela *Xica* as not only racially but also culturally distinct in terms of religious practices (e.g., belief in African Orixás), linguistic dialects (use of slang and "low-class" speech), cultural celebrations (e.g., distinct wedding ceremonies), sexual mores (e.g., presence of not only rape and abuse but also lust for the white other) has made the genre a target of criticism for putting forward a biased and racist representation of the slave and former slave population. However, following Baldwin's (1984) critique of Wright's *Native Son* as a form of essentializing fiction and Kureishi's (1985) assessment of ethnic representations, these telenovelas seems to struggle to represent in a historically and culturally convincing manner the social persona not only of the black but also of the white/European population, particularly the latter's envy of the slaves' greater sexual freedom. As Kureishi (1985: 14) notes, this is not the easiest of undertakings in "politically correct" times, when the writer is seen as "a public relations officer, as a hired liar": "If there is to be a serious attempt to understand [Latin America] today, with its mix of races and colours, its hysteria and despair, then, writing about it has to be complex. It can't apologize or idealize. It can't sentimentalize and it can't represent only one group as having a monopoly on virtue."

Following this lead, it would seem that telenovelas "know what [they are] doing, as the[y] cross those frontiers between gender, race, ethnicity, sexuality and class" (Hall 1993: 449). Thus we must be careful in assessing their critical value. It is not a question of arguing about whether they are good or bad or even a realistic contemporary representation of the colonial past. It is not even a question of arguing the value or worth of soap operas in general. Rather, critical assessment should emphasize the value of the representation itself, the cultural implications, power effects, social and political ramifications, of the melodramatic representation afforded by the soap opera. As Stuart Hall (1993: 448) says in his public conversation with Salman Rushdie of new black cinema in Britain, it is not about defining something as good; rather, it is a question of how these new examples open avenues of critical discourse and challenge the traditional subjects and regimes of representation. This, I believe, is where the telenovela's and the narco-drama's contributions need to be assessed, how they open new spaces in the regime of popular cultural representation, even when the genres are still heavily embedded (how could they not be?) in the political and cultural constraints of their melodramatic medium—what Linda Williams (2001: 8) refers to as "melodrama's almost incalculable influence on American attitudes towards race."

MELODRAMATIC THEORY AND LATIN AMERICA: THE INFLUENCE OF JESÚS MARTÍN-BARBERO

Martín-Barbero (1987), among others (see Brooks 2005; Gledhill 1987, 1991), has explored the history and role of melodrama in the production of popular culture in Latin America. For Martín-Barbero this particular mode of representation in Latin America was created in opposition to that of the established theater, which helped express and maintain the views of the elite class and the educated bourgeoisie. In contrast to the theater, melodrama made very little use of dialogue. Instead, it relied on the overdramatization of scenes through use of the body and the repetitive use of music as a mood stimulus. In this process, the characters' emphasis was less on their full development as people than on their use as symbolic embodiments of ethical values such as good versus evil (see Brooks 2005).

These historical characteristics of the melodrama—overdramatization, emphasis on emotion rather than logic, use of music to mark key relationships, characters as symbols of ethical values—are still the key elements of telenovelas throughout the Americas and therefore are also part of all these telenovelas' cultural and historical representation as well. What is also interesting is the underlying and reified opposition between the media of high art, such as the theater's reliance on intellectual logic and verbal agility, and the media of popular culture, such as telenovelas' emphasis on emotions and "overacting." This dichotomy is maintained in the description of telenovelas as bad or low cultural expressions, for example, as *bobonovelas* (dumb soap operas), or in the explanation given when something illogical happens only because it is a telenovela.

This discriminatory stance, however, is not unanimous. In recent years there has been a significant appeal from established writers to value and credit the work of soap opera artists. Instrumental in this regard have been the tributes and writing prizes given to soap opera writers like Corín Tellado, including a well-publicized interview by the established Peruvian writer and former presidential candidate Mario Vargas Llosa. Even Colombia's Nobel laureate, Gabriel García Márquez, has made public a wish to write a soap opera because of its far greater popular appeal than any other form of writing in Latin America (Rowe and Schelling 1992).

Notwithstanding this recent tolerance, the members of the elite seem to have been less concerned with a channel or outlet for their emotions than with a manner of expressing the education of the emotions as a marker of "higher" civilization. This repressive element is essential, since, for many, the bourgeoisie is indicated by its control of emotions and its need to separate sentiment from social setting, thus internalizing emotions and re-creating them as "private schemes" (Martín-Barbero 1987: 125). This opposition between the public display and the repression of emotion in elite cultural representations is, for Martín-Barbero, key to the production of hegemonic devices in the consumption of melodramatic portraits. It is the ambivalent role of the emotions as explicit or implicit vehicles of representation that allows the mass production and consumption of "popular" culture. Telenovelas and narco-dramas allow a form of "emotional democracy" that nurtures their popularity and at the same time reifies the social distance between "real art" (which is what the elite consumes) and the melodrama as the main form of popular entertainment (Martín-Barbero 1987).

According to Martín-Barbero (1987), this hegemonic structure is also related to the preference given in the melodrama to two forms of imagery: familial relationships, and social excess. These are an integral part of all Latin American telenovelas. They move the plot from a moment of not knowing to one of knowing again, of gaining and establishing one's true identity once the moral judgment at the end of the melodrama is expressed. Plot development is typically exemplified by things that happen to family members (e.g., lost children and family members, confused paternity, lost inheritances) or situations in which family members find themselves (e.g., marriage, sibling relationships, engagements) that are not what they seem or are supposed to be. The melodrama becomes an exercise in seeing beyond appearances, going past how things should be, to seeing what they actually are. Through this recourse the melodrama appeals to the public's sense of life's contradictions and follies, especially for the less economically well off, who know firsthand of social and emotional hardship. In this manner, the melodrama uses family imagery to "understand and express the complexity and opacity that the new social relations embody" (Martín-Barbero 1987: 131).

The second element is recourse to the rhetoric of excess. To quote Martín-Barbero, who succinctly outlines this particular approach (1987: 131; emphasis mine), "Everything in the melodrama tends to excess. From an initial scene that exaggerates the visual and musical contrasts to a dramatic structure and form of acting that demand a constant effect of emotions and a response of laughs, tears, sweat, and chills from the public at all times. Judged as degrading and excessive by a *cultivated* sensibility, this excess contains a victory over repression and a particular economy of order that emphasizes bourgeois notions of saving and safeguarding." It is, ultimately, through its critique of, and latent attacks on, the safeguarding of sexual and social mores that the telenovela most convincingly provides a new assessment of the colonial legacies and desires that permeate contemporary Latin America. As I argue throughout the book, these melodramatic representations are about offering the Latin American social body a realistic sense of redemption and revelation. It is precisely through these often contrived images that the audience is able to understand itself and its social surroundings in a much more dynamic fashion.

For Linda Williams (2001) melodrama provides a wonderful example of the cultural resurgence of media images being reused. She uses the metaphor of a "leaping fish" to describe the intricate, slippery content that melodrama uses to embody its powerful reworking of national cultural assumptions. It is this insight that allows both Williams and Gledhill (1987) to argue for "a general study of melodrama as a broadly important cultural mode" (in L. Williams 2001: 17). It is this medium of excess (as normative visual pleasure) that best expresses the "entertainment needs of a modern, rationalist, democratic, capitalist, industrial, and now post-industrial society seeking moral legibility under new conditions of moral ambiguity" (L. Williams 2001: 23). Ultimately, what new historical melodramas about the West reflect is that the genre is more about reinscribing and constituting a lost past of victimization when one has been the conqueror (L. Williams 2001).

In many ways, Gledhill (2003, 1991, 1987) foregrounds several of these arguments in her studies of melodrama. She recognizes the resistance to bourgeois norms that pervades the parody of emotions and sentiments throughout the form. She also rightly highlights the power of late-nineteenth-century productions of popular culture that were developed as melodramatic vignettes. For Gledhill, as for Brooks (2005), melodrama signifies a new secular order that looks to incorporate notions of the sacred and the power of social control within contemporary characteristics of the individual and a modern moral order socially reconstituted under a (post)modern democratic façade.

BETWEEN TWO GOLDEN AGES
IN MEXICO: CINEMA, CULTURE,
AND SOCIAL TRANSFORMATION

This book also engages with a melodramatic production particular to Mexican cinema, the narco-drama, since its beginnings in the 1970s to the present, especially in terms of its relationship to the greater transformation of Mexican and Latin American politics and culture (see Medrano Platas 1999; Rodríguez Cruz 2000; Trelles Plazaola 1991). From 1970 to 1995, Mexican cinema hit a supposed creative lull that distanced it from its earlier golden age (1930–1960) and from the most recent rich cinematic explosion in the late 1990s. It is interesting to note that, during this supposed period of cinematic "crisis," other cultural expressions such as music, literature, social theory, essay writing, and sports, particularly soccer, found some of their highest national expressions. It is also telling that in this period was laid the social groundwork that would serve to destabilize Mexico's one-party rule, ending in the PRI's (Partido Revolucionario Institucional, Institutional Revolutionary Party) being deposed after almost eighty years. My research assesses the relationship between cinematic production and the sociopolitical and cultural transformations that both influenced and were influenced by it.

Mexico in general and Mexican cinema in particular have had an enormous influence on the rest of Latin America. Mexican movies visually represent an American Third World country which has been seen as stronger and more vibrant than the rest of its Latin American counterparts (Agrasánchez 2001). This symbolic strength has been expressed in Mexico's ability, with however many disappointing results, to challenge U.S. imperialism and stand up to that country's overwhelming cultural influence. Mexican cinema's golden age was central in this enterprise, offering an alternative way of life to that presented in Hollywood's Tinseltown expressions even when it was being fueled by similar economic resources (see Fein 2002). Despite, or perhaps because of, the heterogeneous U.S. backing of Mexico's golden age, these movies were able to provide a cinematic vision which was also closer to the cultural and racial realities of Latin America.

This film boom produced actors such as Dolores del Río (Ramón 1997), Anthony Quinn, and Rita Hayworth who also succeeded in the U.S. film industry. However, it also enabled a large group of Mexican artists, such as María Félix, Pedro Armendáriz (García 1997), Jorge Negrete (Serna 1993), Cantinflas, and Pedro Infante, who represented different film genres and were honored at international film festivals and glittered in film houses throughout the Americas. This golden age was not to be revisited until recently, though, with the success of such films as *El crimen del Padre Amaro* (Father Amaro's crime), *Amores perros* (Love's a bitch), *Lucía, Lucía,* and *Y tu mamá también* (And your mother, too).

The period in between (1970–1995), which is the object of my research, saw the development of a B-movie industry that, abandoning the higher cultural ground, looked to entertain and to be commercially viable by representing more day-to-day Mexican characters and reality. Several other genres besides narco-drama arose during this period, including sex comedies (*películas picantes/picarescas*), romantic melodramas, and even a wrestling film series about El Santo (The saint), a strutting urban hero and defender of the poor. The romantic melodramas were close to the content of the telenovela and have been blamed for the decline of the early golden age. *Nosotros los pobres* (We the poor) has been hailed as the precursor of this genre (de la Peza 1998). This and other movies integrated many of the melodramatic elements of the telenovela into a concise two (or fewer) hours of film and many times even managed to transform them into musicals, letting the songs carry much of the tragic/dramatic story.

In many ways, Pedro Infante was one of the most emblematic figures in this transition between early golden age cinema and the production of romantic melodramas and musicals. Perhaps the intense melodrama of his life, including his tragic death, contributed not only to his early film success but also to the continued fascination of the Mexican, and Latin American, public with his life (see Rubenstein 2002).

The sex comedies are another melodramatic variant, with specific gender-related scenarios. Most of these films are structured around two or more male friends who somehow manage to get involved in and escape one thorny situation after another while surrounding themselves with gorgeous women in all states of undress. The beautiful women stand out in these movies precisely because most of the leading men, well-known comedians, are relatively unattractive and fully clothed. The film series *La india María* is an interesting reversal of this patriarchal melodramatic structure in which María (like her male counterparts) is the unattractive and foolish ethnic character who is able to survive difficult situations and somehow always surround herself with good-looking men.

NARCO-DRAMA

In many ways, narco-drama can be seen as falling between these other melodramatic film genres. Most narco-films elaborate a story contained within the larger context of the drug trade and incorporate both a violent Mafia ethos and the martial arts. They almost always present a patriarchal power structure and beautiful women parading themselves as sexual objects and exploit a melodramatic structure of excessive sentiment, musical cues for the development of the plot, and a moral metanarrative of local good versus global evil.

It is quite important to remember that, in keeping with good melodrama, these films immediately set up an alternative moral structure to the officializing discourse of the nation. For example, the state and its representatives, that is, politicians, law enforcement, bureaucrats, and soldiers, are seldom portrayed as the good guys; the heroes are either Lone Ranger types or misunderstood, repentant drug dealers. This alternative reading of the drug war has made narco-drama particularly difficult for the state and the elite to tolerate but has further secured its success as a more realistic reading of life in Latin America.

Narco-drama is the visual end product of a long process of cultural revalorization in Mexico, particularly in terms of translocal identity. Along with the production of these films there are other cultural elements, like narco-*corridos* (songs which are central to many of the films and played by hundreds of bands including the renowned Los Tigres del Norte and Los Tucanes), fashions (exotic-leather boots, worked [*piteada*] belts, and silk shirts), and values (a brutally violent code of honor) that share the narco-sensibility (see Astorga 2003, 1996, 1995; see also A. González 2004; Paredes 1958). The films portray narcos (drug dealers) as ambivalent subjects who, although involved in the illegal drug trade, maintain strong social and personal commitments to their local communities, family members, and friends. At the same time, these films contain a high level of regional specificity and interaction. As they are a regional expression of Mexico's northern frontier, they represent the broader picture of the migrant condition as well as that of the impact of the drug trade on the migrant communities. In many ways, narco-culture maintains an inherent relationship with its Colombian counterparts, the continent's initial drug producers and the group from which Mexican cartels clearly learned their trade (and bested). As Colombian writer Laura Restrepo argues (2004), one of the ways that Colombia managed to free itself a bit from the drug trade was by exporting it to Mexico.

COLOMBIA'S PARTICIPATION

The illegal or subversive elements in these films concerning the drug trade (as well as their ambiguous representation of official and cultural authority) are essential to the public's fascination with them and their success. Unlike narco-*corridos,* neither official nor private venues have been able to ban these films even when the hostility toward them is intense. Another important element in this ambiguous state-cinema relationship is the role of Colombia and that nation's drug enterprise in the education of Mexican cartels and in the latter's representation in melodrama. It is not surprising to find a collaborative relationship in terms of media and film production, including the telenovela hit *Pasión de gavilanes* (see Chap. 5). This telenovela, although supposedly taking place in Colombia with Colombian actors, uses the Mexican version of *cumbias* and *rancheras* as the musical backdrop.

The Colombian connection thus links the earliest influences of narco-representation and the geographically specific Mexican film genre to the rest of the Spanish-speaking American continent. In many ways, even with the very specific thematic of narco-dramas, Mexico has not lost its cultural influence on the rest of the continent and is, in many respects, determining the material to be discussed and highlighted.

Colombia's participation as one of the earliest centers of the drug trade (probably along with Peru), however, marks a distinct form of social interaction that expresses a more symbiotic exchange of cultural materials. It was most probably the development of several regional centers of sophisticated drug marketing (as opposed to mere production) that marked Colombia's violent expansion into Mexico and the Caribbean in order to export drugs to the United States (Cajas 2004). These elements, along with the serious crisis of the Shining Path and Tupac Amaru guerrilla insurgencies in Peru, marked Colombia's divergent evolution and speedy dominance of drug production and trade on the continent, and arguably even worldwide.

It would not be long, however, before this particular model of strong family-run cartels coupled with extreme violence and severe codes of honor, all pointing to a dangerous and fast lifestyle, became the model for the Mexican drug industry. Mexicans, particularly in the northern states from where the drug is introduced into the U.S. market, unlike their Caribbean counterparts, stopped being mere intermediaries between the two markets and claimed a stake in drug production and trade, independent of the Colombian cartels.

This shift, in many ways, demanded a serious reworking of more traditional and established forms of social relationships and even of the national ethos. Drug production in Mexico was able to cut off the dependency on Andean drug production. This meant several things, including the growth of contestatory agrarian politics among northern rural peasants, who were ready to connect to one of the most troublesome legacies of the PRI's redistribution of Mexico's revolution. These northern transformations were part of the region's continuous historical heritage of opposition to the official (and hypocritical) one proclaimed by the central government in Mexico City (Vanderwood 2004).

At the same time, these newly founded Mexican cartels and drug lords also had at least a century-long history of outlaw and criminal behavior to fall back on, as the murders of young women in Juárez and Chihuahua in the early part of the twenty-first century clearly attest. For Astorga (1995) the image of the Mexican narco goes back all the way to the 1920s, when Mexicans were already trading illegally across the border to support not only themselves but whole communities that were being left out of the state's redistributional practices. Thus the more lucrative (and dangerous) drug trade introduced by Colombian cartels only imported a more dramatic content to an already burgeoning network of informal entrepreneurs and well-intentioned laborer/Lone Ranger types in the area.

These shifts in the social relationship also reworked the more traditional representation of Mexicans as a peaceful and quiet people (or even stupid or lazy, as is expressed in U.S. caricatures) to a population more violent and prone to gang activity as well as involved in illegal and criminal behavior (Vanderwood 2004). This shift has been encouraged if not created by an urban, xenophobic discourse in the United States and anti-immigration policy. One must wonder, therefore, if the development and success of narcos in widely popular films is a way of producing an image of illegality in a much more ambiguous and nuanced form than that imposed by both Mexico's official discourse and that of the historically violent and overpowering colonizer of the north.

CULTURAL HYBRIDITY

Along with these new social markers and shifting relationships, hybridity in all its cultural variations takes on much greater significance. Prime among these variations are cultural border crossings (what Anzaldúa [1987] refers to as the "borderlands," symbolically speaking) and musical hybridity, particularly but not exclusively the *cumbia*. In general, Mexican bands like Café Tacuba, Molotov, Maldita Vecindad and South American bands such as Fabulosos Cadillacs, Bacilos, Los Amigos Invisibles, and Aterciopelados all play a contemporary form of hybrid music that mixes a wide range of Latin rhythms from rock and punk to *rancheras* and *boleros*. However, the musical transformation of Colombian *cumbia* to Mexican is most probably somewhat independent of this shift, marking it as a particular type of transnational reconfiguration of a cultural musical identity.

Cumbias, themselves a mixture of Spanish and Andean rhythms, are a long-standing tradition in the northern Andes, although they have always been recognized as Colombia's national musical genre. In the 1970s, this musical rhythm was introduced into the Mexican market, where it went through a transformation into a totally different genre, Mexican *cumbia*. As they had done previously with *salsa,* Mexicans took the original *cumbia* lyrics and shifted the genre's musical structure to one faster and leveled with pointed stops. At the same time that Mexicans adapted *cumbia* to different musical instruments and band styles, a new dance version also developed, different from the Colombian *cumbia* dance.

This musical hybridization not only relates to but also marks the form of narco-sensibility made possible by the Colombian drug trade and its new melodramatic form, a form that no longer offered the official discourse and hegemonizing sentiments as the norm of decency in these motion pictures. I argue that these sociocultural transformations, cultural hybridity, and cinematic evolution influenced each other, that the supposed creative lull in Mexican cinema might have provided an organic way for the population to represent itself on the screen, as it was doing with music (in the infamous narco-*corridos* and the appropriation of *cumbia*) and literature (with major continental figures like Octavio Paz and Carlos Fuentes, but also Elena Poniatowska and Laura Esquivel). After all, it was also during this troubled period—1970–1990—that large-scale government corruption, increased drug trading, greater social upheaval, and the growing pauperization of the population marked a new era of cultural emergence for Mexico as well as for the rest of Latin America (see Monsiváis 2000, 1997).

POSTMODERNITY IN LATIN AMERICA

To a significant degree, the last three decades of the twentieth century were marked by the continent's return to pseudo-democratic forms of government, a reworking of neoliberal models of economic development, and a profound desire to come to terms with brutal military dictatorships and the aftermath of their overthrow (see Guillermoprieto 2004; Sábato 1998). It was in this dynamic context of political and social movements, artistic ventures (including a vibrant Latino rock movement), and state-led economic experiments that melodrama developed and reigned. And that, for some scholars, marked a new postmodern form of identification for the Americas (Yudice, Franco, and Flores 1992). Left behind were more traditional forms of representation such as peasant movements and workers' unions, and personal identity became resignified as a form of contestatory politics (see Escobar and Álvarez 1987).

Indians, women, environmental workers, and homosexuals (to mention the most salient) became the central agents of social change and redefined the traditional identities of workers and peasants in powerful ways and beyond their initial national parameters. Internal migration and the stronger pull to the north (i.e., to the United States) were also an important element of resignification, making any understanding of popular movements and cultural production obsolete unless they were seen in a transnational, even global, context. The more developed and established nations of Brazil, Argentina, and Venezuela (which, along with Mexico, had always been the countries with the greatest cultural and economic clout on the continent) were no longer capable of supporting their populations, which generated a large influx of their citizens to the United States and Europe. This only intensified the migration started decades before by smaller nations like Puerto Rico, Ecuador, and Panama.

This is the context in which the melodrama developed. It soon became one of the most successful forms of cultural representation throughout Latin America. This does not imply that melodrama is the only, or even an authentic, form for expressing Latin America culture; it is simply one of the most successful. This is important, as it clearly is a waste of time (and energy) to wonder about authentic representational traditions, since almost always the ones we choose will lose the popular support of those they are supposed to represent. Rather, it seems important to assess the varying success of popular representations instead of arguing about their authenticity from a particular, officializing standpoint.

Similar to Anderson's (1991) notion of styles of imagined communities as the most salient question in terms of the nation, it might be important to understand why some forms of representation become more viable than others, and what the mechanisms are that enable these particular cultural representations. There is no doubt that telenovelas and narco-dramas, mediated as they are by a transnational media market of local and global consumption, have succeeded where many other loftier—and less-lofty—ventures have failed to give voice to unequal and biased groups. Therefore, we must ask about the different voices and agents being artic-ulated and frustrated within these two forms of melodramatic develop-ment. How do these two melodramatic genres define and integrate the cultural markers they are trying to represent? How are they contained by these markers, and how do they make money from them? These and many other essential questions about the role that melodrama has played in Latin America's postmodern existence pervade my research.

The production of melodrama in Latin America today is big business and earns big money. This is possible only because culture is already part of the essential melodramatic representational structure.

CHAPTER OVERVIEW

The book is divided into two parts: the first addresses melodramatic production in one Brazilian and three Colombian tele-novelas; the second addresses the cultural politics of the narco-drama. Chapter 2 concentrates on the 1998 production *Xica*. While Brazil is one of the first centers of telenovela production (alongside Venezuela and Argentina), it has also produced by far the most provocative and chal-lenging telenovelas in terms of sexual explicitness. This powerful tele-novela is based on the historical figure Xica da Silva, a slave during the eighteenth-century diamond boom in Brazil. She managed to seduce a top official and through this romantic liaison to gain freedom for her and her children and became the most powerful woman in the region. The multiple issues of colonial desire and race, particularly among those of African and European descent, makes *Xica* an invaluable source for exploring the postcolonial transformation of the continent.

Chapter 3 assesses the powerful social effects of the telenovela's melo-dramatic representation in the transnational reworking and transformation of Latin American identity. Once again I will engage *Xica* to analyze the role of envy as a postcolonial tool of social leveling. I also use the breakthrough Colombian telenovela *Betty la fea,* which boosted Colombia's contribution in the Latin America telenovela market, to assess the role of seduction in the constitution of both postcolonial identity and consumer markets. For this endeavor, I use the work of two postcolonial thinkers, Frantz Fanon and James Baldwin, to better contextualize the different postcolonial discourses successfully used in these telenovelas' globalizing ventures.

Chapters 4 and 5 both assess two other hit Colombian telenovelas that address problematics of class, gender, and race. Both telenovelas, *Adrián está de visita* and *Pasión de gavilanes,* explore problems of personal and political identity. The former presents a provocative reworking of the Hollywood film *Guess Who's Coming to Dinner* with an Afro-Colombian man not only as main character but also as the plot catalyst. *Pasión de gavilanes'* plot offers a complex rendering of the interclass marriages of three brothers to three sisters, which enables the role of the sisters' mother as both cultural victim and victimizer. In many respects, both of these productions are emblematic as much for what they do as for what they choose to hide or silence, even as they develop a subtle and successful rearticulation of transnational and transracial identities.

The next four chapters are concerned with the narco-drama. Chapter 6 traces the historical evolution of narco-character and narco-sensibility, particularly as it has been outlined by Mexican scholars such as Luis Astorga, Roger Bartra, and Carlos Monsiváis, to name a few. The chapter assesses both the historical evolution of a narco-melodramatic representation and the national undertones that such a representation has elicited.

Chapter 7 concentrates on migration, border crossing, and the production of two icons, Juan Soldado and Jesús Malverde. Both of these figures, canonized by their popular appeal albeit not by the Catholic Church, are intermixed with the fluid movement of people and identities at the Mexican/Latin American–U.S. border. I use both of these folk saints to assess and interrogate the discourses of migration, transnational identity, and vulnerability, which mark all border crossings, metaphorical or not.

Chapter 8 marks another significant variation of transnational and gender identification. *La reina del sur,* a novel written by the Spanish author Arturo Pérez-Reverte, became an international best seller narrating the story of a female drug trafficker from the Mexican state of Sinaloa who worked in southern Spain. The author spent several months in Sinaloa interviewing a wide variety of individuals, which lends the novel cultural conviction. The book's popularity was enhanced when one of the most popular bands, Los Tigres del Norte, composed an infamous narco-*corrido* to raise to the status of myth the life and times of the main protagonist, Teresa Mendoza. I explore both the central role of a female and her conscious crossing of Mexico's borders, along with the enormous resentment and mixed emotions with which Sinaloans have met these cultural representations.

Finally, Chapter 9 and the conclusion (Chap. 10) synthesize many of the elements elaborated in the book. Chapter 9 in particular looks to understand the hybrid nature of narco-dramas as objects of both fascination and psychoanalytic reflection. What is it about sexual desire, the drug culture, and *cumbia* music that resonates so powerfully with a border(ing) culture and a larger border (i.e., Latino) population in the United States? And ultimately, what does this new postcolonial and postmodern form of Latin American identification say about the specific production of culture in the Americas today, and the role of melodrama in affecting and being affected by these same cultural productions and representational endeavors? This is a particularly haunting question that is not lost on conservative academics in the United States today (see Huntington 2004).

Chapter 10 assesses many of the same issues for both the narco-drama and the telenovela, synthesizing many of their central discourses. Three of the most important issues addressed in this chapter are transnational identity and globalization, the politics of postcolonial melodramatic representation, and perhaps most important, the daily struggle to earn a living in Latin America today. I explore how these elements intertwine to make one of the most tragic places in the world also one of the most exotic and provocative. I examine the central role of melodrama in bridging the gap between tragedy and pleasure and the transgressively constitutive nature of desire in reaffirming a viable postcolonial identity. The central question I reflect on is how one makes personal assets out of global tragedies and then not only represents them as pleasurable and fun but also exports them to earn social capital and economic gain. Melodrama thus constitutes (or not) a new way of being and seeing postcolonial Latin America in its reconfiguration from a modern to a postmodern identity.

PART I

Two

SEEING *XICA* AND THE MELODRAMATIC UNVEILING OF COLONIAL DESIRE

Don't you dare tell me what you want or do not want.
—MRS. CIELO TO HER DAUGHTER, XICA

As one of the characters in the Brazilian soap opera *Xica* declares prophetically, "The best way to forget about the past is to not mention it, to not even talk about it" (all translations are mine unless otherwise noted). This statement by the male patriarch of a well-to-do family concerned with hiding the family's Jewish ancestry could as easily be interpreted as an expression of the anxiety over the colonial past that haunts contemporary Latin America (and the colonizing European powers, as well). Since the 1800s, Latin American nation-states have consistently strived to escape the relations of domination and exploitation that marked colonial social relationships. Colonialism, however, much like an ailing person who refuses to die, hangs on in government practices, bureaucratic corruption and inefficiency, and in strict racial and social hierarchies and familial obligations. Over and over again, colonialism raises its Medusa-like head to remind all of us of its ubiquitous position in the formation of many of the essential characteristics of the continent's legacy. It would seem as if the coffin in which colonialism was buried was not carefully nailed shut, and, as portrayed in Yoruba tradition, coffins that are not nailed tightly allow the dead to loom large in life again. It is this particular colonial dynamic that is the focal point of the latest Brazilian soap opera to have caused a stir throughout the Americas.

This chapter explores *Xica*'s contribution to the problematics of postcoloniality throughout Latin America, in particular, the ambivalent role played by melodrama and the popular media in empowering colonial desire in a postcolonial setting. It is not my objective merely to analyze *Xica* as a telenovela, as a reflection of popular Brazilian racial discourse, or as part of a larger cinematographic tradition of cultural representation. Such an analysis within the context of Brazil's extensive cultural and cinematic production, although needed, would not only warrant a separate and lengthy treatment (see Bastide 1971; Freyre 1963, 1946; and Ribeiro 1988, 1972 for an introduction to this subject) but would also be particularly limiting in assessing this telenovela's popularity outside Brazil's borders. Several authors (see Johnson 1987; Johnson and Stam 1982; Rowe and Schelling 1992; and Stam 1997) have studied Brazil's popular cinematographic culture and the paradigmatic role played by race in that culture.

The racial ambiguity featured in *Xica* may have furthered the program's popularity throughout the continent, a popularity which exceeded initial expectations (and saved the production company from bankruptcy) and made the program into the latest (and largest) sexy Brazilian soap opera to be successfully exported throughout the Americas. Perhaps another reason for the telenovela's popularity is that *Xica* was able to tap into the ambiguous legacy of colonialism in the daily life of Latin Americans. For example, the *comendador*'s carriage was one of the most popular floats in the 2000 Dominican heritage parade in New York City ("Los dominicanos desfilaron" 2000); the four-hour visit by Tais Araújo (who plays Xica) and Víctor Wagner (the *comendador*) to the Museo del Barrio in East (Spanish) Harlem far exceeded the institution's expectations and forced it to block further admission because of the large turnout. Even the North American (and English) mainstream magazine *Vanity Fair* ("Channel This" 2000: 182) highly recommended this "campy Brazilian soap opera" to its English-speaking audience, stating that as "part *Roots* and part soft-core porn you will hardly care that you can't understand what anyone is saying."

The success of the soap opera speaks to both the contemporary relevance of its subject matter and the pivotal role of melodrama in resolving (or at least stating) the contradictions inherited from centuries of foreign domination, racial discrimination, and slavery. There is no doubt that colonialism's influence is far from over in Latin America, as a brief assessment of contemporary politics or even kin relationships will testify.

As previously stated, this chapter looks at the cultural tenets of the Brazilian soap opera *Xica* and their implications for the logic of colonial desire prevalent on the continent. *Xica* was originally aired in Brazil in 1996 and has been exported to several countries throughout the Americas including, in the year 2000, the United States. The telenovela is loosely based on the life of Xica da Silva, a former slave (a mulatta, the daughter of a wealthy plantation owner) during the Brazilian diamond boom of the early 1700s who used her wit and sexual charm to become one of the wealthiest women of the period as the *comendador*'s concubine (Malatesta and Kiernan 1999).

One of the particularly rich elements of the telenovela is the portrayal of Xica as the child born of the rape of a house slave by one of the wealthiest male plantation owners. Due to skewed genealogical and property relations as portrayed in the telenovela, Xica's status as a slave is never questioned, but her mixed heritage clearly comes into play in the issues raised by her volatile character. Unlike traditional representations of Xica, as being a member of an enslaved population, her mixed heritage aids the telenovela's questioning of racial identity and race relations and their productive, phantasmagorical representations (Butler 1997). At the same time, her mixed heritage provides for an interesting rupture of the national imaginary (not only in Brazil but throughout the rest of the Americas where the telenovela did so well) of the cohesive family with little discord or as a conglomerate of neat racial groups devoid of intense interracial desire and sexual reproduction.

Perhaps one of the biggest elements implied by Xica's mixed heritage is the exposure of the traditional desire of white males (particularly elite males) for the bodies of young black or mulatta women. This exceptionally contentious issue, still present in contemporary elite white households with young black or mulatta maids, has always been at the core of the arguments of female coalitions struggling for their rights. Xica's mixed heritage also speaks to the rivalry between women of different races and the powerful role of envy as a highly charged leveling mechanism used by oppressed populations, including women (see Giddings 1984). Therefore, it seems clear that the ambiguity of Xica's mixed racial identity resonated with a public enthralled by her questioning of not only her rightful heritage but also the denial of her humanity and the sterile social competition in which the majority of the continent's impoverished population is caught.

One the best-known representations of Xica's character is a 1976 Brazilian film, also entitled *Xica,* directed by Carlos Diegues. Interestingly enough, the person who played Xica's mother in the telenovela, the renowned Brazilian actress Zezé Motta, starred in the movie as Xica. Although the film is not the subject of this chapter, it is important to note that, despite the complete lack of biographical resources that the director had to contend with (a limitation shared by the telenovela's producers), the film was a popular success and was seen by over eight million people in its first three months (Johnson 1987). Perhaps this success is marked less by its supposedly "carnivalesque celebration" (see Johnson 1987) than by a greater discourse of racial and cultural ambiguity central to the contested role of politics in artistic production throughout Brazil and the rest of Latin America (see Calvino 1986).

Therefore, *Xica* is not the first representation of this colonial heroine's life or even the first time that a telenovela has located itself within the logic of colonial society; the telenovela *La esclava Isaura* (Isaura the slave), for example, had a similar setting. However, *Xica* does utilize elements that makes this soap opera unique among melodramatic representations. Key in this respect is its understanding and metaphysical transformation of colonial memory. As in all telenovelas the audience is invited to identify with the main protagonist, who in this case is not only a poor woman but also one who happens to be both a former slave and of African descent. This element by itself, having a nonwhite (or non-European) in the leading role, is a novel turn in the melodramatic representation of popular culture on the continent. This is particularly striking in light of the prevalence of an ingrained racial hierarchy in which blacks still occupy the lowest tier of the social structure throughout the Americas. And though *Xica* takes place in Brazil, the racial hierarchy, Catholic religious hegemony, and the class structure clearly resemble that of most, if not all, of the other South American territories and former colonies.

The melodrama develops an economy of representation in which emotions and sentiment, as opposed to rational or logical thought, are primary. The characters' personae exemplify these emotions through overdramatization and overidentification with the viewer. Thus, typically, four characters are presented as basic to the economy of the melodrama: the traitor (Violante, Xica's amorous and social rival), representing the evil and dark forces at play; the victim (Xica herself), typically a poor yet strong-willed woman who embodies good; the trickster or jokester (José María, Xica's "gay" confidante), the dumb fool who provides comic relief; and the vigilante (Xica's lover, the *comendador*), who orders the moral outcome of the story and permits good to triumph over evil.

What may also be an original melodramatic turn in *Xica* is a greater number of characters and subplots. Paramount among these are women who express the gender struggle imposed on their sex: María Dolores (the sergeant's daughter, who is imprisoned, tortured, and condemned to death for having sex out of wedlock); Elvira (alienated from the elite and forced to become the only white prostitute in the Tijuco, who finds true happiness with her gay husband and shares him with a faithful slave who fathers half of their children); Countess (who, although being the highest-ranking woman in the telenovela, complains about her lack of freedom and authority and engages in orgiastic sex with male slaves as her only form of empowerment); Úrsula (who seduces one of the wealthiest young bachelors in town, then accuses him of rape and forces him to marry her, all the while viewed as a living saint by the conservative members of the Tijuco); and, finally, Mikaela (forced into marriage to the army commander but who flees with his son and kills her husband, his father, in the process). There is also a long list of male characters and of children, which further complicates the plot, although it is its reliance on traditional melodramatic options that sustains the soap opera.

THE POSTCOLONIAL POLITICS OF DESIRE

Until the day when the fire of desire occupies all of our life and makes everything clear
—THE (FORMER) NUN

The topic of desire takes central stage in *Xica*. It is the theme underlying most, if not all, of the telenovela's character development and the characters' relationships with one another. Different forms of desire—social, sexual, class, and so on—permeate both the characters' actions and the motivations behind them. However, it is undoubtedly sexual desire that is used most of the time to represent the characters' daily struggle. Overt sexual representations and explicit nudity (as well as lovemaking) are used to sell the telenovela to the public and to increase its ratings. Even though Brazilian soap operas are infamous for their high tolerance of sexual explicitness, *Xica* seems to have gone beyond what has traditionally been tolerated ("Tais Araújo" 2000; "Xica" 2000).

This higher level of sexual imagery is not the most daring element in the telenovela's representation of desire, however. Most audacious is the colonial context in which the explicit sexual scenes take place. From the outset the telenovela locates itself in a problematic historical period, the reign of José I of Portugal, with an entrenched local elite that both responds to a repressive religious machine (the Catholic Church) and holds a large African population as slaves. Significantly, Indians (i.e., Native

Americans) are absent from the telenovela. This colonial context is disquieting as a setting for entertainment, especially as the colonial period is not acknowledged in the program in any conclusive manner. A plausible comparison would be an Israeli production company establishing a concentration camp as the setting for a popular and steamy soap opera.

But in a way it is the fact that the colonial legacy is far from extinct in Latin America that makes this setting, albeit problematic, also an extremely provocative one in which to explore contemporary notions of desire, sexuality, gender, class, and all forms of social hierarchy. That the colonial legacy is still present in Latin America is easily evidenced by many social markers in Latin America, for example, the presence of racial hierarchy, marked gender biases and entrenched patriarchy, and the established Catholic religious norm. However, there are more subtle norms that are also a result of colonialism that are explored by the telenovela and that are an established way of being and behaving on the continent. These include the role of envy as a leveling mechanism, family structure replicating colonial relationships, and whiteness as a normative (and yet invisible) identity. It is these explicit and subtle elements, all the baggage of colonialism, that a contemporary postcolonial identity in Latin America struggles with and that *Xica,* if not necessarily successfully, at least directly engages.

One level of this sexual desire is marked, as one would expect, by a fascination with the other. In this case, since the European subject is established as normative, the nonwhite, in this case, the African, is established as the exotic other. And the telenovela is quick to explore and express this fascination with the other's body, when one of the "respectable" characters is reproached "for not being able to control himself when in the presence of somebody with dark skin" or when José María is chastised because "he still misses that black man."

Significantly, it is the love (and sexual) relationship between a European (Portuguese) man and an American (of African descent) woman that is the central theme of the telenovela. However, the program does not shy away from the unequal power relations marked in these sexual relationships in scenes of sexual violence we are invited to witness. These uneven exchanges are acted out and possibly give us a glimpse of how they have been "normalized."

One of the most brutal scenes is a rape, or the unwilling abuse of a slave's body for the sexual pleasure of her white master. Both female and male slaves are used to pleasure their owners, but the injustice and violation resulting from these actions are never consciously expressed by the characters committing the violent acts. However, there are subtle differences in that the male slaves are more eager to engage in sexual liaisons with their white heterosexual (and nonheterosexual) partners. It is always clear, though, that the slaves have very little agency in initiating, establishing, or maintaining these interracial and unequal sexual relationships. Thus most male slaves (as well as some female ones) happily satisfy their own sexual desires with white partners but are always reminded of their enslaved status and are verbally and physically threatened when they show reticence or an unwillingness to comply.

In many regards, these gender biases resemble Fanon's (1967) critique of the colonial logic afforded, according to him, by a black man involved with a white woman, although not by a white man involved with a black woman. Fanon and many other contemporary scholars (Anzaldúa 1987; Mallon 1996; Morraga 1994, 1986) have established the primacy of the female other's body as central to the mechanism of sexual control and through it of political and imperial domination. It is the female native's (African or Indian/Native American) body that is literally raped, symbolizing the rape of the land by the European (male) aggressor to install his descendants (plant his seed) and establish his power over the territory. This is why the sexual control of white women by black men supposedly would, in a postcolonial context, reclaim the balance lost in the colonial debacle whereas the black woman's submission to the white man for whatever reason, forced or not, only reestablishes colonial dependency and exploitation. It is this logic that allowed Fanon (and his brother) to marry white Frenchwomen while condemning Mayote Capécia for wanting and desiring to do the same (Fanon 1967: 41–62 passim).

Fanon's (1967) description of the sexual nature of colonial domination is useful for both its insights and its shortcomings. Fanon is thus an interesting and a controversial icon, considered by some as one of the strongest anticolonial figures of his time. Contemporary scholars have taken Fanon's colonial model further and, not denying the centrality of female sexuality in colonial domination, asked, What if that same female sexuality is possessed with social agency? What if both the male colonizer and the male colonized are fighting against (not for) the colonized female? In other words, what if the colonized woman is fighting for herself instead of reliving the western colonial fantasy of having her men fight for her? In such a case, according to many of these scholars, the "earth shakes" and the "categories crumble," since the colonial structure loses its most vital internal logic (Mallon 1996: 177–179). What is left is a new postcolonial chaos where neither the former colonizers nor the colonized can easily establish political domination by controlling the native woman and her sexuality.

Xica presents an interesting scenario in which to explore this issue. The attraction of this telenovela is established by its central character's being a native/other woman who, far from submitting to (either white or black) men's desires, is in complete (and therefore transgressive) control of her body and emotions. And, rather than denying the nature of her emotions and desires, she plays them out against the social structure that she is forced to deal with.

It is telling that in most soap operas women more than men are the central protagonists, which, to some degree, expresses something that (most male) social scientists might have been slow to understand: that women, elite or not, have (and have had) much more agency than anybody would want to admit. It is legitimate to ask whether the difficulty in admitting woman's agency in colonial societies might not be a result of the dreaded impact of such findings not only on our historical understanding of these societies but also on the restructuring of our contemporary relationships because of it (see Stoler 1996).

The "fierce," undominated woman (see de la Cuadra 1985) genre presents an attractive protagonist with whom the public readily relates, a needed element if the purpose is to export telenovelas throughout the Americas. Women, who are the main consumers of soap operas, can easily identify with the rags-to-riches plot line but even more so with a protagonist who, as they do, suffers from the unjust and institutionalized political system of domination characteristic of contemporary Latin America.

But men are not exempted from an attraction to melodrama. Many Latin American men watch soap operas as well and, like women, are also enticed by a volatile female as the main protagonist, especially one as alluring and unrelenting as Xica. In this manner, the fearless woman also conveniently plays into the colonial male fantasy of the woman challenging the man and patriarchal domination.

A telling moment in this telenovela is when the *comendador,* under the impression that Xica has been unfaithful to him, throws her out of the house and orders her to stay in town until she gives birth to his son. He pretends to no longer be concerned with her or her body (which the audience knows to be a lie) but only with the seed that he has planted in her womb. He is worried about his son as his rightful heir and, most tellingly, the son is the only "thing" about whom he can express interest and worry.

This scene is revealing in many regards. It exemplifies the typical colonial structure in which domination over the female body is the manner in which power is inscribed, making the offspring (the son) the primary point of the sexual/social relationship. At the same time, this overt
concern for the son clearly points to the political linkage between sexual
(even familial) concerns and the broader notions of social norms and
hegemonic devices. The scene also provides an insight into the fragility of the hegemonic structure of colonial society and the role of desire
in that particular political process. The fact that the *comendador* cannot
express his desire for Xica because of his code of honor and sense of
dignity (two more subtle colonial normative agents), limits him to a
social structure that he governs, since he is the highest representative of
it in town. He may thus express, in a restrained (and male engendered/
imprisoned) way, only his concern for his progeny. This was one of the
pitfalls of colonial desire, that, if expressed, would bring about tragic
consequences, the most likely one, the unraveling of the colonial structure itself and with it the collapse of all established identity categories
into chaos. It is this oscillation between hegemonic identity and chaotic
reality that is most clearly referred to by both Baldwin and Wilde (1964)
(not coincidentally, both queer writers) as the legacy of postcolonial societies. As Baldwin (1984: 20–21) elaborates:

> Now as then, we find ourselves bound, first without, then
> within, by the nature of our categorization. And escape is
> not effected through a bitter railing against this trap; it is
> as though this very striving were the only motion needed
> to spring the trap upon us. We take our shape, it is true,
> within and against that cage of reality bequeathed us at our
> birth; and yet it is precisely through our dependence on
> this reality that we are most endlessly betrayed. Society is
> held together by our need; we bind it together with legend,
> myth, coercion, fearing that without it we will be hurled
> into that void, within which, like the earth before the Word
> was spoken, the foundations of society are hidden. From
> this void—ourselves—it is the function of society to protect
> us; but it is only this void, our unknown selves, demanding,
> forever, a new act of creation, which can save us— "from
> the evil that is in the world." With the same motion, at the
> same time, it is this toward which we endlessly struggle and
> from which, endlessly we struggle to escape.

This is the unstated danger of desire, especially within a colonial setting. Colonial desire speaks to the emotions and sentiments of those caught up in the different ranks of power and domination, and in that regard is completely opposite the rational Western political project that has been so painstakingly constructed to secure the future of foreign elites at the expense of local populations. That is why in colonial settings desire, particularly sexual desire, possibly because it is presented as uncontrollable, is strongly demarcated and the system is vigilant against its expression. In this case, it seems that melodrama more than any other artistic or academic venture would be the most likely medium in which to express the ambiguous nature of colonial desire, since melodrama in itself is invested in exploring the emotions and sentiments, not the hidden rationality behind human relationships and interactions.

And as a medium in which to express the ambivalent and explosive nature of colonial desire, *Xica* is at its best. The telenovela explores not only the archetypal interest of the white for the other, the reified notion of "jungle fever," but also whites' as well as blacks' desire for whiteness, homosexual male and female desire, repressed religious desire, and, perhaps most disturbing, female desire. In *Xica,* women, both white and black, are far from the docile sexual partners that colonial historiography and fantasy have constructed. They are women clearly affected by their sexual drive, who want at all costs to have sex with men (Elvira with José María), who enjoy sexual pleasure (María Dolores), who are not satisfied with one man (the Countess), who want to have sex with other women (the former nun), and who consciously repress their own sexual desire in exchange for social power (Violante).

In El Tijuco colonial desire is behind every door, in every breath, even in the stones that people walk over. It is this perceived reality that allows the Inquisidor to state toward the end of the telenovela: "Battling the devil so closely, I have learned to smell desire as I perceive it in your breath, as the candles and incense that burn at the altar." Everybody knows, especially those enmeshed in the social structure, that a move that allows any kind of desire to hold primacy would shake the foundation of the society from which they benefit. As Violante recognizes, "desire is bad, it is very bad." After all, she should know, since all her actions are motivated by her desire (and the hiding of it) for a man (the *comendador*) who is always beyond her grasp. It is because of this that the death of a lover, the hanging of an innocent woman, the abuse of other human beings because they are slaves, and so on, are all a small price to pay for the maintenance of the status quo.

This is also why the *comendador* cannot express his desire for Xica unless he articulates it in a contained, controlled, and state-sanctioned manner as lust and whim, not caring and love. It is this love "that is hidden and
hard to follow" which is prophetically criticized by Eugenia, one of the
psychics in the telenovela, as "making the future become dark and forcing one to lose all power." All the characters in *Xica,* as in postcolonial
societies, are under threat of destruction unless they keep their desire—
and their love—under control or present it as something else. Thus,
Úrsula passes as a saint, José María denies his love for his male slave, Mikaela lies about loving her stepson, and Santiago refuses to act on his love
for Elvira because she is a prostitute.

And yet it is that same desire that reminds them of life, of blood
rushing through their veins, of the extreme fragility of the structure in
which they live, and of the constant fear that a step toward that desire
is a transgression of the way things should be and of the social structure
that gives them a place and defines their existence. However fragile their
identity might be, it is still a rooted identity rather than the dreaded chaos
and insecurity that transgression would afford. As Foucault (1998: 73)
has outlined it, to transgress is

> to take on the limit to its unnatural evolution, to force the
> limit to look at its disappearance, to make it see what it does
> not want to see, what it excludes. It is an act of violence,
> aggression that attacks with cruelty the limit it is cross-
> ing. In other words, transgression owes the fullness of its
> experience to the limit it is effacing; It is constituted by the
> limit's dissolution. Transgression uproots or disturbs the
> limited certainties with such an immediate violence that any
> thought or action is ineffectual as soon as it attempt to seize
> them. Transgression affirms the limited being, that is, it in
> actuality affirms the limitlessness into which it leaps as it
> opens this zone to existence for the first time.

This genuine desire—for who one is, for what one wants—reified by
one's transgression, is the real diamond for which all are mining in the
Tijuco without knowing it, and which in one scene Xica accuses the
comendador of not being able to offer her: "The only diamond I wanted
was the one that I thought you had in your heart, but now I see it is
only full of ravines and abysses." It is in this same vein that Mikaela can
scream at her hostile stepdaughter, Violante, "I have myself and I will

see more horizons than you have any idea even exist. You are just like dry flour, where even beans would not grow." It is also this allure, of the transgressive possibility of living out one's desire, even for an hour a day while watching television, that makes *Xica* such seductive entertainment for postcolonial subjects who know on some level that society does not excuse or forgive the transgression of desire.

THE FAMILY AS AMBIGUOUS SIGNIFIER

When it comes to our own family it is very hard to see,
and when you see, it is impossible to understand.
—MRS. BIENVENIDA

The generic role of the family in postcolonial societies is imbued with ambiguous economic and social significations. In many regards, melodrama makes use of this ambiguity to stage its own representation of social reality. As Martín-Barbero (in Rowe and Schelling 1992: 232–233) states, "Melodramatizing everything, through family relationships, the popular classes take revenge, in their own way, upon the abstraction imposed by the commodification of life and dreams." In this particular reading, the family is hailed as a sanctum free of commercial or economic exploitation and a nurturing place for communal existence and care. However, this somewhat traditional representation of the family and its moral values is not devoid of glaring contradictions. It is the ambivalent roles expressed in familial relationships that are most adequately met by melodramatic representation and that pervade *Xica*'s portrayal of the family in the colonial past.

Fanon (1967) was one of the first postcolonial writers to theorize about the effect of colonial relationships on the structure of the family. According to this initial model, the postcolonial subject is torn between a reified, colonizing paternal presence and a colonized maternal image that structures the child's identity. At the same time, this greater political division has a direct impact on the gendered construction of both males and females in significantly different ways: while males are burdened with a colonized Oedipus complex model of wanting to kill the oppressive father to replace and take his place, females are the object of contestation and severely judged if they claim any agency in their own futures.

Jamaica Kincaid (1997) has explored the colonial impact on family structure in the postcolonial setting of the Caribbean. Her family memoir of Antigua makes clear the personal analysis of her family as intertwined with the political domination and control of the island by European powers. The haunting description of her childhood and nuclear family in Antigua reminds one of the assessment of another Caribbean writer, Jean Rhys, of the horrendous impact of colonialism on familial (and personal) relationships. Both in Rhys' (1982a) *Wide Sargasso Sea* and Kincaid's (1997) *My Brother,* one is privy to how a patriarchal structure, misogynistic tendencies, authoritarian domination of children, smothering of independent activity, individualization of emotions, the socially leveling role of envy, and a strategic use of martyrdom and victimization reinforce colonial power and are used similarly within the family for control. Understanding the impact of political structures on a socially essential reproductive unit like the family makes it is easier to comprehend the interest that a colonial regime would have in reordering family structure. This is particularly so when, in the Western tradition in the Americas, the family is hailed as the locus of moral education and good manners (*buenas costumbres*).

As a colonial melodrama, *Xica* elaborates a cohesive narrative of the family and its complicity in the power mechanisms of political domination. This narrative—as demonstrated by the telenovela's popularity—reverberates quite strongly in the contemporary postcolonial family context. One of the most striking elements in *Xica*'s representation of the family is the ambiguous role of women in general but also, in particular, in the family setting. Even though the majority of viewers are women (or possibly because of it), the women fighting for social and personal agency in the telenovela are continually punished for their independent and free-thinking demeanor. It is not hard to understand the attraction that women fighting within systems of tight colonial power and control would have for contemporary women throughout the continent, especially when many of the engendered systems of domination have not significantly changed in the last two centuries of postcolonial existence.

As one of the telenovela's characters, Doña Cielo, sighs to her husband (the town's highest-ranking military official, who might have been murdered by his own daughter), "What would I know? I am just a poor woman who is debating between what she should do and what she should not do." The misogyny prevalent throughout the telenovela expresses the official position of the period and is most succinctly expressed by this military man: "I feel no sympathy for women. Women have been

made to procreate, and with her death [referring to his daughter's sched-
uled execution] my name will be cleared."

This complete submission of women to a man's authority is played out
in the control of daughters by their authoritarian parents, particularly
their fathers. In one scene a daughter is smilingly (and eerily) reminded
by her mother that "you have nothing to worry about concerning your
wedding. The only people making the decisions will be your father and I."
This "flawed" existence as daughters is also expressed in a rare moment
of shared confidences between two noblewomen, the Countess (the *comendador's* fiancée) and Violante (who is also in love with the *comendador*): "We are noblewomen, daughters of good family, and they treat us
like the colonized. We are used as simple merchandise." This is also the
betrayal experienced by Violante when she realizes that in his will her
father, with whom she was (almost incestuously) close, bequeathed all
his wealth away and left her under the control of her older brother, Luis
Felipe.

Once again, the retelling of the submission of women to fathers' and
other men's misogynistic control is not surprising. What is jarring is the
at times explicit manner in which this control is exercised and expressed
through both words and actions, for example, imprisonment, beatings,
and even failed executions. Also surprising is *Xica's* explicit depiction
of this disturbing power regime, an explicitness that is not so easy to
represent or take in during these politically correct times. It would seem
that one of the telenovela's attributes and, consequently, a reason for its
success, is the freedom that the characters have to express what they
think and feel and to do what they want to do. Thus the characters
express something that, because of a numbing political correctness or
strategic hegemonic devices, is kept hidden from contemporary viewers,
both male and female, and not freely acknowledged. In this regard, *Xica*
expresses contemporary situations that are suppressed and silenced, not
talked about for reasons of control, but that are aired in the telenovela
because it is supposedly about a period that ended centuries ago.

Xica also cunningly expresses the other side of this oppressive reality, that is, that if so many mechanisms of control are necessary, then
women and daughters are not as silent and devoid of opinion as they
are portrayed as being. If women were so naturally voiceless, colonial society would not have developed the means—paramount among
them the family as the guardian of moral and social (including sexual)
mores and norms—to silence them and keep them in line. In a way,
this is a functional solution to a complex problem; only the weight of

internal domination (see, e.g., Foucault 1990) could control something as volatile as human nature (in the sense of how human nature has been constructed). Thus it is the keeping of *buenas costumbres* and common decency that works to keep colonial order in check.

Xica, however, exposes this familial domination, thereby providing insights (and cracks) into the hegemonic constitution of the colonial family. One of these insights concerns Xica's relationship with her son, whom the governor repeatedly claims as his, to the point that he has pardoned her and will not send her into exile until after the child is born. Xica ferociously insists on keeping the baby after it is born, even though this will mean a complete overturn of the established order. One can only wonder whether it is Xica's marginality that makes her willing to meet the system head on and not give in to the established norms and principles that guide people in the Tijuco.

One must also take into account the twofold rebellion in Xica's struggle to keep her son (first, as a woman, and, second, as a former slave). Were she still a slave there would have been no question about her keeping her child with her. The child would have been property and as such it would have been left to the "master's" discretion as to what should be done with "it."

There are at least three more interesting elements that result from this particular melodramatic instance. The first is the constant referral to a "son" even when the sex of the child is unknown and will continue to be so until the moment of birth. To some degree one can blame the language for this constant referral to a son instead of the use of a more gender-neutral term. However, it is in this linguistic burden—using the male to represent the whole—that one can even more keenly understand the misogynistic tendencies of the colonial order and how language itself has been shaped and continues to shape these engendered relationships.

The second element is the dramatic difference in terms of who has rights over offspring. In contemporary society it is no longer the norm for the father to have absolute rights over the child; on the contrary, it is traditionally the woman, with or without the support of the courts, who has the responsibility for the child's upbringing. However, even though this is a significant change, the underlying structure remains the same; that is, the sex of the child continues to play a similar role in the future of the family's standing. While the birth of a girl continues to evoke stereotypical concerns about her sexuality (read, her virginity) and marriage, the birth of a boy is pervaded with ideas of honor and support of the family and its name. This particular *machista* structure, pervasive throughout the continent, is even more revealing when one takes into consideration that there is nothing "normative" in a day-to-day existence based on these attitudes. And more important, as *Xica* and colonial accounts show, these gender prescriptions have never really been the norm, not even during the colonial period, when, because of this contradiction, they had to be enforced with cruelty and sadism.

Finally, Xica's ambiguous standing in terms of not having a "real" family, due to her having been born in bondage, may also play a role in her liberated behavior. Without the heightened family restrictions, Xica is in a much better position to carry out her own wishes and desires, even when they go against the social norms of family and decent behavior. This freedom, however, is a fragile one in the sense that she is free of direct familial obligations but not of the overt norms imposed by society at large, including her own partner/lover, the *comendador*. At the same time, familial freedom has come at the price of having been born into bondage, seeing her family bought and sold, and having to struggle to become a (free) human being. Xica's struggle can be seen as striving to re-create the family she never had (e.g., by allowing all her friends and persecuted people in town to live with her). This type of family could not have existed in her time or in contemporary Latin America, that is, a family created out of honest love and sincere desires that would not open a fissure in the oppressive cultural structure of Latin America.

In an archetypal and provocative fashion the two major protagonists, Violante and Xica, are women and daughters who in reality are extremely far from living down to what is expected of them. Both of them have greatly exceeded their "place" in the colonial setting in which they live. However, since this is not only not permissible but also unheard of (and therefore nonexistent), both Xica and Violante must find different ways of disguising (which is not the same as hiding) their active participation in their own lives.

There are several instances in which these women's agency is paramount. The women in *Xica,* possibly because they are the most but, by far, not the only ones oppressed by familial obligations, manipulate everything in their reach to exercise their own freedom and agency, which ultimately translates into power. The more power they have in this colonial context the more freedom they are endowed with, and vice versa. An example of this is seen when the Countess visits the town with her husband, who is there on official business for the Portuguese crown.

The Countess loses no time is sleeping with every slave in Xica's household, including bathing with six of them at the same time. She even allows herself to admit that "the darker they are the more appetizing she finds the men." Because of her status, she and her husband are above the rules of the church's morality, and yet she uses those rules to maintain her prestige and legitimization.

The Countess and Xica have a lot in common in the sense that both allow themselves freely to exert their most sincere and provocative desires, sexual or not. Their freedom, interestingly enough, is afforded from having been born at opposite ends of the social ladder, which allows them to escape the most oppressive normative obligations. However, the rest of the women in town, who are caught somewhere in between required "decent" behavior and their passionate desires, do not passively submit to their husbands or to society's whims either. They utilize the same normative propriety and decorum to gain as much freedom and power as is possible without losing their reputation and life in the process.

In this sense, their lives are a gamble, as they push as hard as they can against the odds with the cards life has dealt them. The telenovela's characters, like Violante, Sra. Cielo, and Úrsula, are by no means the passive women that colonial society instructs them to be. They have had premarital sex, plotted to murder their enemies (including their own offspring), attempted to seduce the priest, and are in charge of the wealthiest families in town. It is interesting to assess whether these atypical women are seen by viewers for what they are, a more realistic portrayal of female (and male) agency under the burdensome requirements of both colonial and contemporary Latino culture. It is clear that they use not only their marginality but every aspect of their daily lives, as women do today, to live out their passions and express their agency.

Once again, melodrama's appeal to familial representation is sustained by a market economy that has sought to outdate kinship organization. Latin Americans are living in a setting where, more and more, according to Martín-Barbero (1987: 245), "the transformation wrought by capitalism in the labor force and recreation schedules, the commodification of street and domestic time, and even of the most primary social relationships, seems to have abolished the primacy of the family." It would seem that, in direct reaction to this, melodrama is able to lobby its viewers to hold onto another, less stereotypical, form of social being and feeling. The melodrama, *Xica* included, allows a great number of Latin Americans to take revenge on the capitalist forms of production of which they are an active part and to revisit the ambiguity of familial obligation as both the upholder of a "moral economy" and the safe haven from a market economy that seeks to commodify all of their existence.

If this is true, then we need to ask, along with Martín-Barbero (1987: 131), whether "these broad and complex familial relationships, which stand as the infrastructure of the melodrama, are not the manner in which the people [*lo popular*] understand the complexity and obscurity of modern market relationships. Is this [family] anachronism not a metaphor, a 'new' old way of symbolizing the social[?]"

The ambiguous standing of the family, however, continues in the fact that melodrama itself is yet another form of commodification and of the transnational economy. Possibly, however, in this instance the roles are inverted, and this time the melodrama serves as an export and not something being imported from beyond the continent's borders. Maybe melodrama allows revenge through the inversion of colonial relationships, or at least a representation of such.

CONCLUSION: THINGS ARE WHAT THEY ARE, NOT WHAT THEY SEEM TO BE

Everything always ends up being wrong. That is what I see.
Everything in life always turns out wrong.
—LITTLE GIRL

According to Martín-Barbero (1987: 244; emphasis in original), one of the principal objectives of the melodrama is to know or *re*know (*reconocer*), to go beyond the mere appearances. The successful melodrama "looks to struggle against all the wrongdoing, the façades, against everything that hides and disguises reality: *it is a struggle to make oneself known.*" In this respect *Xica*'s central plot is completely in line not only with the genre's expectations but also with a willing continent of identifying viewers. It is easy to see the appeal of *Xica* and other telenovelas to an audience that very much sees itself as invisible, hidden from global view unless it is in exotic (e.g., as a vacation spot or a place in which to live out sexual fantasies) or macabre and culturally backward (e.g., primitive practices and political structures) references.

Telenovelas like *Xica* allow viewers to reconnect with a social being different from the one daily presented to them in newspapers, educational institutions, and other "civilizing" mediums. Identification with the melodrama speaks directly to a continent still searching for its own historicity and sensing its having been left out of the global order. It is not a coincidence that many market economists, social scientists, and other professionalizing agencies have dismissed Latin America (as part of the larger "Third World") as an insignificant force in directing its future or that of the world; since the colonial encounter, Europe has usurped this role for itself and its most vivid imitators, the United States and Japan.

The role-playing and dislodging of disguises central to the melodrama would seem the natural setting in which a Latin American could envision a reality more in tune with his or her own. The melodrama, contradictorily enough, more realistically represents people's day-to-day existence. The telenovela reflects the immediacy of people's life and speaks to their own logic of existence and not to the one historically afforded by the colonial encounter. And it is telling in this regard that this lived-in product would be the one that, unlike the majority of the continent's production, is most important for global exportation.

The primary characters' role-playing, Violante's and Xica's, for example, provides for self-identification of who one really is as opposed to what one should be, is supposed to be, or is judged as being. Thus, on the one hand, Violante, as she is reminded by one of the priests, uses the church to disguise her need for power and social influence. Through this religious disguise she is afforded agency: she can proposition a priest, disregard the death of her brother, and plot to harm the reputations of her enemies.

On the other hand, Xica's use of disguise is subtle and therefore more complicated. At a basic level, Xica makes use of her "charm" (sexual or not) to get away with what she wants and is less willing to disguise her own desires and wishes or her readiness to act on them. This exposure of her desires, this "realness" of sorts, is the disguise that transforms Xica into the heroine. And to some degree this position is afforded by her original bondage, during which she had very little to lose, since the most essential of all colonial characteristics, one's dignity as a person, had already been stripped from her. However, this structure changes when she becomes the richest woman in town yet continues to act the way she wants to, even if it means going against the established norms.

This behavior is telling because, just as the colonial order is based on the exclusion or repudiation of feelings and passion to safeguard *buenas costumbres,* Xica's livelihood is based on the exclusion of these *buenas costumbres* themselves. The logic is the same; the contents are inverted. Linda Williams' (2004) analysis of the colonial relationship between white wife and black mistress in the U.S. melodrama *Mandingo* (1975) also provides similar insights into the racial dynamics of desire and identity and, ultimately, of romantic belonging.

In *Xica* there is also a carnivalesque ethos that almost creates a free-for-all aura. At one level, this repudiates the status quo and justifies daily existence; at another, it leaves the structure intact and makes explicit the real forces (both external/national and internal/psychological) that are at play. It is this ambivalent identification, rather than any "realistic" elements, which makes the telenovela such a social success: "It is not the representation of the concrete and specific facts that produces in fiction the sense of reality but rather a certain generality that looks both ways and supports doubly the particular facts of the real [world] as well as the fictitious one" (Magnani in Martín-Barbero 1987: 246).

I would argue that *Xica* portrays a reality much more complex and untidy than the one traditionally expressed in either official or alternative representations. It is these "freedoms" that have afforded it such widespread popular appeal and made it a lucrative product for export. This double "success" does not excuse it from limitations and the commodification it is a part of. However, *Xica* still does violence by representing Latin American reality; that reality is possibly, however, less limiting than that offered by traditional social science and the high arts, and is more willing to engage with the chaos and despair intrinsic in the continent's present. One can see in *Xica*'s melodrama a sustained excess which strives to overturn the bourgeois notions of safety and repression (Martín-Barbero 1987: 131). As one of the characters, keenly aware of the political and personal danger hidden in the moral order, says to another, "You are very dangerous because you do not say what you feel." And this is clearly one of those lessons that no postcolonial subject in Latin America has ever forgotten.

The telenovela *Xica* ambiguously addresses the long-dead spirits that spring out of colonialism's coffin. *Xica* uses its melodramatic façade and its disguise as entertainment to touch on one of the central nerves of the continent's colonial legacy: desire. Clearly, the ambivalent role of desire (sexual and otherwise) is pivotal in balancing the effects of power at all levels, especially a social power that is largely based on obvious misreadings and misreconstructions of its colonial past. It is this explicit acknowledgment in *Xica* that allows its protagonists to agree that "it is of no use to go to the [political] authorities; they never solve anything."

Yet far from feeling utter despair, contemporary Latin Americans, like Violante, continue to reconstruct their postcolonial reality in a way that will allow them "to not go insane from their not understanding the reason for so much pain in their hearts." In this way melodrama may be not only an efficient medium through which to assess a dramatically conflicting Latin American existence but also one less scrutinized by the officializing hegemonic devices of normative Latin culture. After all, these are just telenovelas, and commodified for export at that.

Three

PRODUCING THE GLOBAL WEST THROUGH LATIN TALES OF SEDUCTION AND ENVY

*And in one sense, if I were asked for a definition of myself,
I would say that I am one who waits; I investigate my
surroundings, I interpret everything in terms of what
I discover, I become sensitive.*
—FRANTZ FANON, *BLACK SKIN, WHITE MASKS*

FRANTZ FANON AND THE RESIGNIFICATION OF THE WESTERN OTHER

In his soul-searching book on the geopolitics of colonial oppression, *Black Skin, White Masks,* Frantz Fanon (1966) elaborates on the difficulties of living within contested social, national, and personal identities. In one of the more personal accounts he declares that if his son's fingernails (or skin, height, language, and physical disposition) were carefully examined to define his identity, they would reflect how the mythologies Fanon is trying to expose would have survived intact. In this, and other equally moving passages, he explores the contesting discourses of the west (and the nonwest), global and local, and the ethnic identity struggles that are an integral part of the modern world system that frames our contemporary social interactions.

Fanon's portrayal of his son's identity, along with his judgmental scrutiny of Mayote Capécia's (and, by extension, black women's) fascination with the colonizing white male other, is not lost on feminist critiques of his work. These are not unrelated to his color blindness toward his son's mother, who was white and French, or the fact that he so vehemently argues for the release of his son from the same constraining colonial discourse that denigrated his own identity. It is also relevant that Fanon's son was born during the struggle for Algerian liberation in which Fanon aligned himself with his colonized Arab (br)others in an all-out war against France for national independence.

And yet, half a century after discourse limitations and national liberation wars, our fingernails and skin hue (along with everything else) continue to be used to define our postcolonial identity (see Scott 2004; Žižek 2002). More problematical, it is also through these processes of racial and ethnic definition that we are to be welcomed, or not, into the global west, although it is still unclear what exactly this place/name "west" means, or where it is located.

I use Fanon's (1967, 1966, 1965) work in this chapter to introduce the contemporary conundrum of global identity and postcolonial existence. His work, however limited, highlights an initial preoccupation with what is referred to today as the "postcolonial debate," and which, since the 1950s, has produced a fruitful inquiry (see McClintock, Mufti, and Shohat 1997; Said 2000; Spivak 1999). The postcolonial debate— in many cases aligned with critical cultural studies agendas—has been resourceful in questioning the nature of identity in the aftermath of colonial liberation and the expansion of capitalist forms of economic globalization (Gilroy 2000, 1987). Primary among these concerns have been notions of the west, which are more problematic today than they were during the period of national liberation in the 1950s or even the 1960s.

It is particularly challenging to wonder what would be the west's opposite. If it is the east, does an east exist without a qualification of "Far," "Middle," or "Near"? Or do these geographical adjectives reflect theoretical idealizations rather than bounded territorial or cultural realities (see Gupta and Ferguson 1997)? Perhaps the west's opposite is less global in scale, so that, instead of opposing a global east to the global west, we can only oppose contesting localities?

Thus notions of Asian, Latino, African American (and other geographically defined social categories) are better seen as antitheses to the west. Although the constraining articulations—at times, explicit racism— of such reified categories claiming a global identity for the west but not for others are not lost on postcolonial scholars, who have outlined the subtle hierarchical process established by this unequal identity production (e.g., Said 2000, 1989, 1978). A more effective approach, however, would be to discontinue problematizing nonwestern identities and reassess why it is, or possibly how, this western identity has been afforded such a hegemonic hold on our own global existence and exchanges. Stuart Hall (1997b) has been most adamant about recognizing the west for what it is: a "local global." It is this particular analysis that most promisingly attacks western mythologies, or the myths implicit in the production of the "west," including those in Latin American telenovelas.

Two lines of inquiry immediately arise. The first is the need to go beyond the simplistic explanation that the west's stronghold is a result merely of economic relations of exploitation. That many of these unequal relations of economic exchange exist is a fact, no longer a topic of profound scholarly debate. That these socioeconomic inequalities are denied by western governments is hardly cause for surprise nor should it warrant much academic attention. However unfair these relations are, though, they still do not account on their own for our contemporary system of complex identity production. Rather, it would seem necessary to establish a genealogy of these economic relations as globally and locally intertwined; that is, we need to ask how is it that our global economic relations developed the way they have (and continue to develop) and how they are so essential in hiding their own social figuration. This inquiry must also extend itself forward, in terms of a "history of the vanishing present" (see Foucault 1990; Spivak 1999), and assess how these economic processes, contradictorily, produce and integrate cultural practices from hair braiding to parent-child expectations and sustain them as markers for authentic forms of identity.

The second element is the seeming ease with which a western identity establishes itself as a global one. This is particularly problematic from an anthropological perspective, since there is nothing naturally global about either Europe or North America other than their constant presentation and reification of themselves as such. Therefore, instead of beginning with the assumption of a global western identity, it makes more sense to question the source of this narrative and the representational power that allows the west to claim an almost uncontested identity as the global other. What are the mechanisms in place that enable the advance of an identity so unflinching in its missionary enterprise but, even more telling, blind to its own social boundaries and local grounding? It would also be equally imprecise to explain away the west's global existence merely with a historical retelling of Europe's colonial enterprise; colonial exploitation would then constitute itself as more of a question than an answer. However, this simplistic articulation might be essential to the question itself. How is it that the racial, economic, and, above all, moral collusion inherent in the colonial enterprise remained intact for centuries and still colors our world system of development and democratic ideals (Escobar 1995; Ferguson 1990; Mignolo 2000)?

In this regard, to define contemporary global and postcolonial identities as mere epiphenomena of economic domination or colonial oppression is to belittle the efforts of millions of Latin Americans who engage this question every day of their lives. Who are the "they" and the "we," and how do "we" approach a basic understanding of the ever-changing nature of identity production? It is with regard to this question that economic domination (including capitalism and globalization) and political domination (mainly neocolonialism and the development discourse) are essential conditions of the contemporary problematic of identity—but in no way exclusive determining factors.

Rather, from these initial lines of inquiry we are able to further explore a landscape that cannot be monolithically defined, and yet continues to be imagined and represented, for its own benefit, as if it were. It is this contradiction—of being who we are, and not; the need to be identified and ravaging that identity at one and the same time; the claiming of a western identity and proving it otherwise in our daily acts—that demands closer attention ("David Scott by Stuart Hall" 2004).

JAMES BALDWIN: THE CONTRADICTIONS OF WESTERN IDENTITY (OR NOT)

Now as then, we find ourselves bound, first without, then within, by the nature of our categorization. And escape is not effected through a bitter railing against this trap; it is as though this very striving were the only motion needed to spring the trap upon us. We take our shape, it is true, within and against that cage of reality bequeathed us at our birth; and yet it is precisely through our dependence on this reality that we are most endlessly betrayed. Society is held together by our need; we bind it together with legend, myth, coercion, fearing that without it we will be hurled into that void, within which, like the earth before the Word was spoken, the foundations of society are hidden. From this void—ourselves—it is the function of society to protect us; but it is only this void, our unknown selves, demanding, forever, a new act of creation, which can

save us—"from the evil that is in the world." With the same
motion, at the same time, it is this toward which we endlessly
struggle and from which, endlessly we struggle to escape.
—JAMES BALDWIN, *NOTES OF A NATIVE SON*

I have quoted again at length from this passage because in
it Baldwin (1984) identifies the conundrums (one of his favorite words)
of identity and, even more specifically, that of western identity. It is not
surprising that the book carries the provocative title of *Notes of a Native Son* and continues to play with the ambivalent signifier of "native
son" used by Richard Wright to describe somebody born in the most
powerful representative of the west, the United States. Throughout the
book, Baldwin outlines his own problematized identity and wonders
about his fleeing the United States only to realize that he was its most
precious offspring, or how European castles and histories meant and signified more than the African narratives he so much desired and wished
to embody (see also Angelou 1986). It is this striking realization which
awakens Baldwin, and us as well, to the full, contradictory, circle of his
existence and our local/global identity.

The realization, for Baldwin, that after years of embracing a black
identity he had to accept that he was as American (culturally constructed
to mean the United States of America as opposed to the rest of the continent) as apple pie was a painful one. Moreover, Baldwin recognized
that being black in the United States was more American than apple pie,
and that this truth was what had to be kept a secret. In its place the "apple pie" was offered as the sacrificial lie (see also Baldwin 1998). Meanwhile, the price of these secrets and lies had been paid with the skin and
bodies of Baldwin and others, both "black" and "white." But each price
paid was different, each body ransomed at a different cost, and each of
those ransoms contained rich personal histories of a struggle caused by
unequal identity production.

There are several other instructive elements in Baldwin's questioning
of western identity. The first, not necessarily highlighted by Baldwin
himself but not any the less powerful because of this, is his initial insight
into western identity as problematic and fractured. For Baldwin, this
particular version of westernness is underscored by the genocide and
ethnocide expressed by lynching and various other forms of oppression
in the United States. In Baldwin's analysis, an American identity is a local, particular form of westernness; he recognizes that there is no global
west (and never really has been) but, rather, a series of fractured identi-

ties that hide their "fracturation" in the hopes of surviving their own embittered chaotic existence and resultingly disjointed identities. Black identity, for Baldwin, serves as the destabilizing other whose existence has been so patently and necessarily denied in order to maintain a singular American identity (see also Morrison 1993; West 1994), since without that fracturation no singular American identity can be afforded: not only would the apple pie have no taste but the simile itself would never have come into existence.

Obviously, there can be no white identity without a black one, yet the ways in which each racial identity produces the other in unequal exchanges of power and social narrative are not as easily contained within this symbiosis. This is where Baldwin's contribution is particularly intuitive in that he creates a double narrative, essential in assessing not only the constitutive nature of fracturation within the west but, even more important, also the cost of this fracturation, which he constantly refers to as "the price of the ticket" (Thorsen 1991).

A provocative twist to his identity narrative is the fact that in it both Americans and blacks lose their hegemonic power as meta-identities: neither is singular; neither is complete; and neither exists independently of the other. A second narrative twist is afforded by the evidence on which these identity truths are based. The evidence espoused by Baldwin is not that of his own hegemonic predecessors or of empirical proof. Rather, it is that afforded by his own lived experience. These are no longer the stories of his slave and/or putative plantation-owner ancestors. This is Baldwin's own story, intertwined with that of his ancestors, along with those who articulate similar experiences in the legacy of their own identity. The strength of his experience was such that it exiled Baldwin from the United States for most of his life. Yet "the evidence of things not seen" is the key argument against the innocence so anxiously forwarded by U.S. society at large to disprove its guilty western identity.

Thus we have two elements to be further explored to gain insight into our ambivalent construction of globalization and an extremely unequal articulation of culture and power. The first is the reification of a local west, hidden in a collective unconscious of racial differentiation by its own narrative of global capital. The second element is provided by the elevation of personal experience to political and social analysis. Baldwin always knew he was at a disadvantage. It was this profound knowledge of his unequal status that allowed him to struggle for and construct a personal truth. Thus he was never completely fooled by (or full of) the history of his own people (either as Americans or as blacks) and successfully strived to maintain an ambivalent identification with the official dissemination of history.

The degree to which Baldwin was able to escape official history and identify exclusively with the intellectual elite was also the degree to which he was able to produce an alternative social discourse on identity during his own life, one explicitly focused on those fractures that are so systematically denied. When asked in a televised interview for his credentials for becoming a writer, Baldwin's unflinching response was, "I was born poor, negro, and a homosexual, what better training could I have received?" Once again, contained within this response is a particular way of seeing the world that enriched his writing and allowed him insights unavailable to many intellectuals of his (and our) generation. Through his life and work he offered the combined wisdom of emotional knowledge that can further our assessment of the problematics of a "local/global" (Hall 1997a) western identity, an identity that hegemonizes its disruption and in so doing hides its local genealogy in the energy of convincing us of its global characteristics.

Like Baldwin, other scholars have questioned this western identity, most explicitly during national liberation wars and guerrilla warfare (mainly but not exclusively in Latin America). However, many of these scholars have critiqued the idea of a global west as if they were outside of its realm. Therefore, and without any consciousness on their parts, they have also created that which they were fighting against: a global west. In their resistance to and liberation from the west they have furthered a fractured west as exclusively global and looked to distance themselves from this disrupted global construction. In exchange for their own, purer (or, at least, supposedly more authentic) identity they also created a more cohesive west—one that in many ways inspired the sources of their education and political ideals.

This particular form of resistance to colonialism, engaged in at different moments by scholars such as Fanon (1967, 1966, 1965), Memmi (1991), Cabral (1974a, 1974b), Freire (1992), and even Baldwin (1988), made their situation, struggles, and identity much more ambiguously productive. Perhaps because of his nationality, for Baldwin, this ambivalence became a much more central part of his intellectual production. To an enormous degree, it limited the power of his identification as a pure native unspoiled by western action; in another, more ambivalently productive way he made it the source of his work, and therefore of his identity. His ideas were not tools with which to attack the master's house (to paraphrase Audre Lorde's [1997] metaphor) from the outside but, rather, to dismantle it from the inside. This is particularly problematic because it constitutes a form of spitting up on oneself; that is, when the master's house comes tumbling down it is enough to comprehend the chaos that ensues, but the chaos is amplified when it comes down on one's own head.

Because of this, Baldwin's writing is both courageous and powerful, constituting a form of resistance for other intellectuals/artists to follow. In this regard, resistance is articulated in a different manner, not as the simple pounding on the master's house but as understanding the collusion implicit in supporting that fantasy house in the first place. However dreadful the master's house is, it has always constituted a reference point for masters and slaves alike. And no matter how disquieting a plantation can be, not being sure what would arise in its place brings its own terrifying nightmares. Or as Baldwin (1988: 20) elaborates, "Any upheaval in the universe is terrifying because it so profoundly attacks one's sense of one's own reality."

I am not arguing that oppression is better than not but, rather, that the destruction of oppression as though it took place only in the master's house and does not form an essential part of one's identity is yet another form of illusion or fantasy, one not that far removed from that imbuing the master's realm with hegemonizing power. Identity production, and its transformation, never occurs in a void (see Kureishi 2001, 1990). At the same time, it is clear this is one of the most painfully intimate lessons of the postcolonial debacle since the 1950s. Many colonies liberated themselves from the oppressing other but were unable to liberate themselves from their foundational oppressive relations, that is, their fictions. Meanwhile, these relations of unequal production constitute who these postcolonial subjects are in essence, and what they want to be, that is, the seductive object of their desire. It is in this manner that a coloniality of power is indelibly connected to the national identity production of postcolonial subjects (see Quijano 1993).

THE ARTIST'S WAY:
BORDERLANDS AND SEDUCTION

Many artists and scholars have grappled with the constitutive nature of desire within the political realm. Several French writers have utilized a Lacanian understanding of desire to explore its constitutive role in the self, and how it relates to its social surroundings in the production of specifically exploitative political relationships (Bataille 2000, 1991, 1988, 1987, 1986; Duras 1985; Kristeva 1991). For example, Duras (1985), pointing to the reason why so many purely academic assessments of the political have failed to both predict and transform, has readily elaborated the pitfalls of understanding the political as devoid of the personal. In its stead, Duras' work analyzes in its own way yet another powerful production of the local west, this time in its French incarnation. In *The Ravishing of Lol Stein* (1967), Duras explores how the mental/emotional breakdown of a woman facing her own oppression/ exploitation is analogous to the national experience of people who have experienced their own social alienation. For Duras, having been born in Indochina, no other disruption can exemplify this alienation more than coming to terms with the French oppression of millions of people all over the world, from Indochina to Algeria and back to Paris.

I believe Duras' insight is useful when applied to the Latin American landscape, and to the ambivalent production of the particularly problematic western identity of *latinidad* (Latinness). There is much to be explored in terms of desire's constitutive place in the articulation of Latino identities in the United States and its hierarchical political grounding. This ambivalent desire is also central to several other political enterprises, including Europe's expansion and plausible constitution as a global west through denial of its own local practices and the uneven reconfiguration of neocolonial relationships in the Americas since the 1800s. Many have taken this preoccupation with desire as a central issue to be wrestled with in their own lives and work. It is this committed approach that figures in both the social and the professional identities of activists, scholars, intellectuals, professors, or simply human beings trying to come to terms with the political complexity of their existence (see, e.g., Castillo 1996, 1994, 1992; Martínez 2001, 1998, 1992; R. Rodriguez 2002, 1992).

Within the Latino ethnoscape, several artists/scholars stand out as representative of this particularly productive way of looking at the complexity of identity production. Paramount among them are three who have received both national and international recognition: Guillermo Gómez-Peña (1996, 1994, 1993, 1991), Coco Fusco (1995, 1994), and Gloria Anzaldúa (1990). The titles of these authors' main works (*Warrior for Gringostroika* [Gómez-Peña 1993], *English Is Broken Here* [Fusco 1995], and *Borderlands/La Frontera* [Anzaldúa 1987]) express both the complexity of their production and their willingness to entertain a multiple tension in their exploration of Latino identities.

Each of these author/scholar/artists in his or her own way spells out the complex contradiction that being Latino/as in this new world order entails. Ambiguously, Latinos are constituted as westerners only when they escape the national American (U.S., that is) fold and become the object of a steady, envious glare from their Latin American counterparts. Latinos are seen as having been seduced (and accepting that seduction) by the United States and, therefore, by everything that is in opposition to their authentic Latin American existence. However, instead of being punished for this transgression (which puts them in Latin America's public realm), they become the envied signifier of what Latin Americans really would want to be if given the chance. But it is important, as these authors explain, that this ambivalent (as all identities are) western identity of seduction and envy (transformative elements of desire) is assumed at a specific price, that is, not being seen as westerners in their country of origin (or the place they call home), the United States.

Latinos, I argue, in some profound ways constitute another site of western production and, as such, are continuously contributing to essay collections of "notes of native sons (and daughters)," now in the plural and more gender integrated (Cortez 1999; Ray González 1996; Guerra 1999; Santiago and Davidow 2000). Anzaldúa has, possibly, been the most illuminating in her assessment, probably because of her exploration of a specific Latina identity and not an abstract, generalized Latino one. She has produced a model of borderlands within which to talk about the hidden incongruity in words/identities like "west," "American," and "Latina." Her production is even more profoundly affected if we take into account language's doubly Calibanesque wounding of western identity: the opposition of a formerly colonizing language like Spanish against the newly colonizing American English. And yet, what does one do when these colonizing elements make up the liberated self that one envisions and that is vehemently exported in telenovelas, when, to paraphrase Kincaid (1989), even the language fails us because it is so embedded in the same exploitative relationships from which we are striving to free ourselves (see Kristeva 1991).

BETTY LA FEA:
ENVY-STRICKEN CONSUMPTION

Betty la fea embodies two very different processes of hegemonic ambiguity. The first is a hegemonic national representation in the highly competitive market of international media companies. In this regard, other national productions, such as those from Colombia, provide a more diverse market and, with it, yet another hegemonic reconfiguration of the global economic order as it is locally reified in Latin America. The second process of hegemonic ambiguity is much more subtle, and because of its less obvious problematics I shall discuss it below.

As Martín-Barbero (1987) points out, the melodramatic content in telenovelas is key to their popular following and commercial success. The fact that they are described as an inferior form of entertainment and labeled lowbrow by elites is but a useful mask behind which they can exert their powerful influence without being questioned in terms of content or appropriate social message. As does *Xica* (see below), *Betty la fea* shows an enormous brashness in the elements that it utilizes for public reflection, and if the plot itself does not seem original, the elements used to tell the story in many ways surpass the typical content of the story. One could argue that it is these characteristics that justified its 2006 offshoot in Mexico, *La fea más bella,* and in the United States, *Ugly Betty* (see Postscript).

The first major shift is the physical makeup of the characters themselves. This is the first time that a telenovela features characters who are regionally different from previously established ones. In this instance, it is Andean-looking people, regionally distinct from the traditional Venezuelan stylized bodies, the darker bodies of Brazilian characters, and the white European features of Argentineans, who made their way onto the continent's television sets. This subtle change of type may seem minuscule, but for the continental reworking of concepts of beauty and the allocation of television time for new types, the implications are manifold.

This shift in image production is further driven by the fact that the protagonist as well as her group of friends are referred to as *las feas* (the ugly ones). This categorization as ugly is contingent on the main plot, which is a modern reworking of Hans Christian Andersen's story of the ugly duckling and is set within the confines of the modern offices of a traditional, affluent Colombian family's textile corporation. The fact that Betty and her cohort are defined as ugly is further highlighted by their constant opposition to a blonde bombshell who plays the dumb, malicious, and capriciously narcissistic self to the last sensual drop.

The ugliness of Betty and her friends (all mestizas and one Afro-Colombian woman), however, is not due only to their race, their older age, and bigger body size but also to their emphasized "common" behavior. Highlighting this behavior is Betty's ridiculous and irritating signature laugh, but it is exemplified as well by the braces on her teeth, her geeky outfits, and her naïveté. All of these characteristics are shared to a greater or lesser degree by her counterparts and her nerdy first boyfriend; all are identified by their gossipy behavior, clumsy body movements, and lowbrow talk. The campiness is further sustained by an explicitly homosexual character in the company who, stereotypically, is also the fashion designer. This flamboyantly gay designer is able to ambivalently explore continually irritating campy behavior while constantly deriding the ugly characters and scoffing at their less-than-privileged status, thus signifying a distinction between elite and nonelite identifying behaviors. This distinction is not lost on class-ridden Latin Americans, who know how the same behavior carried out by different social players will not mean the same nor provoke the same reaction from the public or the authorities. In other words, being elite or upper class allows social and sexual freedom, including homosexuality, not even imaginable for the lower or working class.

The explicit campiness in *Betty la fea* is an interesting and refreshing melodramatic recourse that seems to have had a positive impact on the national and international consumption of the soap opera. Unlike other telenovelas that strive for an authenticity that can never be truly achieved—which is what makes them telenovelas, after all—*Betty la fea* utilizes campiness to question the moral structure of the company and, through it, the characters' personal lives. In this light, the equation of Ecomoda to Colombia itself elucidates interesting questions about the morality of the nation. It is clear to all viewers that *las feas* (Betty included) are not real people—nobody is that ugly or campy. And there is no doubt that *las feas* (particularly Betty) are the heroines of the story. At the same time, they, *las feas,* subtly exemplify a real identification with the majority of Latin Americans, who have considered themselves ugly from the moment they were born, or, more significant, have that image imposed on them by modernizing development projects of the powerful west.

Thus campiness allows for a cultural resignification that otherwise could not take place. Nobody would consciously identify themselves as *fea* or with the *feas,* since no one is really ugly in that overproduced way or laughs in that manner. Yet it is this "realistic" distance which affords a "real" proximity to the emotional identification with the characters that most viewers feel, an emotional proximity that has to be consciously denied but that allowed *Betty la fea*'s economic success, including the development of a spin-off. The telenovela was such a surprising success in fact that new episodes that developed the central plot further than was initially planned were written to take advantage of the show's triumph.

Beyond the central plot of ugly (duckling) assistant transforming herself into her boss's boss and making him pine for her, another interesting element is the role that social envy plays throughout. The competition between the two groups of women, the "successful" blonde and the "ugly" ones, is marked by a complicit relationship of envy that is played out at every turn. The beginning of the soap opera features the envious behavior of the mistreated ugly employees and their constant struggle to break out of their subordinate positions. However, this particular behavior is in reaction to the successful woman's attempt to keep them in that subordinate position and to mark their inferiority as inherent to their class, race, and physical appearance. This relationship is inverted at the end of the soap opera, providing the moral lesson and allowing Betty to be celebrated as the real heroine.

The ambivalent relationship between envy and transformation is crucial to the process of cultural resignification afforded by *Betty la fea*. Betty, as the heroine, has to step out of these envy-driven relationships and limit her personal need for vengeance. Once she is able to claim the power that is the source of the need for retaliation, as exemplified by her former boss' public display of love and therefore unmanly humiliation, she can put envy aside. In doing so she is allowing the flip side of envious relationships—seduction—to develop, which is powerfully consummated in her "true" love relationship.

In this way, telenovelas give Latin viewers myriad levels of seductive identification: love, revenge, and power. Yet it is the last which I believe most closely addresses the telenovelas' ambivalent production of a totalizing global west. This particular process of westernization is obvious to any Latin American who has suffered social oppression, as is the case for most of the continent's population. The struggle between beauty and ugliness is incorporated not only in the ever-present melodramatic conflict between good and evil but also in the "modern" struggle between the global west and the local nonwest. The successful characters represent a modernized, developed world toward which the ugly locals, or premodern Latin natives, strive. The native/ugly women are not "at home" in the modern world of offices and finance, which is what makes Betty powerful. She is able to shine in their "developed" world of high finance and flashy looks, and on their own terms. *Betty la fea* thus establishes envy as the motive and engine for these women. And all Latin natives can ambivalently identify with this, since they are aware of what they lack and will do everything in their power to obtain this modern image, this developed existence, as Betty does.

Betty achieves a powerful transformative identity: she is no longer ugly (i.e., local, native), since she is one of them, yet at heart she is still one of the locals, making her the moral heroine of the melodramatic entanglement. However, she is also the best example of successful western seduction, since she, more than any of the others, "buys" into the promises of a developed/modern identity. Her ambivalent victory also signifies the result of five centuries of a coloniality of power that marks (our own) seduction by a western identity.

It was this process that was avidly followed by Latin Americans, perhaps even more so by Latinos, because it is Latinos, as commercially exported, who embody Betty to their southern counterparts, as the ambivalent markers of a global west while constantly living the local production of this western existence. What could be more seductive than a telenovela that inscribes a web of love around our deepest unacknowledged life's desires. Yet we can conveniently remind ourselves that it is merely a telenovela, not related to our own reality or to that of anybody around us.

XICA: THE SEDUCTION OF COLONIAL DESIRE

The successful Brazilian telenovela *Xica* is also marked by ambiguous cultural signifiers powerfully inscribed in the production of a localized global western identity (see Chap. 2). It is this particular resignification that made *Xica* so popular throughout the Americas, including among Latino/as in the United States. As previously discussed, *Xica*'s popularity might be explained by a series of factors, including its quite successfully ambiguous handling of a colonial legacy that still figures centrally in the way Latin Americans envision themselves and how they feel the world—wrongly—envisions them. It is also this ambivalent colonial legacy that allows for these subtly seductive elements to express a traditionally hidden agenda. The most powerful seductive force in *Xica* is native black sexuality, with its parade of sexualized male and female bodies seducing both the population of the Tijuco and viewers. Yet, although black sexuality is definitely highlighted, white sexuality is also obscurely signified through the political incorrectness of whites who express their ambivalent sexual need (through envy and seduction) for what they do not and can never possess (a black identity), and of blacks in their ideal-ization of and desire for whiteness, a more developed/modern existence, and the social recognition of their humanity and right to freedom.

It is this relationship of mutual envy, captured most powerfully in the sexual discourse of the telenovela (as in contemporary postcolonial Latin American societies) that is commercially exploited by *Xica* and has made it a huge success. However, it is not only sexuality which has made *Xica* a success, as sexually explicit images in Brazilian soap operas are the norm and have never been the sole cause of a telenovela's becoming a hit. It is more likely that a powerful discourse of colonial inequality, still alive on the continent, coupled with the centrality of the oppressed sexuality of both blacks and women account for *Xica*'s success. It is also this reconfiguration of colonial desire that has enabled a powerful resig-nification of western identity markers, with seduction and envy being central to this cultural-political reconfiguration.

Violante and Xica, the two leading female characters, highlight this process of resignification. Within the typical order of melodramatic structure, the two protagonists embody the moral struggle fought in the Tijuco between the forces of evil and good, as well as the more con-temporary forces embodied in this morality play: a threatening global modernity versus a local nondeveloped world identity. Violante, in the role of a white Portuguese woman, is the antiheroine, emblematic of all the "proper" morals and values that a colonial world envisions. She represents what is right and correct within the confines of official mo-rality as sanctioned by the Catholic Church and the colonial political structure. In opposition to this official morality stands the character of Xica, a former slave, who rivals Violante in striving to obtain ulti-mate public approval and, most important, an inner sense of agency and power.

Of course, the most ambivalent marker of this power struggle is (in keeping with the telenovela's melodramatic structure) the love object of both women: the white (also Portuguese) *comendador* and the power that his high office and status signify. Xica, as Violante's former slave, is able to win the *comendador*'s love, though he was Violante's fiancé, but Violante holds the official cards in her hand. Xica might be the one the *comendador* loves, but it is only Violante whom he can marry and recog-nize as his wife in the officially constrained social structure of colonial (and postcolonial) life. It is in the struggle between these two women, who encapsulate the town's aspirations for a pain-free existence, that the moral conflict of the telenovela unfolds. It is also in these complex and overburdened relationships that the telenovela is able to ensure its commercial commodification and its cultural resignification.

The telenovela visits a number of significant sites of contestation, impossible to outline (see Spivak 1999 for the issue of uncontainment within postcolonial analysis). The outcome for both "heroines" could not be more distinct. Contrary to the subversive element of the plot, it is Violante, not Xica, who ultimately marries the *comendador* and thus obtains the official status that she so consistently works for throughout the telenovela. It is Xica who is left behind in Portugal's colony, Brazil, with the *comendador's* children and his love but, significantly, without his body, his power, or the protection of his status and wealth.

Yet, in the final scenes these apparent resolutions are inverted (or resignified) over and over again. Even though Violante gets her wish and marries the *comendador,* whom she thinks she loves (though even the possibility of her being able to love is questioned throughout the telenovela), and, most important, gets the social recognition that she has striven for, she is abandoned by the *comendador,* who imprisons her in a mansion, never to see her again. We are reminded of the fate of the white Creole Bertha, who in Brontë's (2003) *Jane Eyre* is doomed to live in the attic for the rest of her life (see discussion below). We last see Violante running frantically around in circles in her plush prison before finally, with no more strategic resources at hand, accepting utter defeat and the maddening realization of the existence that colonial society has prescribed for her. Once again, the similarity between Violante and Bertha is staggering (see Spivak 1999). What if the greatest seduction is the promise of achieving what you have always wanted and finding it to be the most profound postcolonial nightmare?

On the flip side, Xica is unable to marry the love of her life, who comes one last passion-driven time to see her in Brazil before he is forced by political commitments to spend the rest of his life in Lisbon. She is left a free woman, with enough wealth to live comfortably, and with two children, a boy and a girl, who are the only emotional connections to her relationship with the *comendador.* But it is clear that she also has to pay the price for being who she is and for questioning being born into "historical relationships not of her making." This is the price of her ticket (in the Baldwinian sense): to live the rest of her days a single woman, without the one person who could quench her unending desire to love and be loved and, most important, recognize her as human.

In *Xica* we see modern and western productions of identity set against the backdrop of premodern and native existence. If Violante is representative of an officially powerful modern and white existence, Xica is the emblem of the local, postcolonial persona. It is not hard to imagine the varied identifications that these protagonists, and the whole melodramatic structure of *Xica,* evoke in a Latin American population oppressed since the sixteenth century. However, the semantic structures of the soap opera allow for even finer cultural distributions: unlike in *Betty la fea,* the modern ideal represented by Violante is neither morally right nor illusory in its traditionally exemplary mode.

Xica urges resistance to this modern ideal, representing it for what it is: mere nakedness behind the emperor's new clothes (see Sayer 1994). There is a direct line of evidence, as exemplified by Violante's madness, that buying into the official, developed ideal can only lead to hypocrisy in even the best of cases, and death (symbolic or "real"; see Žižek 2002; see also Butler, Laclau, and Žižek 2000) in the worst. In this case, the values are inverted, and it seems better to stay in one's original (supposedly authentic) identity than to play with these "civilizing" ideologies of seduction, death, and destruction.

But even this inversion is subtly disarticulated. The fact is that Xica ends far from the colonial subject portrayed at the beginning of the soap opera: she is no longer a slave; she is the wealthiest woman in town and, in the process, has overturned the two most traditional barriers of social identification, race and gender.

It is this process of resignification that is the single most seductive indication of the telenovela's commercial success and commodification. Xica is transformed at the end from the "traditional" postcolonial subject because that in itself was always an illusion and also because, and most important, her own envy of and seduction by the trappings of the west (European modernity and development) marked her whole existence, from the moment of her birth. And there is a price for this seductive transgression, for her envious desire to have what the others (civilized whites) have: she must live without her love object for the rest of her life. It is through this seductive process of envious desire that Xica is constituted as Xica, and so she is marked as yet another localized version, this time a Brazilian one, of a globalized western identity. It is to this ambivalent production of a local west (as all western identities truly are) that the last scene speaks with the marriage of Xica's daughter to the wealthiest bachelor in town in a ceremony performed by Xica's son, who is now a priest in the same church that condemned her to nonhuman oblivion. And this is also, perhaps, the reason for Xica's laugh, as her character merges with her daughter's in the last shot, to resignify the unending cycle of postcolonial subjection and ambivalent western identification. The audience sees Xica in her daughter's wedding dress, finally obtaining her fondest wish of human recognition.

THE (IN)CONCLUSIONS
OF WESTERN IDENTITY

All the mad conflicting emotions had gone and left me worried
and empty. Sane.
  I was tired of these people. I disliked their laughter and
their tears, their flattery and envy, conceit and deceit. And I
hated the place.
  I hated the mountains and the hills, the river and the rain.
I hated the sunsets of whatever colour, I hated its beauty and
its magic and the secret I would never know. I hated its indif-
ference and the cruelty which was part of its loveliness. Above
all I hated her. For she belonged to the magic and loveliness.
She had left me thirsty and all my life would be thirst and
longing for what I had lost before I found it.
—JEAN RHYS, *WIDE SARGASSO SEA*

This chapter posits the central complexity of western identity in its myriad forms. At an initial level we must explore the contradictions within the constitution of the west as an unquestioned (at least in public) and therefore unquestionable (as a result of this initial repression) global identity, even though, like all identities, especially hegemonic ones, this one is produced by contesting cultural scenarios and socioeconomic negotiations (see Gupta and Ferguson 1997). Hall (1997a, 1997b), among others (e.g., Mignolo 2000), has suggested the inextricable complexity of this local production that is so "successfully" effaced in the west's self-representation.

It is this twofold process of the local production of the west and the effacing of its local production that I have termed "fracturation." I use this term quite purposely to describe what I see as an inherently coupled process of western cultural production. Therefore, fracturation exposes the multiple incongruencies that are hidden in any attempt at creating a homogeneous identity: the process that is an essential component (as counterhegemonic strands are to hegemonic domination) of identity production (see Wylie 1995), and fracturation because it allows us to unveil that local production of western identity before it becomes a global west. This analysis is particularly difficult because the shift from local west to global west is not a tangible shift but, rather, an almost imperceptible moment of inherent reconstitution (see Butler 1997).

In their own provocatively insightful ways, however, both Fanon and Baldwin (as discussed above) address this "inherent reconstitution" not only in their work but in their lives as well. Thus, as with many other postcolonial thinkers who have taken on similar political interests and constraints, it is impossible to separate their work and their lives. It is also in this vein that the production and the analysis of a Latino/a subject in the latter part of the twentieth century may help us understand the local west's historical production (Anzaldúa 1987; Fusco 1995; Gómez-Peña 1996) along with the ambivalent resignification of Latin American telenovelas as a deeper understanding of western identity production.

In assessing the production of western Latino identity in the United States, however, I merely want to highlight, not enshrine as unique, a process that has been central to the constitution of Latin American identity, yet another form of local western identity. In this discussion of the ambivalent production of a Latino identity and the supposed incongruency between a globalizing west (i.e., the United States) and a local nonwest (i.e., Latin America), I wish to emphasize the role played by seduction and envy—that is, the desire for what one does not have and therefore what one is not—in the contested sites of localized western production.

This seduction is clearly present not only in the production of telenovelas but also in their successful commodification and reception by Latin American audiences throughout the continent. In them, through the use of melodrama, we see a particular form of western identity being produced in a local manifestation and then transformed into a global form of consumption or production. In both *Betty la fea* and *Xica* there is the seductive image of modernity, civilization, and a narrative of capital inscribed in the plots and bodies of those represented. At the same time, these scripts of capital themselves become the objects of desire. As a seductive reflection of their wants and needs, this global form of normalized existence compels audiences to watch. The assumption that we all want modernity and money is what best expresses melodrama's allure.

But it is important to point out that the audience does not suffer this seduction passively. Rather, viewers are agents in this process of envy and desire, since it is through them that the observed roles are lodged within local western production and transformed into a global western entity. The seduction does not occur outside of the production of a Latin American or Latino existence. This seduction allows its subjects to become who they are: people who want and desire to be something that they are not or cannot see themselves as being, that is, fully modern. In this sense, a Latino identity is a mirror of Latin American identity and what this particularly hybrid identity has meant for Native Americans for over five centuries. Therefore, what becomes important is not to distinguish the west from an absolute opposite but, rather, to understand how the west comprises differences which are later effaced by its seductive claim to global singularity.

This process is central to both the production of identities that, ambivalently, encompass their western and not-western elements and the west's production of itself. As I have stated, I do not believe this process of otherness, seduction, and envy or desire to be new. Jean Rhys permits the British employer of Jane Eyre, Rochester, to express it in his desire to be rid of the Caribbean reality (see the epigraph on page 63). It is only fitting to end this chapter with the opening lines from Rhys' (1982b: 7) *Voyage in the Dark,* as they reflect the voyage of a Caribbean woman to the metropolis, London. The lines express that effaced shift from local to global west which is so subtly hidden because it is at the core of west and nonwest identity production: "It was as if a curtain had fallen, hiding everything I had ever known. It was almost like being born again. The colours were different, the smells different, the feeling things gave you right down inside yourself was different. Not just the difference between heat, cold; light, darkness; purple, grey. But a difference in the way I was frightened and the way I was happy. I didn't like England at first."

This difference constitutes the slow but certain shift from local west to a global western existence. But it is also this difference that marks the hegemonic success and fracturation of the west, since, without difference, there could be no west. Betty's and Xica's characters succeed because they are able to obtain those things deemed desirable by the modern world, but their success comes at the cost of the fracturation of their previous identities and their ultimate seduction by a global other, that is, the west, as a "rightful" expression of the modern. It is in this seduction by desire that political relationships are inscribed, but it is also in the impossibility of ever fulfilling this seductive desire that the western project fails to completely efface all difference and at the same time secures its continuous production through these differences. It is also this ambivalent process of western production that is secured in the telenovela's successful cultural resignification of *latinidad* in the United States.

It is not a coincidence that oppressed groups like women, blacks, and homosexuals embody racialized desire and suffer the harsh backlash of desire's lack of fulfillment. Latin American and Latino identities are no different in this regard. If anything, a Latino identity is the latest to be constituted as not western in the global west, even as the latter is being constituted as a local by most of the populations of the world, including Latin Americans. It is this shift, so provocatively addressed in telenovelas, that needs to be further explored. However, questioning this identity shift is not so safe, as the troubled lives of Frantz Fanon, James Baldwin, and Jean Rhys, among others, demonstrate. It is not a simple endeavor to excavate one's identity and history only to learn that one has been the west's most treasured secret all these years, and that by fighting that identity one has succeeded only in anchoring oneself even more firmly to the global west's mythical production of itself, and through that process, of oneself, as well.

Four

KAREN'S SEDUCTION

The Racial Politics of Appropriate Dinner Guests

Colombian melodramatic production has seen a re-surgence since the 1980s, evidenced in the manufacture and export to the rest of the continent of a myriad of successful telenovelas. Among the most popular are *Pobre diablo* (Poor devil), *Adrián está de visita,* and *Pasión de gavilanes,* all three of which were preceded by the overwhelming success of *Betty la fea* (see Chaps. 1 and 2). *Betty la fea* opened up spaces not traditionally available to Colombian media. Its success was used to justify extending its run and to produce a sequel, *Ecomoda,* a highly atypical move.

Not surprisingly, *Ecomoda* did not enjoy its predecessor's success. However, these two, as well as all other Colombian telenovela productions, are indebted to an even earlier hybrid media experiment, an extremely successful, telenovela-like television series of the late 1980s called *Escalona.*

Escalona clearly marks a new stage in melodramatic representation, not only for Colombia specifically or the Andes in general, but for South America as a whole. *Escalona* was not a telenovela per se even though it built on the melodramatic format of telenovelas as well as on the rural musical tradition of the *vallenato.* The program also catapulted the main male actor, Carlos Vives, to international fame and sexual icon status, boosting his career first as a *vallenato* artist and currently as one of the most popular singers of tropical music on the continent.

Escalona differs from telenovelas in two main regards: it was not offered as a daily show but, rather, as a weekly hour-long program, televised on Sunday nights, and provided livelier outdoor settings than traditional telenovelas had done, using tragic outbursts only to highlight problematic situations rather than making a dark, tragic setting the main scenario for the plot line. *Escalona*'s main story is similar to the story line of telenovelas in that it develops a forbidden love affair between Rafael (played by Carlos Vives) and Maggi, which culminated in an eventful ending. Music (in the form of *vallenatos*) is central in developing the chief plot line, since Rafael is a songwriter/musician by profession. At the same time, this lower-class professional identity sets up a traditional class disparity that resonated loudly with Andean audiences, helping make *Escalona* a regional hit. The program would prove particularly innovative in this regard, since it introduced an Andean sensibility into the melodrama, an awareness that was lacking in the traditional Venezuelan, Brazilian, and Argentinean productions. As a hybrid, *Escalona* also introduces other literary elements, such as powerful magical realism (central to Colombia's and other South American literary landscapes) in the form of a scary, playful devil character, and a nostalgic rememorialization of a detached rural colonial landscape (see Rulfo 2003).

The success of *Escalona* is even more surprising when we take into account that the Colombian nation-state was immersed in one of the most violent civil struggles on the continent during the program's run. The presence of black characters is a major contribution to a different, and arguably a more realistic, representation of the Latin American melodramatic landscape. Unlike in previous telenovelas, in *Escalona* the black characters are not maids or servants, nor do they merely play the victim in a rags-to-riches story. Rather, the Afro-Colombian characters led a more "normalized" (in the sense of being both good and bad) existence, which again resounded powerfully with the large black population of the two other northern Andean nations, Peru and Ecuador.

A black character in a central role resurfaces in a more recent Colombian hit, *Adrián está de visita* (televised in the United States in 2002). In this instance, Adrián (an Afro-Colombian character played by a black actor) intrudes into a middle-class white household and questions their most deeply held social beliefs about class, race, sex, and normative decency. *Adrián está de visita* follows in *Escalona*'s footsteps in another way as well: by portraying a less-violent country in which colonial memory has been erased in the lush homes of the middle and upper class. However, this time the melodrama takes place in an urban setting in a sanitized version of a rural past that explodes into farce only during key dramatic moments. These perilous but measured interruptions in the melodrama also highlight the dangerous amnesia of the family (and, by correlation, most of the country's middle-class population) with regard to their colonial origins and legacies.

GUESS WHO'S COMING
TO DINNER, ANDEAN STYLE

One could easily argue that *Adrián está de visita* is loosely based on the 1967 Hollywood film *Guess Who's Coming to Dinner,* in which Katharine Hepburn and Spencer Tracy play the parents of a liberal household who are shocked by their own racism and elitist sense of middle-class privilege. In the Colombian telenovela, as in the film, the conflict is initiated by the white daughter's bringing her new love, a mysteriously successful black man, to dinner so he can meet the family. Of course, the initial reaction of the family, composed in *Adrián está de visita* of father, mother, brother, female cousin, maids, and an over-the-top blind aunt, is priceless in its melodramatization of an anti-black racism coupled with politically correct behavior. But if this luscious moment is prime for melodrama, Adrián's announcement that he does not love Karen, the daughter, that he has used her only to come into the family's home, and most important, that he is her half-brother only heightens the racial encounter and sets the central plot line of the telenovela in a twenty-first-century Andean context.

The telenovela presents Adrián, the central character, as the father's son by a former black lover, murdered under mysterious circumstances several decades before. The newfound son says that all he wants is to live in the same household as his father (and his family) to make up for his lifelong loss of economic and emotional support. The family's initial shock and resistance are defeated by Adrián's blackmail: if he is not allowed to live with them he will destroy the father's honor by letting everybody know of his forbidden sexual entanglement.

As the story advances, each family member is mesmerized and somehow shocked into "becoming alive" (in an emotional way that defies their previous sense of normative decency) by Adrián's inquisitive and mysterious presence. At the same time, Adrián's role is metaphorically enriched by its being represented in the opening credits of the telenovela by his shadow as well as by a threatening black cat walking in the garden, or even by his physically saving the niece from drowning.

With regard to the murder of Adrián's mother, initially we are privy only to a repetitive image of her being shot. The mystery progresses further with each family member's powerful emotional resolution. Karen's brother comes out as a gay man and falls in love with the maid's son (an extreme melodramatic opportunity used to exploit both men's beautiful physiques); the shy female cousin/niece turns into a fashion model and marries Karen's former fiancé, leaving behind her life of martyrdom and familial obligation; the mother remarries her high-school sweetheart, who, unlike her husband (Adrián's supposed father), is a faithful, loving, and supportive man. Meanwhile, it could be argued that Karen, the whitest representative of the family, is, ambivalently, saved from her nymphomaniacal tendencies and left wondering about her incestuous desire for her black sibling.

The father and the blind aunt, as the two main evil characters, provide different melodramatic characteristics in their ultimate demise. The blind aunt is killed by the police when she tries to shoot Adrián (she has secretly recovered her eyesight and not told anyone) after he discovers that it was she who murdered his mother. She committed the murder in an outburst of jealousy for the father's love and wrecked the car as she fled the crime scene. As a result of this crash she lost her eyesight and was (supposedly) condemned to blindness for the rest of her life (to be read as a spark of divine justice).

The drama, on the other hand, is too much for the father, whose continuous ordeal of trying to be the perfect Latin American man (i.e., "el hombre de Buchanan," or the Marlboro Man, as expressed in television commercials in the 1970s) while sustaining harsh professional and sexual schedules with little emotional outlet, kills him. He dies of a heart attack, but not before repenting for his unjust treatment of his family.

The telenovela presents a visiting Adrián who disrupts the social tranquillity and normative decency that this white middle-class family is feigning. At the same time, Adrián is able to restore the whole family to a lifestyle more in tune with their real desires (even if those desires are unconscious). Thus he sacrifices himself (the black man) for the good of the family (mainstream white society).

In many ways, however, *Adrián está de visita* allows an alternative reading in which one can read Adrián as the rightful master of the house, lord of his own emotions because he is acutely aware of his desires and unrelenting in his thirst for an authentic life and honest human relationships. The seduction of Karen, therefore, in both racial and sexual terms, provides a postmodern model for the acknowledgment of whites' colonial intrusion into the household of poor Indians and blacks throughout the Andes. It is not surprising and quite insightful that the large Indian population throughout the Andes is still absent from this telenovela's melodrama (and that of most others).

THE RACE QUESTION:
WHO IS VISITING WHOM?

Problematically perhaps, the manner in which the action is developed in *Adrián está de visita* would seem to favor understanding the white middle-class family as the rightful owner and Adrián as being the usurper of place and status. However, the melodrama's structure and its final outcome would seem to indicate otherwise. As Martín-Barbero (1987) highlights, telenovelas are about bringing the rightful or hidden identity to the surface and, through this process of rediscovery, recognizing the protagonists' "real" identity. Taking into account this melodramatic element helps to shift the initial superficial racial reading of the telenovela and allows a much more subversive understanding of the race politics implicitly determined by the program's structure and the audience's attraction to it. It is therefore both the family's and Adrián's initial identities that are hidden and subsumed and that need to be rescued from behind the social façade.

The final outcome also seems to signify an inversion of the traditional white hegemonic racial structure, since it is Adrián who not only brings the disaster down on the family but who, while doing so, also survives the family's demise. This particular development is significant in that it would be precisely the family member who grew up (supposedly) without a family support system and who (also supposedly) comes into the family's fold to feel the love and care that he has been forced to live without who is the strongest and the most aware of the demands of love within the family structure. The truth is that, even throughout the devastation of the family's downfall, it is Adrián who becomes the single trustworthy confidante of mother, brother, and niece alike. Even the father forgives him and repents his callous behavior in having denied his bastard child, literally, his black offspring, his love and support.

In many respects, however, it is Karen who carries the burden of the normative white racial structure. Her being the only blonde in the family seems to highlight a class and racial behavior routinely associated with white superiority. Among her white social markers are her job at a fashion magazine (one must remember that this is still war-torn Colombia) and her complete disdain (along with a concomitant fascination) for anybody below her racial/social status. This contempt for anybody with nonwhite racial features is so strong that, though she never questions her brother's homosexuality, she does protest his having chosen the maid's son for his lover. And yet it is this same contempt/attraction that makes her seek out two racially inferior lovers: Adrián, the prohibited black man; and her father's driver/bodyguard, who possesses strong *cholo* (mixed-Indian and Spanish heritage) characteristics.

Therefore, Karen's racial and sexual seduction is made even more symbolically forceful by the fact that it is she, the superior blonde female, who falls for precisely those defiled subjects whom she believes herself to be above and for whom she constantly (must) express contempt. Yet in many ways it is most telling that unlike the other family members, she is the one, as the whitest of them all, who is most vulnerable to the perils of her prohibited desires. It is also quite meaningful that, in making an attractive woman carry the burden of her race, *Adrián está de visita* also affords a series of seductive sexual images that help project the public's fantasy-filled representation of a seduced whiteness.

Karen's extreme racial representation is interesting in many ways, including its being women throughout the world who are typically made the representatives of their race (see Mallon 1996). This is expressed not so much in phenotypical depictions as in the meaning of traditional clothing. Even in the Andes it is the Indian woman who must wear traditional dress while the men are much freer to choose Western clothing.

The gender division of racial representation is also enacted by the father to a limited degree. As a man, and a Latin American man at that, he is able to have extramarital affairs without any public condemnation. Although it is clear that his unfaithfulness is not a topic for polite conversation, there is an ambiguous element in the recognition of his transgressive behavior. Therefore, even though his extramarital affairs are seen as transgressions that are made worse by his preference for black women, they are also in many ways his right not only as a man but as the head of the household. It is this transgressive sexual behavior, made more explicit by his racial preference for black women, that constitutes his vulnerable male identity. That identity entraps him to such a degree that it allows only one plausible resolution: his death.

This same gendered racial division of a representative burden is visible in the father's virulent reaction to his son's homosexuality and explains why it is not his son's lifestyle but his own honor that is on the line. The fragile male postcolonial identity has been provocatively engaged in both postcolonial academic and literary contexts and is one of the centerpieces of *Adrián está de visita*'s melodramatic attraction. The father's sexual transgressions, when compared to Karen's, let him off the hook quite easily if one looks at his not having to hide them or being worried about being shot by a spurned lover, as his daughter is. Yet the telenovela's resolution is based on the father's premarital racial/sexual transgression, since the family's demise has already been determined by his refusal to follow his heart, marry the woman he truly loves, and care for the child he knows is his.

The telenovela's dénouement is marked as much by the father's repentance as by the revelation that it was the aunt who murdered his lover (Adrián's mother). The aunt committed this murder out of envy and jealousy and without the father knowing about the crime or of her love for him. So again, it is the father who represents the most fragile gender on which the telenovela's melodramatic resolution depends. He appears to represent heterosexual men as having little room for negotiation. This depiction would seem to prove particularly seductive to a female audience, which, as the main viewers of telenovelas, knows gender discrimination so intimately. But precisely because of this gender inequality, women have much less to lose, and therefore a greater realm of negotiation and agency, because they do not rely on this absolute (and false) proud representation for the constitution of their gender.

This seduction of racialized black bodies, as performed by Karen and her father, however, also marks a deeper racialized understanding of the idea of rightful owners and visitors, as highlighted in the title of the telenovela. The brother is also caught in this particular racial/sexual seduction, but its enactment within a homosexual relationship serves only to further imply the hidden danger and darkness of love and forbidden desires (see the next section). As in many other postcolonial representations and mediums, the nagging colonial question of rightful ownership, memory, and historical inheritance is ever present in *Adrián está de visita*.

The fragile structure of this white family represents its unfair claim to the power and status that it has carefully crafted and strived to maintain. Even further, its need to protect itself from contaminating race and class markers belies its brittle position as master not only of its destiny but also of all those human beings under its social control. In many, and contradictory, ways it is the nonwhite character, in this case, Adrián, who serves as the psychoanalytic looking glass in which all the others see the reflection of their oppressive behaviors. It is ultimately, or should be, the self-knowledge gained from recognizing its savageness, cruelty, and sadism that will be the family's route to salvation. Once again we see a central concern of postcolonial identity reconstitution: What is one to do with a legacy of violence when one has internalized a vision of the violent colonizer as the civilized hero? This contradiction is further betrayed by the revolutionary fervor of many nativecentric postcolonial struggles (see Memmi 1991).

Therefore, the racialized representation in *Adrián está de visita* provides for an understanding of the postcolonial setting different from what one would initially understand from a superficial reading of mainstream popular images. The white family has everything to hide, including the fact that it has built a comfortable existence on lies and the exploitation of others and, more significant, on the repression of its own desires and a denial of its innate humanity. Thus all the family members must choose to reinforce their typically corrupt behavior or to use this moment of psychoanalytic disruption to live their lives in a more open and therefore more realistic manner. Yet for that internal shift, they must come down from Mount Olympus, where they have sat for ages passing judgment on everyone except themselves. It is this denial of their self-righteousness and perfect judgment that is, ultimately, too much for the father to bear, and for the aunt to survive.

The rest of the family, however, does choose to correct and amend its privileged, "colonizing" behavior. In the process, each family member accepts the need to violate her or his own sense of what had been assumed to be normative decency, which relates more to an austere sense of almost Victorian pride than to Latin American cultural norms. The brother must abandon the heterosexual male fantasy, which he never fully inhabited; the mother must accept the necessity of remarrying and allow herself to be vulnerable and an object of seduction; the niece must marry her cousin's former fiancé and prepare herself to be seen as a usurper even when she knows that not to be the case. It is this violent denial of their traditional way of life that allows the three to escape death (emotional or physical) and live for the first time with the acceptance of their desires and a closer approximation to who they truly are.

Only once they have made the ultimate sacrifice—becoming human and vulnerable—are they able to reinhabit their traditional family abode. But then come traps and pitfalls, one after another. Their less-than-pristine behaviors will no longer allow them to engage in their former racial discourse, thereby making it impossible to reclaim a white identity, since whiteness is defined by an inhuman and superior disposition and sensibility. So their newly accepted identities will allow them to live free of these racial constraints but will also mark them as the visitors (and usurpers) that they have always been. Their new and ambivalent social positioning is merely recognition of a former identification of them as the visitors that any true visitor, in this case, the black son, Adrián, can and will expose.

Adrián, however, is not free of racial entrapment, since he was able to "liberate" his family only through his own morally superior, undefiled, and chaste behavior. Because he represents the honest elements of dignity, responsibility, love, abnegation, and care, he is able to sustain himself against the family's aggression and unconscious adverse reactions (i.e., the return of the repressed; see Butler, Laclau, and Žižek 2000; Kristeva 1991; Lacan 1977). It is also this untarnished behavior that allows him to avenge himself on his father, who abandoned him and his mother at birth. It is also this subversive device of untarnished behavior that allows him to reclaim his position as the legitimate son, prodigal in many ways, and the rightful owner of the house, morally speaking.

Yet, the fact that Adrián must also resort to nonhuman, saintly behavior, no matter how honest the melodramatic structure represents it as being, expresses the racial conundrum that being yourself always provokes in postcolonial settings. It is this conundrum that many postcolonial writers and intellectuals feel the constant need to address. And as Baldwin's (1990: 481) last novel so passionately and succinctly notes, when the colonized manage to obtain their social identity/historical authority by recognizing the colonizer's history and nonhuman cultural legacy, "who then in such fearful mathematics is trapped."

THE SEXUAL QUESTION: . . . AND WHO'S REALLY COMING?

As in most contemporary telenovelas, sex and sexuality play a significant role in *Adrián está de visita*. Even though there are plenty of heterosexual encounters between almost every character, it is without a doubt the homosexual relationship between the brother and the maid's son that figures most prominently in the audience's imagination. Male homosexual characters have been more prevalent than female in Brazilian telenovelas, in which sexualized images are not only tolerated but also expected. A homosexual relationship in an Andean telenovela, however, provides a greater melodramatic frame within which to play out the sexual relationship of these two young men, primarily because of the more conservative sexual culture of Andean society and South America in general.

The fact that this homosexual relationship is never judged immoral, dirty, or abnormal further complicates any traditional heteronormative reading of *Adrián está de visita*. At every turn it is those who define homosexuality in harsh terms, the father and the aunt, who are considered the sick or immoral characters. This progressive treatment of male homosexual desire is further heightened by a therapist character who defines (in scientific terms) homosexuality as normal and insists on treating the father's and the aunt's homophobic behavior. It is this melodramatic representation of homosexuality and the fact of a central black character that are the most discussed elements of the telenovela. At the same time, these two elements may be viewed as an important component of the telenovela's transgressive attraction to Andean audiences, to audiences on the rest of the continent, and to U.S. Latinos.

The two male lovers are never seen having sex, touching each other in an erotic fashion, or even kissing each other on the lips. Their homosexual love is represented by a portrayal of male friendship and companionship akin to fraternal love in ancient Greece (see Boswell 1980). Only once are the two men seen in a hotel bed, where they are found by the father after Adrián tips him off. And even then they are fast asleep, as any two heterosexual men sharing the same bed might be.

A question immediately comes to mind: What is the consequence of the centrality of this representation of homosexuality, and why must it be so sanitized to make it a successful melodramatic production? At one level, the taboo on homosexual behavior and the normative homophobia in the Andes and throughout Latin America would seem to warrant this treatment of the material (Horswell 2005; Lancaster 1996; Parker 1991). After all, it is this heteronormative outlook that holds enormous political sway even in the face of tremendous historical reasoning against it (Benavides 2002; Trexler 1995). Yet despite or, more accurately, because of widespread homophobia, a homosexual relationship is an incredibly attractive object for the millions of viewers who are trying to escape this same oppressive normative order, even if it is only for an hour a day.

Thus this particular expression of homosexuality becomes more coherent in its attractive representation of erotic images as not immediately menacing. Melodramatic homosexual relationships are represented as less threatening while still providing an excuse for admiring the beautiful bodies of both male lovers. Interestingly, this male homoerotic relationship is sustained by the presence of two sisters who take the couple in when they are thrown out of their respective homes. These sisters, cabaret singers by profession, are older (both are in their sixties), and their bohemian lifestyle has made them much more tolerant of sexual difference. To the shock of both men, the women have fewer problems with the lovers' homosexuality than even they do.

The presence of these sisters is also telling in several regards. For one thing, it reintroduces an element of sibling alliance or sisterhood/brotherhood as representative of the nation. This national reading is particularly meaningful, since the whole telenovela could be understood as a morality play about the potential danger for a family (or nation) that refuses to accept its sons and daughters because they are black or gay—that is, different—into the fold and instead proclaims them as illegitimate. The playful, wise demeanor of the sisters seems to represent a more mature way in which to live and, more important, serves as a blueprint for the nation. Instead of wasting energy by responding violently to social differences, sexual or otherwise, the sisters' way of life leads one to ask, why not incorporate differences and use them to laugh, sing, and drink to life's follies? This is after all why telenovelas are so popular, because they provide a space for escape from the abundant social hardship in the daily life of Latin Americans.

The other element that the sisters' relationship brings out—incest—is a bit more disturbing. However, this incestuous element also relates to one of the central themes, the incestuous relationship between Karen and Adrián. In many ways, therefore, the two unmarried sisters would seem to represent a sexless lesbian relationship, strongly mirroring the sexless one between the men. However, in the sisters' case, the sex is prohibited by a strong incest taboo that permeates the national (and continental) social body. But once again this particular melodramatic structure is pregnant with meaning, seemingly providing for an asexual understanding of harmonious human relationships marked, significantly, by very strong and stable homosocial ties.

Congenial homosocial relationships, especially in the case of the two men, seem to be in direct conflict with the enormous struggle that the decision to love each other has provoked. It is precisely because the men have chosen to step out of the heteronormative order that they are being punished, however unjustly, as the telenovela takes pains to demonstrate. It is, however, only outside the heteronormative order that they can fulfill their prohibited desires, however chastely those desires are represented. The telenovela uses these homosocial bonds to represent an ambiguous message that is meaningful to an overworked and underrepresented audience: live your greatest desires, however wrong they may be deemed by the strict social conventions. Yet this particular route would seem to mean either sublimating sexual desire or abstaining, which is what same-sex relationships, as less prone to conflict-driven drama, would seem to condemn one to.

It is quite interesting that even a homosexual plot line needs to present a heteronormative structure to transcend the surface representation of this sexual preference. Male–female sexual exchanges are still seen as the most central form of social interaction and reproduction, which is why they are so infused with extreme forms of conflict and violence. So, despite, or contained within, a new, less-violent form of homosocial order a kind of sexual frustration is hidden, since this order would impede not only any form of social reproduction but also any passionate transformation. Endorsing homosexual alliances, then, seems like moot advice, because such an endorsement would represent an alternative, congenial, lifestyle with no relationship to the chaotic ambiguity of real life.

At the same time, it is very meaningful that heterosexuality figures as the only form of social reproduction (not limited to the biological realm), and its representation as infused with conflict is implied but not explicitly addressed in *Adrián está de visita*. Therefore, the violent sexual conflicts arise among the heterosexual characters, who fight, shoot each other, and sully their family's name because of their inability to control their (hetero)sexual desires. Not surprisingly, Adrián is never allowed to be involved with any woman in a meaningful sexual relationship, and the homosexual characters find themselves in a similar situation. The price of a stable social order seems to be a structure in which it is necessary to deny one's sexual desires, desires that can only be heterosexual.

It is within this heteronormative order that one can clearly see the visual economy of representing homosexuality, at least male homosexuality, in such a supposedly progressive manner, since there is no doubt that homosexuality is still being sustained by the dictates of ambivalent homophobic desire. In this instance, once again the ambiguous melodramatic structure succeeds in playing both sides against one another to maintain a melodramatic unity that most of the audience can identify with. So, despite a supposedly blatant homosexual relationship's being presented on television, one has only to scratch the surface to recognize that relationship's unreality and the deeper social structures that produce such an effect of power (see Foucault 1980). These reified structures make it necessary to erase the centrality of the heterosexual relationship and maintain it through the familiar façade of alternative sexual difference. Again, homophobic or not, the homosexual difference is put to the service of heterosexual desire in defining the outcome of all social conflict. This particular device is a profoundly familiar configuration for all those caught in the melodramatic production of telenovelas and people's representation of their own lives throughout Latin America.

But like all successful melodramatic representation, nothing is only one thing all the time. Despite the clear underlying heteronormative structure of the homosexual façade, there are clear alternatives that are represented in the implied approval of the love of these two men. Therefore, the politically correct treatment of their love, the wisdom implied by the sisters' experiences, and the ultimate, more likely, feminine understanding of the homosexual relationship all seem to provide possible escapes from the underlying sexist, postcolonial patriarchy. And again, the telenovela is the perfect vehicle for presenting these disturbing future memories, however contained they wish to or must be represented (Spivak 1999).

DESIRE'S PROBLEMATIC CENTRALITY: THE RETURN OF ONESELF AND THE COLONIAL PAST

Adrián está de visita plays on the ambiguous production of prohibited desire. Like all successful melodramas this Colombian telenovela also makes use of desire, particularly but not exclusively sexual and racial, as its pivotal production piece. The interest shown by Karen toward Adrián frames the initial structure and plot, which revolves around the forbidden love of a white woman for a black man and incestuous desire for a sibling. Knowing that Adrián is her brother does not instantly kill Karen's love and lust for him; rather, it heightens her feelings. It is quite significant that even at the end of the telenovela the last image of Karen is of a woman still deeply troubled by her sexual attraction to a person who might be her brother. Equally important is her ambivalence toward him even after he has caused her demise, that of her family, and of her skewed understanding of herself as a superior white woman.

This portrayal of incestuous desire quickly displaces the notion that falling in love with a family member is not as unlikely as we have been led to believe. Instead of the visceral, almost genetic, avoidance that we expect, *Adrián está de visita* seems to be telling us that there is nothing to stop us from desiring and having sex with immediate family members except the same social norms that limit and frustrate the desires of many viewers. This initial incestuous element is reemphasized by the prevalence of such relationships in Latin American society, especially between fathers/uncles and children who are conveniently erased from people's memory (Amado 1967). Once again, *Adrián está de visita* brings up this prohibited subject in a nonaccusatory way, all the while knowing that it is building on the audience's experience of incestuous relationships in a much friendlier way than is usually tolerated in public.

Again we have the ambiguous attraction of melodrama in that it can present incest without moral judgment and make the incestuous man, in this case, Adrián, the hero. It is clear that Adrián's openness about what he is trying to do, like Macbeth's in his final scene, makes him more appealing to an audience trained to keep its plans and strategies a secret, many times even from itself. It is this postcolonial reality of internalized repression that is kept actively in check by the legacy of social convention, which, as fodder for melodrama, allows pleasurable release.

Karen's incestuous desire and Adrián's honest pursuit of it are similar ways in which to present (and digest) a type of problematic desire that would otherwise be impossible to admit or represent. The central place of desire in our social and self-identification makes it a fruitful element for melodramatic production. In many ways, *Adrián está de visita* addresses the almost daily reality of having to deny one's intimate desires, and therefore oneself, to be able to represent who one should, and has learned, to be. In this case, self-abnegation is even more dramatically enacted when the secret is no longer our own, and the wall that imprisons an almost infinite desire is not as insurmountable as we have convinced ourselves it is.

Adrián está de visita seems to problematize two essential elements traditionally intertwined with desire: desire's central position in defining who we are; and the role of the past in creating that desire. Thus, admitting to desire within the framework of the telenovela allows the characters to face who they really are and to abandon the mask that they have been wearing, almost to the point of exhaustion, most of their lives. One could argue that it is the denial of self which has constituted the characters' lives (see Butler 1997), since in many ways it is these masks that define who the characters are, even if their intimate feelings and attractions are denied. It is also in this manner that desires, both denied and recognized, are equally linked to the particular role that the past has had in shaping a changing sense of self as well as self-projection into the past and future (see Kincaid 1997). When the telenovela addresses the role of desire in incestuous and racial terms, there is undoubtedly a strong reaction among viewers.

The Andes has had, not surprisingly, a different historical evolution from that of other regions of the continent. Like Mexico and Central

America, it participated extensively in the African slave trade but, unlike in Mexico and Central America, the descendants of former slaves are a significant part of the population. Adrián's position as a major character in many ways seems to reflect this Andean reality. Even though the presence of a successful black man is not socially impossible in the Andes, it is rare enough that his image must be sanitized or, more dramatic, tempered with very modern forms of political correctness and containment. There is still, however, an enormous and exotic fascination with this other's body, which, having been vilified and ostracized for centuries, cannot but hold an incredible psychological fascination for those who, ambivalently, deny a prohibited desire.

Adrián está de visita succeeds precisely because it is able to maintain this tension of desire as an element of postcolonial domination without ever engaging it or, even more important, judging it. True to its artistic commitment, the telenovela looks to entertain, but to do so it must hold the public's attention in a way that does not allow viewers to feel rejected by the images. This is the sentiment that the popular *norteña* artist Ana Bárbara succinctly captures in a popular song: "Me gusta, pero me asusta" (I like it, but it scares me; see Chap. 4 for further discussion of *norteña* music, including Mexico's racist reaction to Ana Bárbara's choice of a black Dominican artist, Julio Zavala, as her boyfriend). The beautiful black man's body is placed center stage and, as in the time of slavery, it is he who serves as the catalyst for the production of the social and visual structure that is being created before and within the public at one and the same time.

There is no fear associated with desiring this black man or his body, since what we see now is somebody whose class has been sanitized to make it worthy of our interest. However, Adrián's melodramatic parody of sainthood evidences even further the danger that the black body still holds for Latin Americans' self-image. The crux of the matter is this: this desire still holds an important place in all of the Andean nations' social and ideological reproductive structures, or *Adrián está de visita* would have failed. The telenovela's success marks a racial fault line that represents an ambivalent desire impossible to resolve; a step to either side could mean the transgressor's demise or, most dangerous, the bringing down of the structure that is relying on that desire's ambiguity.

This is the fault line that Karen has crossed and is thus the social boundary that her whiteness has clearly demarcated for her since childhood. Her transgression brings into question her essence, in racial and gendered terms. What comes into play, therefore, is the reproduction of a racial form of whiteness, as a class/status marker comprising its nonhuman lifestyle parameters.

This is where the whole family falters; each member has to save herself or himself, since the fabric of their racial (and therefore) familial relationships and identities has now unraveled. Karen is transformed into a nymphomaniac, which makes sense in the melodrama. The racial transgression is too problematic to bear, so it must be made into an individual mistake even though a couple of episodes before Karen's transformation she exudes the power of white racial representation for the whole family. And she represents the superior whiteness not only in a way that nobody else does but also in a manner which is impossible to sustain after her social demise.

It is this same mistake that Karen's mother makes in a vulnerable moment, when she is seduced by Adrián. As happened with Karen, the same pivotal racial desire is casting its spell, and once again the audience is watching anxiously and with pleasure. However, the mother's "mistake" is only momentary, as she quickly regains her head (and, with it, her place) while we learn that, yet again, this has been a ploy on the self-righteous Adrián's part to release the mother's dormant passion. But his reason is to allow himself to be a catalyst for this passionate awakening but not the object of its ultimate sexual fulfillment; for that the mother will have her new white, middle-class husband.

If the black male body seems to work as a catalyst for awakening all the other characters from their zombielike historical erasure, the image of the murdered black woman also shatters this historical amnesia. In many regards, Adrián's sexual agency can be tolerated, however self-righteous, but a black woman's agency cannot. The murder of Adrián's mother and the father's love for her are melodramatic representations of an equally deep resentment of the agency of black female sexuality. As Mallon (1996) has elaborated (see also Menchú 1998, 1995), throughout the colonial enterprise in Latin America, Indian, mestizo, and black female sexuality served as the tabula rasa on which white and male schemes were inscribed. When either of these racialized and engendered bodies dared move out of its sustaining role, it could only be met with the murderous rage of the mainstream, that is, white people, primarily men, who refused to see their superior positioning upstaged.

This is the central desire on which the telenovela develops its story line: bringing us in and out of the view of the abysmal depths of the colonial encounter between populations of Europeans, Indians, Africans (all in their own ethnically diverse formulations) and from which a new postcolonial reality emerged. But it is to the telenovela's credit that this primal desire is given such a pivotal role and that it refuses to resolve the racial conflict in simplistic and unrealistic terms. Perhaps this is where the incest element helps to maintain the ambivalent desire and the effects of its nonresolution, because resolving the racial conflict would still leave the problem of falling in love with one's brother intact. The problem is what happens when you love your brother (*prójimo*), who is also black and who has been excluded from your line of sight for so long. Karen's last words in the telenovela express her speculation about who Adrián really is. Adrián, her words seem to imply, not only is here to stay but has been here all along.

THE INDIAN IRRESOLUTION
OF AMBIVALENT CONFLICTS

The viewers of *Adrián está de visita* experience an even greater shock at the telenovela's ending. The aunt dies after admitting to the murder of Adrián's mother; the father repents and dies as well; and the whole family drama clears with each individual accepting his or her newfound true state. Only then are we allowed to learn the full truth about Adrián.

As it turns out, Adrián is not really the father's son or Karen's (half) brother. His outright lie doubly confounds all the fears initially expressed concerning accepting a bastard black child as the father's son. For starters, the whole telenovela has progressed on the premise that there is really little reason (other than blatant racism) to deny this unsavory truth. The fact that it turns out to be a lie only dramatizes how much of what we believe to be acceptable is a result of social assumptions (either conservative or progressive) rather than any kind of empirical or objective truths (see Hellmann 1980).

As Adrián explains, he is the son of the murdered woman and a father described as a "good man" whom his mother decided to leave to continue her passionate involvement with Karen's father. Adrián meets his biological father's other son (Adrián's half-brother) just hours before the half-brother dies. His half-brother explains to Adrián how having been abandoned by both his mother and his father condemned him to a life of crime and living on the streets. A life spent in orphanages and gangs and using drugs took its toll, and he is dying at a young age, as many poor young men in Colombia do. As a last wish he asks Adrián to pretend to be him and to take vengeance on his father and his father's family for the love and emotional and economic support which should have been his. Adrián takes up the task with enormous zeal and manages to convince everybody that he is somebody whom he really is not—something Latin Americans do daily.

This surprise is surpassed only by the fact that Adrián is actually a religious novice, and the final scene of the telenovela sees him responding affirmatively to becoming a priest and dedicating himself completely to the Catholic Church. All of his lying, deceit, and sex and the turmoil he has created have been a ploy to test his vocation and lead him to an understanding of how sinful and vain the world truly is. The knowledge that he was never who he portrayed himself to be and was in fact even purer than he appeared further confounds the telenovela's melodramatic production of identity and self-representation. The fact that Adrián is playing a role and hiding who he really is serves as a self-reflective model for what the whole telenovela is doing in terms of melodramatic representation at a more general level.

A surprise ending is fairly standard in telenovelas, although *Adrián está de visita*'s double surprise is more dramatic than most. However, this double reformulation emphasizes the unresolved legacy of identity, plagued as it is by the specters of colonialism and postmodern production. It is this same shifting identity that, provocatively, questions the nature of Latin Americans and how they are stereotypically portrayed in neocolonial media representations to the rest of the world mainly as having corrupt governments and suffering catastrophic events.

The telenovela's outcome securely ties up the loose ends of the initial tensions it proposed, even though some ambiguity remains. As a morality play *Adrián está de visita* visually questions issues of race, family, class, gender, and status as modes of identity production that are vital to both the melodrama's success and the audience's existence. By introducing the audience to an area of uncertain identity and self-representation, *Adrián está de visita* is able to subtly spell out the inconsistencies in Andean social life—ranging from the colonial legacy to the overstrained neocolonial domination of its territory—that constantly vex the population. It is as if these factors, present in daily life, are traditionally excluded from view or forced to be seen in isolation. They cannot be captured in their full complicatedness and confusion, just as happens in real life.

This is clearly one of the glories of successful melodrama, and *Adrián está de visita* is a good example of subverting hegemony by doing what the official rhetoric refuses to acknowledge, thereby recognizing the chaotic and political nature of daily life. And the telenovela is able to do this because its wish to understand the social truths behind the normative façade stems from a displaced sense of entertainment (and pleasure) that must reign supreme if it is to be economically viable.

Yet the double bind is also clear: if the telenovela is to succeed, it must do so by truthfully engaging its audience while at the same time flying under the normative radar of cultural and intellectual production that makes the same arguments in other, more culturally elite, settings obsolete.

Thus this telenovela's handling of racial and (homo)sexual conflict must be done in this twofold manner to subversively capture the audience's ambivalence about the subject but without looking to educate/sermonize in a similarly normative manner. And this is something the telenovela does very well. As discussed earlier, both Adrián and the two men involved in the homosexual affair are presented in such a way that they do not question the most conservative modes of decency. Even though their mere presence sets the scene for subversive unraveling, constant tension is created by the suspense built around how far they will go in each episode, as each program pushes the scenario further but still keeps it from unacceptable transgression. In this matter, this telenovela seems to do what Foucault (1998: 73) elaborates in terms of transgression, that is, recognize the limits of normative behavior by reinserting yet another and new transgressive limit:

> Transgression is an action that involves the limit, that narrow zone of a line where it displays the flash of its passage, but perhaps also its entire trajectory, even its origin; it is likely that transgression has its entire space in the line it crosses. The play of limits and transgression seems to be regulated by a simple obstinacy: transgression incessantly crosses and recrosses a line that closes up behind it in a wave of extremely short duration, and thus it is made to return once more right to the horizon of the uncrossable.

Foucault's (1998) understanding of transgression is particularly useful because it serves to describe that liminal stage of unfulfillment that both subverts and maintains transgression at one and the same time. Transgression is a particular area of productive tension, very clearly outlined by Genet (in both his life and work; see Taussig 1992; White 1993), that serves to reemphasize the contradictorily constitutive nature of cultural production, in particular, the most successfully engaging ones (see Taussig 1992). In many ways, transgression is a key component of *Adrián está de visita,* and by using this particular social mechanism the program constantly maintains the ambivalence between officializing norms, politically correct sermonizing, and seductive ambiguity, all of which only enhance the prohibitive pleasure, entertainment, and objectives of all telenovelas.

Adrián está de visita asks audience members to transgress into personal areas in which their desire for a forsaken black body can be successfully maintained, that is, to a place where that forbidden desire is no longer the object of official censorship and may rival that same normative discourse in terms of normative culture and values. Yet this transgressive scenario is maintained precisely because it is not supposed to be part of daily life but only an entertaining hour of escapist television.

The popularity of such transgressive scenarios, however, marks a "real" understanding that this unspoken desire in many ways marks a constitutive foundation behind the officializing norms they hear daily. This transgressive representation is something the telenovela does quite well and to such a degree that the conflicts of the urban middle-class family in *Adrián está de visita* speak to that transgressive fantasy that is allowed only in the most intimate moments of daily life or in projected forms of pleasurable escape, precisely because that pleasure is marked by the relief that escape allows. It is also an escape that is afforded because the accusatory definition of, from what, or why never has to be spelled out explicitly.

The racialized desire of the other and the constitutive rejection of whiteness as elemental in Andean life are but two of the most salient transgressive elements that *Adrián está de visita* ambiguously projects. Homosexuality, incestuous desire, and sibling love and rivalry are some of the myriad elements that are also constitutive of this melodrama and unevenly maintain the audience's fascination. But we must still ask why the other is constituted by a black and not an Indian (Native American) body, and what the ambivalent elements of enslavement, as opposed to purely genocidal practices, are that are present throughout this melodrama? In other words, why do Andeans still share the continent's melodramatic tendency to not display Indian (Native American) bodies, since it is clearly this silent (or ignored) Indian figure that is framing *Adrián está de visita* and, I would say, all or most Andean telenovelas. There is something quite relaxing about dealing with issues of race and sex, as this telenovela does, that are one step removed from daily life, precisely because the audience is not so removed. Thus a twofold game of representation is being played, not only on the television screen but also in the audience's imagination, where tension between what viewers see and what they know is constantly reproduced and ambivalently maintained.

It is on the absence of this ostracized Indian body that, I would argue, *Adrián está de visita* relies the most for its success. It is also Colombia's position, along with Chile's, of being the Andean country with the smallest Indian population that allows for its particular Latin American view of what Andean society (as a regional expression) is or should be. Again, the melodramatic medium is perfect for this because it does not need nor is it supposed to engage with real life, yet its explicit denial of real life is but another way of directly engaging it at its most chaotic. As Beckett (1976: 25) notes, it is another way of failing again, failing better.

The lack of Indians in *Adrián está de visita* marks the continuing realistic representation of Andean and Latin American audiences in their contemporary historical imagination. It addresses Andeans' and Latin Americans' inability to see themselves in the ways proposed by the globalizing neocolonial demands of the First World. The Indian body is too close to home even to play with, since in many ways it is the nation, not only in the official rhetoric but also in the production of their historical experience as masters and victims of a social process set in motion without their say-so. Adrián and white Europeans might be visiting, but Indians have never left home, and that is a melodramatic secret that is retold in every frame of Andean (and Latin American) telenovelas.

Five

A MOTHER'S WRATH AND THE COMPLEX DISJUNCTURING OF CLASS

*P**asión de gavilanes* is the latest Colombian melodrama to find success throughout the continent. On the air in the early 2000s, it had strong production support from U.S. Latino media based in Miami. This support explains the telenovela's more homogeneous Latin images and the strong Tex-Mex influence on its music and plot.

Pasión de gavilanes takes place in an unidentified rural landscape of large landholdings (haciendas) and familial conflicts. The central plot concerns class conflict between a widowed landholder (and her daughters) and three brothers (the Reyeses) who are seeking revenge for their dead sister. As the story unfolds we learn that the sister was the widow's deceased husband's lover and that after being cruelly treated by him she threw herself off a bridge to her death. The goal of revenge is abandoned, however, when the three brothers fall in love with the family's three beautiful sisters and one by one get involved with then marry them.

The telenovela's subplots, as one would expect, are numerous and complicate the story line even further. The subplots contribute to a shift in which the three brothers become financially successful and are able to buy the land adjoining the hacienda. One by one the daughters, the servants, and the daughter of the mother's best friend end up living on the Reyes brothers' estate. This shift from a traditional estate (that of the widow) to a more progressive one (the one belonging to the Reyeses) seems to take advantage of the myth of modernity and its allure of better living through technology, in this case represented by new wealth and class status. Thus, especially within the violent Andean setting of Colombia, the hacienda appears to represent the enormous socioeconomic shift symbolized by a new class able to acquire wealth and that is questioning the traditional elite structure inherited from colonial times, even though the patriarchal structure seems to be left intact.

Many scholars have addressed this violent socioeconomic shift, particularly in the urban settings of Medellín, Bogotá, and Cali. The drug trade has led to new wealth for oppressed and exploited male urban youth, who have had few other financial options. The drug trade at first also brought about a continuation of and increase in urban political and social violence, inherited from the years of military and guerrilla warfare in most of Colombia's southern hinterlands. Thus, between an ongoing guerrilla offensive aimed at toppling the government and a growing drug trade that opened up a new continental market, violence and the hiring of body guards and hit men became another economic enterprise that allowed poor young men to escape the despair of working- and lower-class existence.

The movies *Rodrigo D. no futuro* (Rodrigo D. no future), and *La virgen de los sicarios* (Our Lady of the Assassins, a dramatization of César Vallejo's novel), released in the late 1980s and in 1994, respectively, capture the anomie and void created by a culture of violence and historical resentment against the traditional elite and middle class. In some ways, the Reyes brothers represent the melodramatic version of this class struggle. They symbolize good boys with a sincere belief in social betterment and political empowerment as a way to help their own kind. It is this reality, viewed in the light of the new economic opportunities offered by the drug trade and associated violence, that allows new forms of upward mobility that many have referred to as an economic democratization of Colombia's resources. *Pasión de gavilanes,* however, because it is a melodrama, is able to represent the good side of this "democratic" process without dwelling on the problematic and negative connotations. In melodrama these darker images are always contained and have greater effects within the narrative, as is the case with *Pasión de gavilanes.*

One such representation is the contemporary historical proximity of Colombia and Mexico as noted in *Pasión de gavilanes'* theme and music. The drug trade and its related culture of violence seem the most obvious link between both countries, particularly Mexico's northern region. It is also this drug link that is most visible in Mexico's production of narco-dramas and the accompanying use of melodrama by both telenovelas and narco-dramas to express in a succinct manner the conundrums and contradictions of contemporary Latin American existence. Prime among these Mexican markers are the music in *Pasión de gavilanes* and the central role played by music in telenovelas in general; this is therefore not a minor correlation.

The Tex-Mex *norteño* and *cumbia* genres are used throughout *Pasión de gavilanes* and in its theme song. This is quite provocative considering that *cumbias* were originally Colombia's primary national musical expression and that a transnational reinterpretation of the genre might have warranted hostile or xenophobic reactions. But the Mexican version of the *cumbia* not only seems to have appealed to the Colombian audience but also to have made the production that much more appealing to a continental market, including Mexicans and the Latino population in the United States. It does not hurt that the *cumbias* accompany the appearance of several voluptuous female cabaret singers as central characters, or that the club where they work is one of the main settings. The club is totally (and eerily) inhabited by Colombians but totally decorated (including musically) with a complete Tex-Mex sensibility. It is as if a plane full of Colombians had landed in the expansive regions of northern Mexico and adapted themselves and their music to the region. This is exactly what, in a melodramatic sense, has happened, and *Pasión de gavilanes* takes advantage of and exploits this metaphor to its last seductive drop.

Rancheras and Mexican-influenced *boleros* are also used to highlight moments of romantic and desire-filled resolution. Prime among these is when the widow decides to marry a younger man and give in to her erotic desires; it is these genres that mark the increased melodramatic tension.

The music emphasizes the transnational relationship between the Colombian and the Mexican realities but it is by no means the only way in which these connections are exemplified. A narco-sensibility of authoritarian behavior (by both males and females), big cars, fancy clothes, and a thug ethos mark *Pasión de gavilanes* throughout. The narco-sensibility is most contradictorily expressed in the fact that the worst thug turns out to be a woman, Dínora Rosales, who, inverting the patriarchal structure, rapes and kills men at will.

The lack of geographical referents makes it even easier to believe that *Pasión de gavilanes* takes place in a mythical location between Colombia and Mexico; the viewer does not have to worry too much where exactly this place is or even if it really, empirically speaking, exists. The most specific national Colombian marker is the actors' accent, but the large hacienda landscape also allows the program to have a general Latin American feel. *Pasión de gavilanes* takes place in a cowboy border landscape of feudal control in which the state's authority and the police, just as in real life, have very little power unless they are complicit in the illegal workings of the gunmen. At the same time, the closely related drug sensibility of Colombian and Mexican counterparts speaks to a much greater realm of melodramatic imagination shared by the continent as a whole, if we look at the configurations of both communities.

One of the most interesting elements in the consumption of this shared historical imagination is that the soap opera is able to cash in on this violent ethos without introducing the problematic elements of drug trafficking or guerrilla warfare, issues that might be too close to home for both Colombians and Mexicans. However, the drug trade–inspired historical imagination is kept alive with the very real presence of violence and shootings. This particular image is embodied in several different characters besides Dínora Rosales, including two very scary thugs/ bodyguards. The bodyguards, although quite intimidating, also provide enormous comic relief by committing their violence in an awkward or jumbled fashion. Thus their death toward the end of the soap opera, as they crash into the car of an old couple (one of whom is completely senile) that they are supposed to kill, makes melodramatic sense.

In equally melodramatic fashion, however, the central violent figure, Dínora Rosales, in some ways echoes her Mexican counterpart, Teresa Mendoza, the main character of the novel *La reina del sur* (see Chap. 8). Dínora is by far the most cold-blooded of all the characters, as well as the strongest. She has murdered, kidnapped, shot at, raped, and intimidated scores of men, but we are privy to her obsession with Juan (the eldest of the Reyes brothers). She is madly in love with him but devastated at being rejected by him. Her violent demeanor is so intimidating and seductive that the two other evil stock male figures are completely enthralled by her (as the audience is also supposed to be).

Dínora Rosales, like Teresa Mendoza, falls into a particular Latin American tradition of strong women (*mujeres fuertes*) who in their own way both empower women and play into the patriarchal male heterosexist fantasy. On the one side, they exemplify the complete subversion of a traditional *machista* reading of society in which women are not men's equals (but are, even worse), when it comes to public (and violent, abusive) behavior. At the same time, however, this voracious, superior (Spider) Woman (the Latin version of Wonder Woman, Mujer Maravilla o Mujer Araña; see Puig 1986) also falls into the descriptive fantasy of what straight men really want: a counterpart stronger than they to subdue them without their having to accept any responsibility (or guilt) for wanting things like love and tenderness, which Latin society has placed out of their masculine, heterosexual reach.

Dínora Rosales, and the telenovela as a whole, expresses a deeper transnational relationship immersed in greater norms and desire for what it is to be a man or a woman in Latin America today, or what it has always supposed to have been. Strong women, like Dínora, allow men to express a hidden side and to publicly fantasize about things so prohibited that even to think about them would be grounds for destroying their idealized manhood. This hidden longing would also make them the target of ridicule for not being the men that they have always presented themselves as being, or what Latin manhood is supposed to be all about. At the same time, however, Dínora also emblematizes a scarier underbelly of the recognition of violence, one in which neither sex has a monopoly over violence but, rather, shares it throughout the continent.

It is violence in its fully gendered expression that is embodied by Dínora Rosales and the men in the soap opera fascinated by her. She is an extreme, fetishized objectification of violence, which in many ways is the central theme of Colombia and Mexico's transnational interaction. It is also the class element, intertwined in this gender ascription, that makes the transnational element that much more real and ambivalently successful. Both gender and class serve as historical markers of needs, wants, and repressed desires that are not only never fully resolved but also, more important, are seldom sincerely examined. It is in this area that melodrama, with its primal turning upside down of events, its gangster women and soft men, is most seductively successful. Class thus continues to be the ambivalent postcolonial specter that is never too far from us and yet always escapes our attention, especially in its most intimately powerful and concrete manifestation of cultural production.

CLASS(IC) DISJUNCTURES

Class, along with race, has been the subject of close scholarly analysis in Latin America since the beginning of the twentieth century. From the work of Marxist scholars such as Mariátegui (1955) to the more current work of poststructural theorists like de la Cadena (2000) and Lancaster (1996), class has served as a tool to assess the historical inequality on which Latin American culture is based. Class differences have also never been overlooked by telenovelas, including *Pasión de gavilanes*. However, what melodrama brings to the table is the much more intimate manner in which it is engaged in this milieu, as class is related both to new (representationally speaking) forms of expression and to a much more fluid, relational (less-static) way of assessing it.

In many regards, the drug trade was enabled by a large population that was ostracized and left out of the middle- and upper-class enjoyment of the nation's resources and wealth. It is not surprising that this new form of class vengeance—of acquiring affluence through an illegal or non-state sanctioned market—was also carried out within the culturally relevant patriarchal or male-dominated structure. This is not to say that women were not part of this class conflict; rather, the transformations took place within male cultural representational parameters of public interaction and violence. That women partook in these supposedly male ventures is clear; otherwise, the strong female images in *Pasión de gavilanes* would not ring true. But most important is the fact that there is nothing masculine about the drug trade and violence other than the historical characterization of it as such.

Pasión de gavilanes insinuates itself into the forays into class disjuncture in a profound and direct manner. As stated above, it makes use of the social results or products of a drug trade experience that opened the door to groups excluded from the nation's wealth. But it does this without explicitly mentioning drugs. At the same time, it is able to deal with class issues, and class' complicated manner of expression, by referring to the strong regional ethnic affiliations that have always sustained the intimate manner in which class differences are maintained and reproduced.

The Reyes brothers are an emblem of young Colombian men who manage to "make themselves" in the traditional macho fashion. In this sense, *Pasión de gavilanes* immediately hits on two very powerful discourses. On the one hand, it reproduces one of the most basic melodramatic recourses, the rags-to-riches story. On the other hand, however, it departs from the more melodramatic production of this plot line by making the protagonists three men rather than the single woman who has been the traditional vehicle of melodrama. The presence of these three brothers, rather than of women, and their continuous rejection by the more traditional elite landholders serve to exemplify many of the pitfalls of class differentiation. In some way, this expresses how the class structure is constantly reproduced in Latin America within the very framework of this and other melodramatic representation.

Throughout the telenovela the Reyes brothers are referred to as thugs (*rufianes*) and are seen as upstarts and therefore as being of a low social class. Thus these men are seen as devoid of class even though they now claim to be the wealthiest and largest landholders of the region. Their constant rejection reflects the powerful hold of a class marker that goes beyond merely having wealth or not, or even the fact of behaving in a civilized way (*tener buenas costumbres*), behavior inherited by the elite since colonial times. Class therefore goes beyond a marker of wealth and civilizing conduct and is, rather, a particular form of identification that excludes others, as do all identifications, without ever having to recognize the rules for or of the exclusion.

In true melodramatic fashion, the Reyes brothers, as the stock good guys, are the emblem of what is good, beautiful, and unhampered by social deception (in true Rousseauian fashion). In this regard, Fernando, Gabriela's young husband, is the exact opposite. Raised with money and "class," he is a gambling womanizer and alcoholic, and Gabriela's downfall (like ours, since we are invited to participate in this identification with her character's struggle) is that she cannot see who he really is. Thus her tragedy—and ours—is missing what is true because of social appearances. In that sense, class is the trickiest element of all to understand, because it comes to represent a conglomerate of racial, regional, and gendered historical attributes condensed into an intimate whole.

The unending judging of the Reyeses as having no class is also enabled by their being seen as outsiders. We learn through flashbacks that they came from a small farming family in another region and lost their parents and home in a fire. This made them migrate and work at different trades, including opening a bakery, until one of them (the youngest) struck it rich by marrying an ugly rich woman obsessed with him who died on their wedding day. This (un)fortunate occurrence provided him with enormous wealth that, in true good spirit, he generously shared with his brothers and friends. The brothers' regional marker is essential in terms of providing an excuse for questioning their inferior class status, particularly after their class cannot be questioned in terms of wealth, education, or even racial attributes (since they are clearly white).

Pasión de gavilanes' class conundrum brings to the forefront many other problems with class and the intimate nature in which it is engaged in daily life throughout Latin America. Perhaps the two characteristics most often associated with class are race and ethnicity. *Pasión de gavilanes* must tackle both problematics in order to fully capture the audience's attention and tap into its forbidden desires. It is telling that no black (Afro-Colombian) character or actor appears, not even in the traditional service or secondary roles, even though Colombia has one of the largest black populations in South America. Thus race in *Pasión de gavilanes* is constructed within a single white racial category in which class, once again, must become the discriminating racial factor.

It is because of this twofold class problematic—somehow incorporating race and ethnicity—that regional affiliation becomes of utmost importance. This is much easier because *Pasión de gavilanes* takes place in the hinterlands, and place and land as a marker of place are introduced as a way to understand regional affiliation as an enormous class marker (and therefore a marker of race and ethnicity as well). It is also not surprising that, as the telenovela takes place in an Andean setting, regional identification takes on enormous weight.

Throughout the Andes, regional affiliation, particularly in the division between highlands and coast, demarcates a quasi-racial identification of *serranos* (people from the highlands) and *costeños* (people from coastal communities). Each of these binary identifications has very strong class and sexual markers as well as the enormously civilizing tone of colonial heritage. While the coastal identification demarcates greater freedom in terms of sexual conduct as well as a more voluptuous way of being (all markers of African ancestry as well), the highlands are defined by a greater tie to an indigenous past (and present) and characterized as more cultured and sophisticated, even though *serranos* possess a more conservative outlook on sexuality (not surprisingly connected to an indigenous representation of the past).

It is these regional markers that are impressed on the characters in *Pasión de gavilanes,* all of whom inhabit some border hinterland but whose ultimately haciendalike businesses and resources claim a closer affiliation to the highlands than to the coast. This also might explain the absence of blacks (even in general shots of the market and bars) and the fantasy-filled production of a single, white racial representation.

It is in this hinterland of landholding elites that the Reyes brothers are seen as foreigners, even though they now claim the same or more wealth and status than the original landholders. All of this allows land and regional identification to take its primary place in terms of an intimate form of class differentiation.

Also not surprising, the three brothers are extremely handsome. This beautification of masculinity also opens a whole new area of melodramatic production apart from both traditional female objectification and sophisticated (suave and worldly) men. These men are beautiful in a raw, "natural" fashion, and in some ways it is that tension between nature's raw beauty in contrast to sophisticated, civilized experience that marks their greatest seductive potential. *Pasión de gavilanes* is a Latin American version of Tarzan's narrative, in which the men possess the best of both nature's and culture's worlds. Their beauty, and the way in which it is handled in the telenovela, also marks an inventive manner in which to peer in (or at) the continent's contemporary assessment of class markers.

The constant excuses the men use to walk around without shirts (and even more naked in sex scenes) are interesting because they serve as windows to this shift from a raw, natural state to one imbued with class, a shift that does not lose "real" and natural seductive power. Male beauty, as well as the signal of this understanding of class (partial or total nakedness), is commercially successful because it occurs mainly toward the beginning of *Pasión de gavilanes;* it is replaced later by suggestive cowboy attire (tight jeans, shirts, hats, etc.) as well as suits and tuxedos. The brothers' ability to carry both off is also emblematic of their superior class status, far beyond the ordinary marker of class—wealth—that the rest of the population in the area seems to accept.

Ultimately, male beauty and natural, raw existence are marked by the title of the telenovela, *Pasión de gavilanes.* The image of *gavilanes* as the markers of passion highlights, on the one hand, lower (almost predatory) class status; on the other, it draws attention to a truer, more natural and real way of being. The title marks the lesson (or wish) that is present beneath all the trappings of class, that there is really nothing superior to natural and rapacious passion ready to be unleashed. It is also ultimately this raw passion that serves as the maximum seduction for those who have been brought up in the constraining order of colonial education and normative upbringing. Thus, caught between the day-to-day existence of civilizing cultural norms, *Pasión de gavilanes* serves to liberate for an hour (or as long as possible) the enabling fantasy of being not who you are taught to be but the person who is caught beneath all the class configurations that have had to be dealt with since birth.

It is also this particular element that causes each of the sisters of the elite household to fall in love with and be seduced by the brothers. It could be argued that this bilateral kinship exchange is a very interesting remake of Hollywood's *Seven Brides for Seven Brothers,* Latin American–style. But perhaps equally important is the fact that it is this natural, and rightful, seduction that puts the sisters at odds with their daughterly obligations toward Gabriela, their mother. It is also this conflict that marks Gabriela's propensity for choosing the wrong man, and therefore satisfying desire in the wrong way by suppressing it for so long that she can no longer recognize the truth about her fascination. It is this conundrum that is presented to the audience as a marker of how to liberate desire from its class(ic) imprisonment, which, from its stronghold, portrays the disjunctures as the liberating forces.

GABRIELA'S WRATH AND
THE SINS OF MOTHERHOOD

Gabriela is the most powerful character in *Pasión de gavilanes*. Her characterization is true to the melodramatic production of the telenovela in various ways. First, it exemplifies one of the telenovela's most important contributions to the Latin American imaginary: making women much more visible than they have been in officializing Latin American political or social statements. Telenovelas incorporate a much more nuanced understanding of Latin American politics and the role that women play in Latin American social reproduction. Contrary to official media representations, women are understood in telenovelas as being vital in the maintenance and reproduction of culture and daily life in Latin America.

In keeping with this particular representation of the female, *Pasión de gavilanes* also takes on women as mothers as being one of the most essential roles given to women through which to express their real, although enormously misunderstood and misrepresented, sense of power. Thus, since the revolutionary contribution of the Mothers of the Plaza de Mayo (Las madres de la Plaza de Mayo), there has been a renewed interest by scholars, particularly feminist ones, in revisiting the powerful, and even contradictory, notions that motherhood has engendered, and continues to engender, for generations of women throughout the continent (Franco 2002, 1989). The recent focus on the genocidal attacks on women in Juárez, Mexico, has also served, tragically, to refocus attention on mothers and their role in standing up to enormous injustices, many times permitted, supported, or carried out by the state and its more violent representatives, like the military or the police.

This newfound acceptance of the political role of mothers in Latin American society, however, also reflects two similar and complicated phenomena. One is the enormous tragedy and virulent repression of the "dirty war" waged by the dictatorships of the Southern Cone; the second is the systematic targeting of young mestiza women not only in Juárez but also throughout other northern Mexican cities. These phenomena may reflect a greater emphasis on systematic violence against women throughout the continent (see Schmidt-Camacho 2004). Thus it is important to emphasize that, although these forms of systematic state violence might seem the exception and therefore warrant a greater public reaction from mothers who have had their children massacred in the interests of national government and globalization, they have also forced those same state and international agencies finally to accept the volatile power of women as mothers in reclaiming their struggle for a truly democratic Latin America.

At the same time, these exceptional representational moments do nothing more than express a more pervasive way of life in which women, and not only as mothers, fulfill a central role in social reproduction that has been systematically silenced for obvious hegemonic reasons. This particular kind of silence, in which men, as fathers and family members, have been unable to struggle alongside them, has been inversely reflected in both Argentina and northern Mexico. In many cases, men have been so damaged by the murders of their loved ones or by persecution by the state that they have been unable to fight without feeling that in some ways they are demeaning themselves in the face of the false ideal of machismo and invulnerable masculinity.

It is interesting that, in many ways, it is now fatherhood, and the hegemonic constraints within which it is constructed, that serves the state's most officializing and conservative reproduction of the traditional social inequality that keeps elite and transnational groups in power. If anything, motherhood, in its more agent-filled capacity, seems to be a positive element (if one can talk in those terms in the face of such widespread tragedy) in the repositioning of gender in social politics on the continent. I believe that it is within this repositioning that the telenovela enters into the discussion.

Since the 1960s, telenovelas have used female characters to reproduce an extremely problematic, but tellingly commercially successful, depiction of women and their social power in daily life. Gabriela's character therefore becomes part of a long tradition of strong women who, however ambiguously or because of their contradictory nature, better express the manner in which women have been misrepresented as not being valuable to daily life.

Gabriela's character also serves as the moral compass of the telenovela. Like everyone else, she must go through a transformation to reflect a newfound humanity. But her struggle is much more intense and painful than that of the rest of the characters precisely because of her greater power and its repressive effects on the people who surround her, even though she is unaware of those consequences. Therefore, while the Reyes brothers must give up their scheme to avenge themselves against the family and the sisters must accept that humanity comes in all shapes and sizes and not only in middle-class packages, for Gabriela the transformation is twofold: she too must give up any revenge and must accept people as they are; and, as a women, she must repress her own desires and needs by using both the good name of her family (including that of her daughters) and the representativeness of *buenas costumbres* to hide her insecurity and vulnerability.

Gabriela's character in many ways is made to represent the landholding elite and its class interests in the face of questioning by the upstart Reyes brothers. This is particularly true once her husband dies, leaving her in charge of the house, the estate, as well as her daughters and her father, a retired military man who is now confined to a wheelchair. Her father's being a former military man is also quite telling, since in many ways this seems to reflect a masculine construction that is dead or physically falling apart and that depends on Gabriela to maintain the masculine ideal with even greater zeal and violence than her husband or father ever did (or needed to). It is that extreme pride that allows her to beat one of her daughters viciously when she finds her having sex with one of the Reyes brothers, to force her daughters (with all the property and family pride that they represent) out of her home, and, ultimately, to see no contradiction in marrying her daughter's former husband.

It is in this marriage to a younger man that Gabriela's lack of judgment is made most explicit and thus warrants her position as the moral compass for the whole melodrama. As she blindly stands by her new husband's side even when he gambles all her money away, sleeps with other women, and even attempts to rape one of her daughters, Gabriela slowly faces the consequences of her dangerously repressed desires. She never relinquishes her power but, rather, allows Fernando, her new husband, to participate in it as an extension of herself, but to the point of artificial fulfillment that leaves her completely empty not only of power but also of the love that she supposedly was seeking. Once again, a double conundrum is established.

It is Fernando who gains total control of the hacienda and all of Gabriela's property, who sends her father to an asylum and locks her in a basement room until she gives him full control of her properties. Interestingly enough, this is also where the other strong woman (*mujer fuerte*), Dínora Rosales, enters the picture, providing Fernando with the support to carry out his Machiavellian plan in a way that he would never be able to do by himself. At the same time, however, Gabriela seems to have pushed herself into this tomblike existence when she thought she was doing the opposite. Her life as prisoner of her own husband in the basement of her own house is really an empirical expression of the same emotional entombment that she has lived her whole life. In a sense, things are easier now because the emotional realm has finally been made understandable.

In a catch-22, as a defender of her class (and race) she has allowed herself to be locked into a nonhuman position in which she is above desire or longing or anything that would make her seem unmasculine in front of her family and employees. She does all of this without realizing that the masculine façade does not make her (or anybody) any stronger but actually weakens her and makes her susceptible to her own repressed desires; it will be that repression that allows her to fall prey to people as nonhuman and ordinary as Fernando and his criminal acquaintances. Yet, contradictorily enough, it is also her role as mother that imprisons her in the part of representative of a class and generation that never really existed except in the cruelest and least-human colonial representations and their resilient legacy.

It is this double conundrum that seems to capture Gabriela's richest contributions to the melodrama. She, as a woman and mother, shares power and social control that are almost absolute in postcolonial structures like Latin America. The more the female contribution and public participation are denied, based on both indigenous and European forms of patriarchal control, the more that female power has been able to subtly permeate the arena of the continent's social reproduction. It is these subterranean devices that make female power, particularly in its motherly expression, so pernicious and at moments even deadly. The feminine power expressed by mothers is obvious enough; what is not is the enormous contortions it must undergo to be able to express itself as what it is. It is this deadly repression, like all repression, that opens mothers and children alike to an enormous and devastating loss of connection and humanity that is accentuated within a postcolonial legacy of civilizing cultural norms and alienating historical markers, particularly within the specific confines of race, gender, and class.

Therefore, Gabriela, instead of following her heart's desire, expresses not only her class' and gender's vulnerability but also that of men, who seem to be trapped in ideas of what is right or wrong. If anything, the lesson Gabriela learns, and that of the melodrama as a whole, is that one is lucky to find out that believing oneself to be what colonial structures over four centuries have claimed one is leads to a desert of feelings in real women and men. Thus Gabriela's transformation is a liberating force that allows her to see herself in a different light and to know that those superficial trappings are not the only way to be. Yet it is to Gabriela's and the melodrama's credit that the telenovela offers a window, however small, to fathoming other ways of being within the parameters of Latin America's postcolonial existence. It is this liberating process that is to be claimed through a more real way of being human, woman or man, and in which the paralyzed former military man who plays her father might be freer than Gabriela ever knew one could be.

THREE BRIDES FOR THREE BROTHERS: KINSHIP'S MIRRORING OF EXCHANGE

Pasión de gavilanes, as I have noted, could be interpreted as a Latin American melodramatic adaptation of the Hollywood musical *Seven Brides for Seven Brothers.* However, one must also take into account the current practice of bilateral exchange throughout the Americas (including the United States), particularly within rural settings. Many somewhat incestuous kinship practices make the more rural southern United States (and the accompanying country music genre) the object of jokes about low levels of cultural production due to the negative effects of inbreeding. Rural (and even urban) Latin America follows similar kinship practices, which have been amply recorded by anthropologists, including in the Andean highlands (see Allen 1988).

The notion of bilateral kinship exchange in the Andes is not as discriminated against as popular expressions in the United States make it out to be there, which explains the ease with which *Pasión de gavilanes* makes use of this particular kinship model to elaborate and complicate its burdened agenda of cultural production. The telenovela sets up two sets of three siblings of opposite sex, so that in opposition to the three Reyes brothers viewers are presented with the three equally beautiful Elizondo sisters. This particular form of kinship arrangement in some ways is a melodramatic delight in its rearticulation of many of the essential cultural elements that contribute to *Pasión de gavilanes'* success and commercial viability. In fact, most of the newcomers in *Pasión de gavilanes* went on to act in other national-hybrid melodramas.

Overarching, in a very general sense, the many melodramatic possibilities of this particular form of kinship arrangement is the tidiness with which this device presents life and its cultural expression. This particularly rigid burdening of both families by having equal numbers of siblings and having all siblings fall in love with each other smacks of high fantasy and romantic idealism in terms of what life one would want one's children to live. It is important to highlight this idealist fetishizing as an enormously burdensome element of postcolonial identity in which the postcolonial subject idealizes life to an absurd extreme and sets the scene for the inevitable disappointment and despair.

At the same time, this kind of neat arrangement, in complete contrast to life's chaos and even more vitally expressed within the poorer parts of Andean society, also heightens the melodrama's most ideal contribution and ideological productivity. The two sets of siblings also spell out a kind of idealized binary expression of opposites that is that useful and poignant because they are a nonrealistic interpretation of what everybody knows life to be like in the Andes and in the rest of the continent. Thus this idealized version of upper-class bilateral exchange permits an economical way to commoditize at the same time that it presents itself as an incredible vehicle for melodramatic tension in the form of the constant internal struggle between good and evil. Even more important, it expresses the ever-present reification of an idealized version of life in its most nonhuman perfection, a version that forever haunts the Andean and Latin American postcolonial landscape not despite but because of its impossible constitution in such a strictly fictitious manner.

Both the Elizondo and the Reyes siblings present a very cohesive unit of familial love, care, and support; even during the most extreme disagreements, conflict (including fistfights between the eldest brother, Juan, and the two other brothers) is an expression, not a denial, of the siblings' concern and depth of feeling. Also in true melodramatic fashion the siblings' relationship moves progressively from initial joyous, almost blissful, birthlike union to a more mature and realistic connection, made possible only through a long, arduous struggle to resolve essential differences and contradictions. Thus toward the end of *Pasión de gavilanes* the siblings are not only extremely loving and caring toward each other but also toward their spouses, producing yet another melodramatic representation of unreal (and yet productively "real") family obligations.

The six siblings thus allow for a disfigured representation not only of familial relationships but also, and more important, of amorous ones. Anyone, therefore, naïvely watching the telenovela would interpret the couples' lack of conflict as the ideal marriage and daily romantic existence. But as any experienced telenovela viewer would argue—and at the same time what secures the telenovelas' popularity—no one would recommend telenovelas as the model for how to live or, even worse, allow telenovelas to influence in any way the decisions one makes to survive daily life.

It is this particular representational tension that, I would argue, is at the heart of the amorous and familial images presented by the two sets of siblings as well as by the use of bilateral exchange as an agent-filled model of social reproduction. Telenovelas, like Hollywood films, never express what life is really like. As the Italian director Michelangelo Antonioni commented on his first visit to the United States, it was thanks to Hollywood films that he knew what not to expect. It is because of the melodramatic nature of these productions that one knows that things seen in films are the things one is least likely to encounter in life. It is this same tension of the Real (Lacan 1977) that Latin American telenovelas take on but, ambiguously, utilize to generate commercial success and to intervene in Latin American popular culture.

Perhaps due to differing historical and socioeconomic realities, and unlike U.S. society's belief in many of the Hollywood myths, Latin America's telenovela success is based on the opposite reaction. Nobody, not even children or mentally challenged adults, would dream of falling into the trap of believing that telenovelas express, represent, or, worse, dictate what life or reality should be or is like. No one would argue that siblings or couples would act in the contained and loving manner portrayed in *Pasión de gavilanes*. Even more important perhaps, it is precisely because the telenovela is so unrealistic that producers enjoy so much commercial success and, as they wish to do, entertain the public. People watch telenovelas to avoid remembering hardships; they look for enough solace to face invincible daily odds due to the ever-present postcolonial legacy and myriad historical inequalities.

It is also this difference between lived-in reality and the reality represented in the telenovelas that makes such a successful representation of the Real (Lacan 1977). Therefore, even though, or despite, *Pasión de gavilanes'* representation of loving siblings and committed heterosexual couples, this is a complete fantasy that manages to reproduce a melodramatic representation that is real in its powerful potential. In other words, by denying the realities of daily life, telenovelas harbor and represent the innermost desire for a social existence devoid of life's constant struggles and challenges. They present larger-than-life struggles between good and evil, and always with a contained, fablelike, moralistic pronouncement at the conclusion.

It is these rarely expressed desires and longings, marked by larger notions of vulnerability and social rejection, that are most succinctly captured by telenovelas. At the same time and despite their utter rejection of daily life, they insert themselves into the very nature of the beast by presenting those things that would make daily life supposedly more pleasurable than everybody knows it to be. In that sense, telenovelas also fulfill the media metaphor of the images being projected in the public subjects' brains. It is in this private setting where the viewer's most intimate fears and terrors, as evidenced in the different forms desire takes, are enacted night after night and thereby allow at least some sense of agency; otherwise, the viewer might experience dementia, schizophrenia, or more exploitative forms of nonhuman interaction.

The melodramatic economy of the Real also allows for a much safer space and way in which to negotiate the prohibited social nature of desire, internalized during centuries of colonialism and postcolonialism. Everybody knows that expressing desire is dangerous business; a safe space for such expression is almost impossible to secure without perhaps leading to the subject's death. It is this process that melodrama is great at negotiating by providing a representational space in which to voice unrealistic transgressions. It is through the telenovela that repressed voices are ridiculed in the most public of ways at the same time that repressed emotions can be articulated and processed without calling down damning judgments.

In the postcolonial game of envy and subject constitution, being ridiculed for watching telenovelas is the least harmful form of discipline and social reproduction. Therefore, one must wonder about telenovelas' enormous cultural contribution in allowing space for Latin America's socially reproductive articulation without the pitfalls of *buenas costumbres* and rejectful constitutions (see Butler 1997), a contribution similar to that of music and literature on the continent but which all the sciences, including the social sciences, have failed to explain in terms of their historical evolution.

It is this melodramatic investment in representation that gets spelled out by sibling relationships and amorous exchanges. The telenovela both maintains the alluring presence of incest without ever calling it incest and mirrors the Latin subject in the model of bilateral kinship exchange. Therefore, once again *Pasión de gavilanes*' success is enabled by the novel use of traditional motifs of kinship marriage structure. It is in this subtle, ambivalent articulation of the emotions traditionally contained in the thorny subject of sibling love that the telenovela, beneath the watchful eyes of the official discourse of *buenas costumbres* and proper behavior, puts forward its "hegemonic articulation" of the struggle of daily life.

COL–MEX MUSIC AND THE HEGEMONIC ORDERING OF TELENOVELA PRODUCTION

There are several salient features of *Pasión de gavilanes,* including its marking of the continued integration of Colombia and the Andean market into telenovela production, the joint effort of Colombian and U.S. Latino producers, and the establishing of a relationship between Colombian and Mexican cultural idioms. In many ways, *Pasión de gavilanes* is very useful for showing or expressing many of the similarities between South American telenovelas and Mexican narco-dramas, and the distinct manner in which both countries have utilized melodrama to offer, since the 1960s, a unique cultural critique of Latin American society. It is therefore important to accept these critiques as a viable commercial enterprise useful for camouflaging the telenovela's much larger cultural agenda, an agenda that is not merely an epiphenomenon created by the use of the medium to create hegemonic media enterprises.

It is in this sense that melodramatic production has also been able to escape official norms by turning them on their head to express what is not only culturally and morally acceptable but also, and most important, what is the best way of representing Latin American culture to Latin America. It is also part of their strategy of flying below the official radar, which allowed telenovelas to avoid serious intellectual or academic scrutiny until the 1990s. It was mainly Jesús Martín-Barbero's (1987) work that put telenovelas squarely on the map as a worthy scholarly pursuit. Martín-Barbero's subsequent scholarship, in particular, has argued the need to understand the revolutionary manner in which telenovelas rearticulate Latin American culture and society while claiming that they do not.

It is as part of this wave of telenovela studies, initiated by Martín-Barbero and others in Latin America (e.g., García Canclini 1999, 1994) and related to the scholarship of popular cultural production in the United States and Europe (Gilroy 1987; Hall 1993) that my analysis follows. It also seems that *Pasión de gavilanes* is part of the successful move of telenovelas into different realms of the cultural exploration of the Latin American landscape. Telenovela production and success at the beginning of the first decade of the twenty-first century mark even greater globalization and essential participation in the world's landscape, including that of Latin America. *Pasión de gavilanes* in various ways marks the transnational element of telenovelas as no longer being for regional or national consumption but as focused, commodified objects being produced for continental and global export.

This transnational element is particularly clear in *Pasión de gavilanes* through the linking of Colombian and Mexican national culture. Therefore, even though it is a Colombian production with Colombian actors, there are very strong Mexican markers. The Mexican contribution is evident not only in a blending of regional rural (cowboyish) attributes but also in the explicit backing of a U.S.-based Latin media enterprise based in a country in which the Mexican population outnumbers that of any other Latin American nationality. It is, however, the music, specifically the Mexican adaptation of Colombian *cumbias,* that marks the hybrid and symbiotic relationship between both countries.

As outlined in the introduction to this chapter, the Colombian connection to Mexican culture has a history several decades old, mainly since the introduction of the Colombian cartels into Mexico's northern region for the purposes of introducing drugs to the United States. However, this does not mean that the drug culture was not already present in Mexico; it has a history there almost as old Mexico itself (see Astorga 1996). Nor does it mean that Colombia's first interaction with Mexico was due to the newfound drug economy's erasing decades of musical and artistic collaboration. Rather, the recent intensification of the Colombian-Mexican relationship (from the 1970s onward) marks a new globalizing enterprise that makes sense because of many historical, regional, and cultural factors that had never before been operationalized like this.

It was in this hybrid globalizing enterprise between Colombia and Mexico that music turned out to be a singular element. The genre's rhythmic tradition completely changed but it also extended *cumbia*'s range of influence and popularity far beyond its original South American frontiers. And it is this same Mexicanization of *cumbia* that *Pasión de gavilanes* utilizes to mark its new transnational product, thereby signaling itself as a recent, exotic Andean production of cultural and regional differentiation. In doing so, the telenovela elaborates a new hegemonic ordering (what I have called in this chapter "hegemonic articulation") that, without being counterhegemonic, manages to introduce different ways of mirroring itself and of being and inhabiting the Latin American subject that is produced on a daily basis.

It is in this way that *Pasión de gavilanes*' use of Tex-Mex music allows for a new ordering of difference, in which the object (in this case, music) is presented again to the public in a slightly different form. It is this reordering that allows for another, similar, way in which to rearticulate knowledge previously utilized to frames one's existence but that now, thanks to this initial rearticulation, allows for a slightly freer manner in which to represent oneself to oneself, and to rearticulate oneself differently again. It is this mode of change that is a powerful aphrodisiac in all successful telenovelas, allowing a representation of the self without entering into the traditional conflict with the official norms which have always had to be contended with for any kind of significant social shift to occur.

Pasión de gavilanes in many ways, but more clearly in its melodramatic usage of Tex-Mex *cumbia*, allows a restructuring of regional difference in agency-filled and slightly liberating ways. It is this representational shift which allows one to see oneself differently in a subtle way (and under the official radar). This shift is the hegemonic ordering that marks not only the telenovela's success but also melodrama's main contribution to the way in which one sees oneself; this presents a more realistic picture of what being and living in Latin America today is all about. It is only by superimposing an obsolete moral order, as melodramas and telenovelas do so well, that one can overcome the obsolete moral order of Latin America's postcolonial existence.

Chapters 2 through 5 mark the ways in which telenovela melodrama affects this hegemonic ordering and permits slightly liberating social spaces or pockets of oxygen and agency. The next four chapters will assess the part of narco-dramas in the melodramatic tradition for the Latinos of the north. As the theme song of *Pasión de gavilanes* constantly and nostalgically reiterates, "That man that you see there will always be mine, precisely because this is not true, and never will be." The melodramatic nostalgia of telenovelas is equally present in narco-dramas, which romanticize an existence that everybody knows never was or never will be, and through which everyone secures his or her daily survival.

PART II

Six

BEING NARCO

The Evolution of a Continental Sensibility

This chapter and Chapters 7–9 engage with a unique form of Mexican melodrama, the narco-drama, and the cultural elements that they express not only in Mexico but throughout Latin America. My analysis of melodrama in Latin America dovetails with my interest in narco-drama, and not only the longer versions in the form of telenovelas. In many ways it was a narco-drama that triggered my concern with the effect that melodrama has on the Latin American imagination and how it translates in the wider transnational project of postcoloniality on the continent.

I remember being enchanted by a narco-drama late at night several years ago as, unable to sleep, I was surfing the television channels. In this particular film the wife was being unfaithful to her cop husband (and the father of her young child). However, as the film progressed (and kept me quite entertained for almost two hours) we found out that her lover was really a powerful drug dealer who was trying to get back at her husband for messing up his narcotics enterprise. Meanwhile, the husband was dealing with a corrupt police force that was trying to keep him down since they were also complicit in the growing regional drug trade. The film revolved around the life of this man as he dealt with all these elements, including the dénouement, when his child was kidnapped by his wife's lover.

Of course, it was the struggle of the antihero, as the honest man (in this case, the husband) fights against all odds and comes out victorious which kept me (and I am quite sure hundreds, if not thousands, of viewers) enthralled and which led me to identify with the main character. It is this same plot line, of impossible odds and regional specificity, that narco-dramas exemplify. With suggestive titles such as *Orquídea sangrienta* (Bloody orchid), *El hijo de Lamberto Quintana* (The son of Lamberto

Quintana), *La venganza del rojo* (Red's vengeance), *La cueva de los alacranes* (The scorpions' cave), and *Clave siete* (Code seven), they all manage to tell a story of drugs, lust, and violence in which it is not the rule of law but the plain, honest man who ultimately wins. Even when the main character is a woman, as in *Orquídea sangrienta,* the plot is the same: corrupt police and army, morally ambivalent drug dealers, and peasants or urban dwellers looking to survive any way they can. But it is the lone individual caught in the patriarchal structure who marks the main character and that is central for understanding the fascination that these films hold for millions of us.

In this sense, narco-dramas are border narratives, as they express the hybrid culture that has flourished in the northern region of Mexico and that continues to provide one of the most productive entry points for tens of thousands of Latin Americans looking for a better life in the United States. Because of both the genre's historical and geographical positioning, the definition of narco-drama has a long genealogy and tradition with varied and powerful implications for regional, national, and transnational circles. Therefore, I would like to explore the central tenets of these films and most particularly their influence on other forms and types of cultural text. Far from exhausting the rich and detailed history of the narco-drama, I would like to emphasize the manner in which this cultural product has come to represent a particular part of Latin America to Latin America itself and to the rest of the world.

As a border dialogue, the narco identity precedes a much older conversation between the United States and its Latin American neighbors. Mexico's northern frontier and being narco do not respond exclusively to a Mexican identity but, rather, to a wider transnational dialogue between the neocolonial U.S. empire and the postcolonial existence of Latin America. It is in this context that an identity that makes one's actions illegal, such as that of narco, permeates the hostile and reluctant relationship between the United States and Latin America. This hostility and reluctance are the latest expression of a long litany of U.S. economic and political injustices toward the south; these have always been, and continue to be, hidden under a façade of democratic rhetoric, personal innocence, and theoretical political goodwill. In many ways, it is out of the frustration with the border scarecrow of a falsely democratic image of the northern empire that the specter of being "illegal," like that of being a narco, is embraced and positively imagined and receives its daily sustenance as well.

It is as a result of this postcolonial encounter that the melodramatic figure of the narco goes beyond its regional construction and is emblematic of the enormously complex and strained relationship between the United States and the rest of Latin America. It is also in this particular form of historical narrative construction that one can see both the impact and the antecedent of Mexico's elevated status in the hierarchy of Latin American cultural production. Throughout the twentieth century only Argentina rivaled the iconic place that Mexico held for the rest of the Spanish-speaking nations of the continent. Although without needing to deny the enormous impact and to some degree equally ambiguous hegemonic pull that Argentina has had on its Latin American neighbors, it never really rivaled the role and status of Mexico as the best road to independent cultural and political development.

Interestingly enough, the narrative separating Mexico and Argentina from each other evolved as a moralistic story of humility and pride in which Mexico always wins because it presents the most seductive combination of both. In general, Argentina has been represented as the most obnoxious manifestation of a personally self-aggrandized national pride. There are many reasons given for Argentineans' supposedly objectionable behavior, including that of the nation's white racial makeup, which allows them more freely to identify with their European ancestors than with any indigenous or African ones. It is of this, his countrymen's nostalgia for Europe as their homeland even though they were not born (or had ever been) there, that Borges (2003) makes fun. It is also this particular European ideological imagining that is compellingly contrasted with the absence of a strong indigenous presence in the country's capital city of Buenos Aires; this also contrasts with Mexico's proud Indian heritage, particularly as it has been officially embalmed by the PRI since 1929.

Mexico has developed an Indian rhetoric without peer in the rest of the continent. Not even Peru, with similar monumental archaeological ruins, has been able to develop an officializing indigenous rhetoric that can as successfully incorporate the Indian past into the nation's present while still mercilessly exploiting the Indian communities within its borders. It is this successful rhetoric of *mestizaje,* Indian pride, and exploitative racial relationships that has seduced the rest of the continent with similar colonial histories. Perhaps the best representative of this ideological façade is José Vasconcelos (1997), who argued for a cosmic race that would be superior precisely because of its mixing of different types of human breeds and temperament.

As has been convincingly argued by many, however, Vasconcelos failed to incorporate the lived-in reality of an Indian population decimated by the colonial powers and a postcolonial legacy that let the whiter and more European-looking people secure the best social positions, education, and resources. One still has to contrast this ideological tool of false hybridity with that proposed by other U.S. and Argentinean ideologues, in which miscegenation is the worst obstacle to development and can barely be mentioned without obvious revulsion and aversion.

It is in this context that one might understand why a rhetorical tool of mythical miscegenation, with all of us mixed now (see Benavides 2004), would prove to be such an attractive object of desire, no matter how obsolete or false its grandiloquent status. Yet not only Mexico but all the other Latin American nation-states that have had to contend with a long history of colonial exploitation and the contemporary presence of Indian and other repressed minority populations have been seduced by this myth. Therefore, even if this was one of the earliest postcolonial discourses to mark Mexico's ideological supremacy on the continent, many others would soon seem to justify the ideological recourse of *mestizaje* proposed by Vasconcelos.

In this regard, melodrama and music, more than any other cultural product (other than perhaps archaeological ruins and pyramids) would seem to legitimize the assertion of a higher cultural ground that a cosmic race seemingly was reckoned to be. This, I believe, is one of the main reasons that Mexico's golden age of cinema maintains such a powerful hold on the rest of the continent's social imagination. Just as Hollywood was securing a stronghold in the United States and the rest of the world, Mexican cinema was producing melodramatic films that expressed sentiments that provided solace for a troubled continent trying for the first time to build homogeneous nation-states out of fragmented communities with violent histories. Thus Hollywood film studios' enormous backing of their Mexican counterparts not only is not surprising but is expected and fairly easy to incorporate into the golden age image necessary for hegemonic control (Fein 2002).

In many ways, it was against the backdrop of the melodrama that two other Mexican elements—music and the incredible allure of the Revolution—made their symbolic power felt; both of them are with us today. Music has had an enormous impact on the psyche of Latin Americans and on sentiments tied to national identity production. Only Puerto Rico has been able to rival Mexico and Mexican musicians and artists in creating a discursive narrative of differing musical genres that interprets and sustains the feelings linked to identity and the struggle for millions of Latin Americans (see Otero Garabís 2000).

This early musical contribution, however, was powerfully incorporated into film musicals as well, starring big names (most of them, significantly, male) such as Jorge Negrete, Pedro Infante, Pedro Armendáriz, and Javier Solís. These stars combined their on-screen presence with superb musical ability and a larger-than-life sex appeal. It is also true that their macho, revolutionary allure (as, e.g., charros) further served to create an iconoclastic, hegemonic rendering of what the future should be like for all of Latin America. It did not hurt that several of these figures died young in plane crashes or led incredibly tragic lives. Even Lucha Villa and Chavela Vargas, two of the female stars, lived harsh, emotional lives that included alcohol and drug abuse and contemplated suicide as they struggled to survive each day. In the 1990s, pictures of a shirtless Pedro Infante were still one of the greatest pulls in a photo exhibition in Mexico City, and the anniversary of his death is still celebrated with almost religious fervor (see Rubenstein 2002).

In many ways, film, as one of the earliest types of melodramatic production, has served as an auto-representation of Mexico's problematic sensibilities and struggles. It was melodrama's dramatic promise that brought not only artists but writers and scholars to Mexico from other parts of the continent and other parts of the world. These films are in many ways the first mirroring of complex postcolonial longings and desires that had not had an outlet. This same ambiguous hegemonic ordering continues in later films, such as narco-dramas, and in the great visual texts of the telenovela, which exploded onto the scene several decades later. Of course, both telenovelas and narco-dramas seem to have perfected the melodramatic production of cheap sentiments and repetitive structure that, far from ostracizing the public, enhance the genres' appeal to vaster audiences than the elite, official golden age cinema reached.

Some scholars propose that these early melodramatic films (see de la Peza 1998) took the easier road of profiting from repetitions and cheap sentimental thrills without looking to bog themselves down with original scripts or genuine emotions. Yet in many ways it was this lesser concern with upper- and middle-class sensibilities that opened the door to the larger lower- and working-class population, which now began to see itself represented on the screen without the buffer of proper (elite) class behavior. It is this democratization of melodrama that the telenovela and the narco-drama were most able to elaborate on. Both once again testified, in a Mexican style, to the aspirations of a poor and struggling population still hungry to have itself represented on the screen, silver or otherwise.

Far from representing only the collapse of Mexico's golden age, tele-novelas and narco-dramas offer a greater opportunity for the "other" Mexican and Latin American to see themselves as protagonists for the first time. And once again, melodrama has proven quite useful in this re-gard by allowing more subtle, subversive, and complicated feelings to be expressed under the oppressive eye of the state without suffering censor-ship. Thus one could argue that the success of these new melodramatic transformations and their contributions to the political reordering of the Mexican (and other Latin American) nation-state occurred because it was in these new configurations that the shifting other of the Mexican nation was no longer only the Indian or even the peasant but the new urban thug and the hybrid Chicano; both of these were now being in-formed with new notions of threat to a middle-class sensibility as well as being imbued with a constant and productive feeling of illegality.

THE ILLEGAL ALLURE
OF BEING OTHERED

Not only Indians but their imagined and many times ro-manticized image were at the core of the "othering" that constituted what it meant to be Mexican—and this at the same time that the rest of the continent saw an option for their own troubled national produc-tions. The 1950s commercial hit *María Candelaria* in many ways captured the differing visions in the troubled focus of the Mexican nation's eye on the victimized beauty of the Indian community. The film's stunning cinematography of Indian customs and geography, with many shots tak-ing place in the Chinampas areas near Mexico City; the virginal beauty of Dolores del Río playing a strong but oppressed Indian woman; and the injustices suffered by her and her male partner all gave credence to the nation's earnest effort to utilize Indians, in the most productive oth-ering, in its homogeneous self-representation.

This initial representation of the nation in terms of its Indian popula-tion was a problem in many ways, three of which are worth discussing for an understanding the emergence of a media-enhanced narco-sensibility since the 1960s. First, the utilization of the indigenous (and lost) past was a very problematic endeavor for Mexico, since the state, particularly after the start of the Revolution of 1910, continuously emphasized that this was not what it was looking to do. Rather, within the long-standing tradition of rural revolutionary ideals, which looked to empower peasants and all of those who worked the land, and the rhetoric of *mestizaje* developed in the first part of the twentieth century, Indians were supposed to be seen as equal members of society and representative of the nation, not as inferior siblings.

Second, the long historical legacy of Indian cultural accomplishments and monumental construction and the ethnocide suffered at the hands of Mexico's colonial European enemies (both Spain and France) were used as motivation to put forward the Indian as the romanticized ideal of what being Mexican was truly about. Quite telling in this regard is that the Aztecs and the mythical land of Aztlán, not any living Indian community, were used as the rhetorical ideal of the Indian and the standard that the Mexican nation should pay homage to and work toward. It is interesting that, in the latter part of the twentieth century, once again it would be the mysterious and enigmatic foundation of Aztlán that the Mexican American and Chicano La Raza movement, the new othered of the Mexican nation, would go back to for re-creating their own mythical production. This time, however, the origin myth was used against the official image (created mainly by the PRI but accepted by all political parties) of the Mexican nation-state.

Third, this pattern of privileging a past representation of the Indian community at the same time that the contemporary community was maintained in virtual slavery and bondage was adopted by some of the countries with a strong Indian presence, which complicated the rhetoric of a homogeneous national identity (Benavides 2004). It is this ideological construction of *mestizaje*, as an inclusive ideology used to exclude everybody but the elite from the political and socioeconomic image of the nation, that Stutzman (1981) in his article's title powerfully defines as an "all inclusive ideology of exclusion" in his paradigmatic article on the *mestizaje* process in Ecuador. But it was Mexico where *mestizaje* was initially presented and reworked to elaborate a rhetorical ideal in which the Indian was supposed to be incorporated into the nation's fold, thereby leaving it, the nation, free to continue exploiting and repressing those same Indian communities while it looked to celebrate their past in museums and scholarly gatherings.

This problematic incorporation of Indian communities through the discourses of *mestizaje* known as *indigenismo* continues to this day, as the Indian-inspired Zapatista uprising in Chiapas and the Indian struggles in places throughout Central and South America demonstrate. However, this discourse, which places the Indian as the sole other of the nation, lost its singular positioning in the 1960s, when other social factors—migration and hybrid identities—found their way into the discursive mainstream of what it meant to be Mexican and Latin American. This factor was highlighted by Mexican writers such as Octavio Paz (1997, 1972) and Carlos Fuentes (2003, 2002, 1991, 1981), who, as part of the larger continental literary boom, began to reflect on the migrant Mexicans and Latin Americans in the United States. Both, in differing political interpretations, wrote about Mexicans who were the other part of the national body, who had somehow violated the homogeneous façade of the nation and proclaimed themselves as illegally subjected to the mainstream production of the nation.

It was perhaps Octavio Paz' essay "El pachuco y otros extremos" (in *El laberinto de la soledad,* 1997) that highlighted this new-old form of nationally ingrained racism in which Indians now shared their oppressive othering position with Chicanos and Mexican Americans, particularly as expressed in the border identity of *pachucos* and *cholos.* It is a testament to the underlying discourse that Paz was able to so successfully express that this essay fueled a national discussion of what it meant to be Mexican (and Latin American) that continues to this day, although successfully dismantled by the contributions of Chicano scholars like Gloria Anzaldúa (1987) and Richard Rodriguez (2002).

Contained within Paz' portrayal of this new othered population were images of urban thugs, criminality, and illegality that defined this different way of being and not being Mexican, images that, of course, Paz and the official state rhetoric found unacceptable to their elite dreams of what the nation should be. Particularly problematic was that this new Mexican community, now living abroad, utilized the same sacred Indian images of Aztlán, la Raza, and rural uprising in the visionary hands of César Chávez to secure a more inclusive, and therefore contestatory image, of what the Mexican nation (-state) had always been.

Lost in this debate were the larger discourses that provided Paz and others with the notion of the illegality of the newfound Chicano other, a notion that initially was attributed to the Indian presence. Paramount among these discourses was that of the border and how, in its criminalization of the new migrant, the official national rhetoric had internalized the same epithets used by the U.S. government, and more immediately

by the xenophobic Border Patrol of the north. If anything, Paz' contribution (I am using Paz only as emblematic of a much larger national
discourse) gave voice to a movement south of the border that ascribed
the same sense of criminality and illegality that had pervaded discourse
in the north since Texas ceased being part of Mexico.

Added to this geographical incorporation of northern racism into
the very foundations of the Mexican nation-state was a new sense of
middle-class norms that saw *pachucos* and all other Mexican Americans
as cultural traitors to the nation. Their betrayal was evidenced in the
fact that they no longer aspired to the same cultural norms and civilized
definitions of the postcolonial revolutionary state and its official, mestizo, rhetoric. If anything, they were using that same rhetoric to express
a new identity that resisted the idea of a homogeneous nation and saw
hybridity and life along the border as a long-standing discourse of what
it meant to be Mexican. They had been betrayed, and not the other way
around (see Corky Gonzales' influential epic poem "Yo soy Joaquín,"
in *Message to Aztlán,* 2001). Mexicans living in the north, from northern
Mexico all the way to Chicago and New York, refused to leave their
Mexican identity behind even while integrating themselves into other
Latin American discourses of being Latino and Hispanic as well as full-
fledged U.S. citizens (see Castillo 1994; Stavans 1998, 1995).

It is this border identity, more independent, but not totally so, of
the official rhetoric of *mestizaje,* that has proven paradigmatic in a new
type of northern regional identity, one that sees itself enshrined in both
music and narco-drama as *norteño* culture (Paredes 1958). The political
and cultural implications of this newfound *norteño* identity are extremely
varied and fertile, including its incorporation into the national myth of
southern Mexico's comprising Indians; the center (mainly Mexico City),
intellectuals; and the north, criminals. But this emblematic image of
the cultural division of the nation was further complicated when large
groups of Mexican Indians from the south migrated to the north, not
only looking to cross the border but also seeking new socioeconomic
possibilities in the northern border cities of Tijuana, Chihuahua, and
even the infamous Juárez (Berumen 2003; García-Canclini 1989; Navia
and Zimmerman 2004).

This new migrant push also saw itself accompanied by a constant
influx of Central and South Americans looking to use these northern
Mexican cities as their base to cross the border into the United States.
It was this same influx of Latin Americans that has motivated the U.S.

government to look at joining Mexico to combat this illegal (according to both governments' positions) influx of Latin Americans using Mexico as their entry point. However, under the shadow of the opulent north, all of Mexico's northern cities have grown exponentially since the 1980s, from small cities into quite large, and at times chaotic, metropolises (see García Canclini 1989; Vanderwood 2004). It was, then, uncontrolled development into a new globalized urban sprawl that supported the view of Tijuana and other border cities as criminalized urban centers that had nothing to do with the true spirit of the Mexican nation, at least as defined by the PRI-controlled state (Monsiváis 2000).

This new northern phenomenon at the southern U.S. border was further affected by the United States' restructuring of its economy within the new global capitalist order. It was this restructuring that supported larger regional alliances such as the one enabled by NAFTA (the North American Free Trade Agreement) and allowed the vigorous creation of maquiladoras throughout the region. This reordering only further influenced *norteño* culture and contributed to greater socioeconomic exploitation and a new gendered division of labor; all of these are partly responsible for the state-sanctioned massacre of young women, whose bodies and lives, no longer just their labor, are seen as objects for the enjoyment and use of the patriarchal structure.

This new phenomenon of global capital coupled with the vision of seeing northern Mexican cities as the playground of U.S. college students and even a place to send the United States' criminals have contributed to an even more subtle reworking of *norteño* identity as an illegal one, although constituted by the racist Mexican and xenophobic North America discourses, looks to contest both at one and the same time. It is in this complex cultural production that melodrama, particularly narco-drama, has both incorporated and contributed new forms of contestatory identity that subtly articulate the Mexican border criminal as the hero who looks to escape corrupt Mexican and North American law enforcement officials, who are always looking to gain the upper hand, economic and otherwise. As a character in a narco-drama notes when a U.S. citizen had been robbed in Mexico, "That is so uncommon, since it is always the other way around." In some ways, as I discuss below, through melodrama, narco-dramas have been able to incorporate the violent and criminal behavior of the Mexican and North American states to find human spaces of liberation and agency, precisely because narco-dramas escape the oppressive and inhumane civilizing norms that have defined existence for much too long.

NARCO-SENSIBILITY AND THE
GLOBAL RETURN OF THE OTHER

Narco-dramas, like good melodrama, fail to live up to the standards of good taste defined by established elite and intellectual cultural norms. Rather, they repeatedly struggle to express and develop the same antinorms and feelings that are continuously criticized and discouraged in all culturally acceptable institutions such as schools, the media, and religious institutions. In this melodramatic genre, violence is at its most extreme, and weapons and thuggish behavior take center stage. The genre thus manages to completely alienate those with supposedly upper- or even middle-class sensibilities who look for subtext, complicated plots, and sophisticated writing in the movies they enjoy. These violent drug lord films, however, manage to disaffect the elite, a small part of the population, while entertaining the rest. At the same time, they manage to offer profound cultural reworkings that are as subtle as they are successful in realigning the complicated hegemonic picture of daily life in Latin America.

To carry out their complicated cultural agenda, narco-dramas immerse themselves in a border culture that profoundly reworks discourses of Latin American identity and reacts to living right next door to the most powerful empire in the world today. It is in this symbiotic setting that a new morality or cosmology is created, in which both national boundaries (or neither) are deemed powerful enough to contain the new forms of cultural behavior and social life. Prime among these factors is the central place of violence, physical as well as other forms, in expressing a new way to relate to the world and its surroundings, including those human beings with whom one is forced to interact. This violence is therefore primal, precisely because it serves both as the figurative symbol with which to express the profound vulnerability of life along the border but also because, like all symbols, it is able to express almost infinite numbers of effects and meanings without being easily depleted.

The violence, which is so explicit and central in narco-dramas, responds to both North American and Mexican (and Latin American) forms of aggression that the narco-drama synthesizes to express a survivor mentality that has made this northern region thrive since the 1960s. In many ways, the pivotal place of narco-drama cannot but reflect the primary role of violence in people's lives along the border as a mechanism of daily survival that has been incorporated at so intimate a level that it creates new cultural products in conjunction with or from it. This is not very surprising considering that border towns, like images of the old West in the United States, and ports have always been thriving but violent places of cultural contact and social imaginary (Genet 1974).

We have seen, since the 1980s, an increase in military surveillance of the border, including the construction of barbed-wire fences and walls, as well as an increase in patrols, all in the hope of keeping immigrants out. Many have noticed this almost paranoid response from the United States, a country that claims to have been built by immigrants, comes at a time when there seems to be a greater migration of people across borders, and the United States and other developed nation-states are looking to increase the flow of goods between transnational spaces. It is almost as if the goods, and not the people, are deemed the only acceptable objects of free trade, which once more emphasizes the essential role of commodities and the commodification of people as an inherent legacy of capitalist expansion.

Intrinsic to this paranoid response from the United States seems to be a complete denial of the same violent and genocidal measures used by the British Empire to rid the land of Native Americans. This denial is also part of the destabilizing claims from any secondary groups, like that of the descendants of enslaved generations of Africans. It is almost as if the United States is precisely scared of allowing other groups to do to it what it did to other world communities. However, if this physical violence would seem to be enough, the greater damage or violence is done through a historical recovery and by the academic intelligentsia, which describes this inhuman destruction with words such as *democracy, freedom, equality,* and *justice.* This supposed innocence is exactly what can be considered the ultimate form of violence practiced on the social subject, and that, according to James Baldwin (1988), is what cannot be denied or forgiven without unfortunate social consequences.

It is this particular form of violence that succeeds in nourishing one side of narco-drama production. As a border product, narco-dramas have been steeped in the discriminatory and racist undertaking of Latin America's neighbors to the north. In many ways, this powerful white (racially speaking) presence has to be treated with enormous care, since it seems that it will go to any lengths not to admit to itself what it knows at heart to be true: that it has equally unsupported claims to the land from which it is excluding others. The same groups' ancestors were murdered and enslaved to assure the nation-state's socioeconomic and political superiority. Thus, having Texas as a neighbor, for example, is no easy matter, with the state's combined sense of historical amnesia and rampant gun culture to defend it. The producers of narco-dramas must be very careful to keep the north's naïve view of life intact or pay the price with their lives.

It is this figure of the United States that makes its way into narco-dramas, mainly as the enforcer of drug laws, and that pretends not to be connected with the drug cartels and to be protecting its borders from Mexican and Latin American criminals. But the problem is that neither position derives from respect. The border-protection position, the supposedly honest one, expresses complete historical blindness and thus alignment with historical violence and denial of social reality. The "bad" U.S. cops are at least being logical in the sense that they are not pretending to be something they are not but, rather, are sincerely looking to make a profit from the situation. Like Macbeth's, their position is clear, and migrants to the north know who and what they are dealing with.

Thus U.S. figures affect narco-drama in different and ambivalent manners. On the one hand, narco-dramas are nothing but a Latin version or reaffirmation of the normative representation of the bad U.S. cop. That is, most of the central heroic figures of narco-drama are drug lords and traffickers, as well as illegal immigrants, but the fact is that they are not really criminals from the Third World perspective from which they are being represented and reenacted. The allure, and seductiveness, of these heroes, mostly men, of course, comes from their not pretending to be innocent players but, rather, taking full responsibility for their illegal trade and violent behavior, and the implications of both. It is this honest acceptance of who they are and have always been (because they have been immersed in a history of violence) that has captured everybody's imagination. As inhabitants of the border (geographically and otherwise), audience members can not only relate to these protagonists but can also know them intimately, from the inside out.

The similarities do not end there, however, as the naïve figure is also incorporated for mirroring purposes and offered as another level of seductive psychic integration. If there is anything that is ultimately recoverable from the way in which the empire of the North looks to historically annihilate its enemies it is the appearance of Lone Ranger figures on which it is impossible to place social blame. Even though these heroes are enshrined in positions of power that are the direct result of their home country's criminal behavior, it is that same contradictory innocence that allows them to be seen as somehow above or free of the constraining and constitutive behavior that has explicitly contributed to making them who they are. Thus it is this contradictory figure who finds himself facing the hero's dilemma in the narco-drama and who is also what allows us to see the hero in a good light, even though he is involved in the drug trade and goes around killing almost everything and everybody in sight.

Therefore, the United States' presence in narco-drama is central, even though it is always (and, for melodramatic reasons, must be) represented by stock figures that fulfill their roles with predictable accuracy to secure the greatest effect. We have a melodramatic genre like narco-drama retrieving decades, if not a century, of imperial policies that have slowly forced it and its *norteño* audience to adapt to a discrete and explicit use of physical and emotional violence to hide its (and the audience's) insecure global moral positioning.

Yet, like all genuine cultural products, narco-dramas have been more than simply reactive. They not only have internalized these global forms of violence and denial of identity but also have utilized these same contrasting images—bad cop and innocent bystander—to turn the tables, so to speak, on the empire.

In carrying out this global melodramatic inversion, however, the narco-drama has developed other implications, including strong national ones that only further enable the genre's cultural potential. It is as if, through these stock characterizations of bad foreigners and local heroes, narco-drama has also been able to escape the official observation of the border from the north. It has done this by portraying the stereotypes that the north expects, all the while ridiculing that same north, which is unaware of its own stereotypes and stock characters. The power of ridicule and irony is no laughing matter, considering the enormous amount of cruelty and pain suffered at the hands of the U.S. Border Patrol and law enforcement. Realizing that one may be smarter and more human than those wielding the power is sometimes the strongest weapon for remaining sane and not losing one's sense of humanity. Staying sane and humane, however, in many cases is not devoid of terror.

The global interaction of narco-drama with North American and other foreign forces is further tempered by the ways in which Mexico's governments have systematically used violence since the beginning of the twentieth century. There are important elements in this regard. First is the patriarchal way in which the state has methodically ignored females' claims to socioeconomic, political, and human equality. At the same time that narco-drama maintains a central patriarchal structure, it manages to relate a "local hero versus giant" plot, which incorporates

many feminist and minority voices that the Mexican state has so successfully annihilated from the cultural picture for its own hegemonic
articulation and survival.

The patriarchal structure, in some sense, is the easiest to see and criti-
cize. However, this same structure is also the most subtly problematic
because of the intimate manner in which patriarchy is lived and articulated daily in Latin America. This is also why and how narco-drama
must be and is embedded in a historical patriarchy that both enables and
gives credence to the constant melodramatic representation of what it
means to live and survive in the cultural borderlands. For this reason, it
is not surprising but, rather, essential for narco-drama to re-create the
frustrating and limiting possibilities of women (and men) in daily life
and to use that limited viability to represent reality in the most real way
through its melodramatic production of it.

Thus narco-dramas are filled with men, all of them at different points
on the moral spectrum within the context of the drug trade and immigrant repression. Women in narco-dramas are secondary characters
in the sense that they seem destined only to be objects of exchange, in a
sort of postmodern interpretation of a Lévi-Straussian or Meillassouxian
redistributionary social structure. Men are the ones with public agency
to control the flow of goods and commodities, and women are seen as
another commodity, but of a sexual nature, to be fought over, won, and
handled. But women are also, in many narco-dramas, the reason for the
development of the plot and the cause of the demise of one or another
heroic (or antiheroic) member of the drug cartels.

As romantic objects of men's public, obsessive desire, women in many
cases figure as the most powerful of subjects, leaving behind their ste-
reotyped positioning as objects. Just as in real life, women in the narco-
drama wield an enormous amount of power, equal to or even beyond
men's, all without having to disrupt their public image as not having
such freedom and agency. The power embedded in personal matters and
the artificial division of public versus private affairs has been amply discussed and deconstructed by feminist scholars in more than one academic discipline.

As in many of these intellectual scenarios, we can see in the narco-
drama very close parallels to the articulation of private/public distinc-
tions. This allows the genre to present a very subtle, yet direct, critique
of patriarchal structures by the simple representation of patriarchy in a
melodramatic parody. In other words, once the most obvious image of
patriarchy is reflected in the narco-drama, its many cracks and incon-

sistencies are obvious and, unlike in other types of social critique or appropriation, there is really little risk of naming them and therefore of suffering the wrath of the emperor being called out for his (and not her) nakedness.

At the same time, this inverted critique of patriarchy steers clear of preaching or disrupting the cultural milieu, a strategy that is not only in keeping with melodramatic structure but that is imperative for the commercial success of most cultural products. Narco-drama, like all successful popular culture objects, must be translatable in direct cultural terms; otherwise, it runs the risk of being irrelevant no matter how truthful or instructive it promises to be. Therefore, what we have is not a call to arms for women's liberation or a scathing critique of men's (and women's) stupidity but, rather, a recognition of the agency and hegemonic articulation which women (alongside men) already wield in the cultural milieu of Mexico's northern frontier.

Because of this preestablished structure of privileged patriarchal representation, disturbing scenarios of female drug cartel leaders, as in *La reina del sur* (see Chap. 8), and ironic rereadings of narco-dramas such as *El mariachi* (see Chap. 9) are able to go beyond being simple intellectual sermons on what is culturally appropriate and to share in the commercial success of the melodrama genre. It is also because of the explicit use of melodramatic inversion of the genre that *La reina del sur* and *El mariachi* are successful in implicitly questioning the inherently stereotypical structure that they are presenting. Just as in narco-drama, and in these two critiques of the genre, the inversion of meaning in the most rational of emotional truths and reality into an absurd image is a delicate matter, and not as easy to do and as lighthearted as the melodramatic approach seems to imply.

In looking at the role of women and of agency in general within the narco-drama, we are also presented with another established melodramatic model: the lone fighter or solitary hero against the overwhelming forces of evil. Of course, the established structure of the (anti)hero as drug trafficker already precludes the idea of a simple good-versus-bad plot; instead, it complicates the story in a more realistic manner. In other words, the antihero as a nonsimplistic, good figure is closer to both the real-life situation of people living in border spaces who have been criminalized (in terms of their space and subjection) and to the border subjects who also must deal with this nonlegal attribution in a realistic manner if they are to survive. As presented in the film *City of God,* a Brazilian version of a Mexican narco-drama, one must shoot and kill (even if one is a little kid killing another little kid) or accept becoming a victim for life.

The local antihero, in this sense, is not somebody who on the surface or even stereotypically fills the role of the good person (something more in line with the telenovela's melodramatic structure; see previous chapters) but somebody who is good deep down inside, even if that goodness is hidden. Within the completely rotten social context of *norteño* culture, only a total idiot or naïf would pretend to be good, since that could mean lifelong victimization or death and perhaps the death of those you love. The central male character (in most cases) is good and heroic not because he does not kill or because he fights drug trafficking but because he does both in a way that looks to harm the fewest people possible, especially if they do not represent the state (Mexican or otherwise) or other drug cartels.

Thus the state is prefigured in the most complete manner but in a way that is mostly marked by its absence (see Abrams 1988). The antihero gets his status and the compassion of the audience because he looks to do the same things that the (Mexican) state(s) does to its citizens— exploit them, kill them, rob them for its own reproduction—and in doing so gets back at the state to a degree beyond any citizen's possibilities for revenge. It is this many times explicit revenge against the state (and its representatives) that is the most satisfying image in the narco-drama and why redemption often requires multiple deaths, since revenge could occur in no other way. But it is also in this complete commitment, even including death, of the central characters that the *norteño* signature of honesty, machismo, and vulnerability (to life's follies) is suggested as the code for all of life's (criminal) endeavors. It is also in this commitment that killing, raping, and even selling drugs can be redeemed as humane in an inhumane context.

The code of honor inherent in many criminal ventures has already made a dramatic appearance in gangster films such as *The Godfather* and is also a central theme in hip-hop, not only in the United States but throughout the world. Perhaps the rap artist Jay-Z's remarks concerning the incredible dishonesty and backstabbing of the music industry are relevant to our discussion, as these characteristics were absent from his previous life as a drug trafficker. It is this same backstabbing, continuously emphasized in narco-drama, that is most succinctly expressed in *La reina del sur* (Pérez-Reverte 2002a: 428), when a local cop belts out, without offering any help to the drug cartel leader, Teresa Mendoza, as she is being shot at by other drug cartel members, "Órale mi narca, show 'em how a Sinoalense girl dies!" (See Chap. 9 for a more detailed discussion of the racial and gender implications of this violent code of honor.)

According to this and other cultural codes, the ultimate bad guy in all narco-dramas appears to be the Mexican state. Because of its legacy of violence, made more violent by a deceptive rhetoric of revolution and liberation, it becomes the poster child for any moral definition of what is bad or acceptable in viable cultural forms. It is also because of the deceptive nature and poor understanding of the Mexican state (and that of all Latin American nation-states) that narco-drama is successful and heralded as a genre of liberation in which a desire to be free of violence and exploitation transcends any actual violence or cruelty. It is not a case of joining the bad guys, the state, in this case, but, rather, of utilizing the same methods to defines one's space and distance from the violent and oppressive state. And this is not an easy or a laughing matter because, as everybody knows, using the master's trade makes one as evil as the master unless one escapes the connection by not naïvely holding on to one's innocence or sense of superiority.

Therefore, the veneration of violence in narco-drama, as in other minority cultural genres like hip-hop and rap, because of the rejection of a naïve sense of moral innocence or righteousness, means the complete opposite of its melodramatic portrayal. The discourse of being above the utterly disastrous social conditions of a society being depleted by its own government and left to suffer at the hands of transnational maquiladoras and border patrols is a rhetoric available only for elite and white (in figurative racial terms) people. That is why narco-drama, above all, is not about the white elite but about "true" Mexicans and what being Mexican is all about.

The narco-drama is therefore a story told by *norteños* about *norteño* culture in which gringos and both the Mexican and the U.S. states may limit and condition the contour of the cultural narrative and daily life but not the scope, essence, and agency of those who have the most at stake in daily border life. Thus narco-drama might be violent, but it is infinitely more humane and realistic than any antidrug campaign or judicial process for massacred women in the area have ever been, or most likely will ever be. *Norteños* (like all disempowered Latin American communities) know that as surely as they know the consequences of crossing the imaginary border that separates them from the north and, ultimately, from themselves.

THE VIOLENT MELODRAMATIC
MOMENT OF A CONTINENT

The narco-drama is perhaps the last Latin American melodramatic expression of the twentieth century. Since the 1970s, it has
filled the Latin American mediascape with antiheroes who, although
immersed in the most violent contexts as expressed in the pervasive nature of the continental drug trade, repression, and extreme poverty, are
able to utilize these same cultural features to reinstate a level of humanity in their lives and to signify an honest level of personal agency. The
narco-drama has been able to fulfill the social imaginary of not only
Mexico's northern region but of the entire nation as well as the rest of
Latin America, perhaps more particularly the millions of Latin Americans who have decided to make the United States their new home.

Therefore, narco-drama affects and is affected by the greater discourses of globalization present in the Americas today. Mexico, as discussed above, has traditionally served as a cultural beacon for the rest
of the continent. First through its music and film, and later through its
literature and political amnesties, Mexico City, along with Paris, has
consistently been where serious Latin American intellectuals go to develop their craft and has figured in the continent's popular imagination
as a nation proud of its Indian heritage in a way previously unheard of.
Mexico has also made use of its revolutionary past to propose progressive social change that, although perhaps not as radical as that of Cuba
and other revolutionary agendas, still provides for a more humane and
peaceful way in which to resolve Latin America's unending postcolonial
legacy of poverty and domination. And it is precisely at these two most
vulnerable points of iconoclastic production and revolutionary legacy
that narco-drama seems to expose the Mexican nation-state's most for-
midable limitations.

The transnational and continental success of narco-drama marks the
manner in which the majority of Mexico's population and the rest of the
Americas become aware of the rhetorical nature of most of the nation-
state's claims. The violent and inhumane environment which narco-
drama and narco-*corrido* so successfully elaborate is far from a simple
commercial enterprise; rather, it is a reflection of a much larger discomfort with and sense of anomie in the face of the consistent offerings of
lies and deceit since the beginning of the twentieth century by a supposedly progressive revolutionary state. Indians in Mexico are as oppressed,

repressed, and exploited as those on the rest of the continent, with the added insult that their historical legacy has been taken from them to support the anachronistic and dubious enterprise of the state's official reproduction. The revolutionary legacy is therefore far from dynamic or honest, as perhaps exemplified by the seldom-visited Museum of the Revolution in Mexico City, the best example of contemporary static efforts at significant improvement in the impoverishment of the country's population.

It is from this vantage point that the narco-drama, far from being a superficial representation of contemporary Latin American existence or even simply a cartoonish veneration of chaotic violence, represents a particularly conflictive moment in the continent's postcolonial history. The development of an illegal market for drugs, including alcohol, in the twentieth century allowed for another way to organize resources and people outside of state control and elite tutelage. The 1970s in particular saw incredible growth in the industry due to the U.S. demand first for marijuana and soon after for cocaine, including the introduction of crack into the inner city and ghettos.

An industry that started in the Andes and was controlled by Colombian cartels really marks a new competitor to rival national economies in assets and financial production and, equally important, also captures the people's imagination as a form of political and economic liberation from the state's traditionally oppressive gaze. In other words, it is a way of finally beating, at their own game and with their own tools, the bad guys who have controlled the state forever—a kind of democratization of the violence that has been experienced only by the continent's poorest. It has also allowed cartel leaders like Pablo Escobar to exact revenge for the poverty that he and so many others have been made to suffer and has allowed Escobar to announce, prophetically, "how poor rich people were in Latin American," when he was able to buy them one after another (Laura Restrepo 2004; see also Bowden 2001).

Narco-drama in many regards is the most authentic melodramatic cultural expression of this influx of economic resources and antistate feelings from the 1970s on. Thus it has secured, and explains, its enormous popularity outside of the northern region of Mexico and why it goes beyond mere national sensibilities to express conflicting feelings about life, gender, race, and the hopes of so many immigrants throughout the continent. Even though it is uniquely Mexican and is an essentially Mexican production infused with machismo, revolutionary fervor, and the code of honor (to mention but a few characteristics), most if not all of these same cultural features have an enormous resonance through-out the rest of Latin America. And this is not a result only of the ped-estal that Mexico has traditionally occupied, because many countries in Latin America have a similarly traumatic history.

The interesting point about the social impact of successful melo-drama, although it is not unique, is that narco-drama once again has raised Mexico in the continent's hierarchy of cultural media production. Even though intellectuals and elites disdain the genre and have even gone as far as to censor narco-*corridos,* both have once again emphasized the leading role of Mexico and its population in expressing the cultural conundrums of the continent. It is ironic that as the same state-sponsored controls persecute the genre, they assure the production of a Mexican imaginary that continues to hold a vital place in Latin Americans' minds and hearts. If one begins to assess the greater hegemonic implications of any cultural production, however, the central hegemonic articula-tion of the narco-drama begins to be less surprising and perhaps more frightening.

The narco-drama is not a single thing at any time or for anybody. It is in its ambiguous hegemonic articulations that it is most successful, both in restructuring the status quo and in reproducing the same old forms of postcolonial exploitation in new-old ways (see Hall 1997a, 1997b). It is in the light of a continental identification of a border imaginary that two of the central religious icons of narco-culture will be discussed in the following chapter; both, in their own way, offer some spiritual sol-ace for immigrants in a context of violent despair and a sea of tears (*valle de lágrimas*).

Seven

SAINTLY FIGURES
AND ICONS

The Migration of a Continental Dream

*The daily faithful make their pilgrimage to the shrine, with
prayers and promises: if successful in making it safely to "the
other side" there shall be due compensation, promises made
and promises kept.*
—WWW.XICANO.COM/JUANSOLDADO

The landscape of Latin America is filled with icons em-
bodying particularly powerful elements that spiritually secure the different communities' survival and well-being. Saintly icons and spiritual
protectors range geographically and culturally from the opulent cemetery in Buenos Aires' upper-class neighborhood of La Recoleta, where
thousands flock every year to pay their respects to Eva Perón, to the
more humble grave site of Juan Soldado in Tijuana, Mexico, where as
many come to ask for protection when crossing to "the other side." Despite their many differences, these folk saints share a great many ideological and spiritual components that have allowed them to become bea-
cons of comfort and hope for the millions of individuals who seek their
guidance, protection, and divine intervention.

Perhaps one of the most salient characteristics of these powerful figures is the fact that all of them have escaped canonization by the Catholic Church or by the state. Despite their different origins and regional
particularities, these icons have been made sacred not by any official
entity but by generations of families and individuals who have found in
them the ideological support not found in institutional hierarchies and
social structures. The opposition of the church and the state has only
increased the popular veneration of these icons and secured their reputation among a large following. In many ways, this reaffirms the popular understanding that the structures of the church and the state will
always oppose anything truly powerful and beneficial for the people.

This largely disconcerting habit of making saints and venerable beings out of downtrodden and even sinful people is open for melodramatic embodiment.

The figures of Juan Soldado and Jesús Malverde, *"el santo bandido"* (the bandit saint), are perhaps the two most important, but not the only, such figures in the *norteño* landscape. Both embody the antihero allure of illegality depicted in narco-drama and are at the center of the production of popular saints. However, and equally important, they also fit the melodramatic narrative requirement for a downtrodden character who is ultimately redeemed in popular memory if not by official recognition. It is significant that Latin America's pantheon of folk saints is not only indifferent to the lack of recognition from normative institutions but most actively in stark opposition to them. In other words, most if not all of these folk saints, and both Juan Soldado and Jesús Malverde fit the description, suffered at the hands of coercive normative institutions, such as the army, the police, or the church, which are traditionally responsible for proclaiming heroic status. Moreover, they lost their lives and were destined to disappear from memory and lose their good name as a result of these oppressive institutions' activities, supposedly carried out to secure the people's well-being.

Examples of rejection range from Eva Perón's corpse's being kidnapped and raped (as many have claimed), in a plot that allegedly involved actors in Argentina and Italy and high-ranking Catholic officials, to the effort to erase the memory of Hermano Gregorio (Brother Gregory), who was shunned by the medical hierarchy in his home country of Venezuela. In similar incidents, both Juan Soldado and Jesús Malverde were killed by the military in the name of the Mexican state. The former was accused of raping and killing a young girl, although many alternative interpretations appeared after his death, including that the crime was committed by his superior, a captain in the army. Malverde was hanged by the governor's order after he proved to be a nuisance, stealing and carrying out illegal trafficking to gain funds for the poor, in a sense, acting as a turn-of-the-twentieth-century Latin American Robin Hood. Thus these two men, their deaths, and their public memorialization provide a realistic scenario in which to create popular veneration for, respectively, migrants and drug traffickers, two of the most essential identities of narco-drama and in the region as a whole. Therefore, Juan Soldado's grave site sees a constant flow of migrant hopefuls in Tijuana, and a similar stream of persons involved in drug trafficking visits Jesús Malverde's tomb in the capital of the state of Sinaloa, Culiacán.

The ideological and spiritual following of both figures has only been heightened over the years by many people who claim that their requests and prayers have been miraculously answered by these icons. Their popular appeal has increased with the constant use of migrant and drug discourses in *corridos* and narco-dramas over the last decades. However, as one might imagine, neither icon is the sole property of migrants or drug traffickers per se but, rather, both display a popular appeal signifying their popularity among the poorest of the region's communities. Further evidence for this is afforded by the fact that there is another shrine to Jesús Malverde in Tijuana, and one can find shrines to Juan Soldado all over northern Mexico and the Southwest (Griffith 2003). Popular veneration is equally as fascinating as the allure of violence, illegality, border crossing, and social rejection.

Juan Soldado and Jesús Malverde provide a useful entry point for understanding some of the larger issues created by the region's melodramatic tradition of expressing and producing a particularly productive popular cultural identity, productive to such a degree that, although extremely grounded in local traditions, it serves to highlight and reveal similar historical legacies throughout the continent. It is in this manner, and a testament to the powerful discourses at play, that both icons have proved to be so appealing to communities that have had to construct an identity without protection from their governments and other powerful social institutions. It is to these postcolonial markers of abandonment that the maintenance and continuing memorialization of these two icons (who were assassinated in the early part of the twentieth century) speak.

The borderland component is powerful in both folk saints' public devotion as well. It is expressed as a socially chaotic existence in which the law and norms are not seen as the rightful heirs to an accepted form of civilized life but as markers of political coercion and manipulation. This discourse, therefore, is central to the veneration of both men as a kind of social vengeance for their deaths and a belief (almost a hope) that all is not lost even when one becomes a victim of those more powerful than oneself, particularly the state. Therefore, the borderland imaginary is intertwined with that of marginality, of barely surviving on the outskirts of a geographical border; this imaginary, far from being unique, turns out to be the most empirical symptom of a much broader kind of social or symbolic liminality. It is in this place that making it to the other side becomes of prime importance and acquires meanings that are essential to where one lives and, more important, to the production of one's identity.

These markers—of borderland, marginality, and illegality—are part of a wide array of social discourses that make explicit a much more profoundly symbolic way of living and relating to one's surroundings than is captured by the culture's official scripts. In a sense, it is the very things that escape censorship that are most severely burdened with meaning and that are useful in creating a cosmology that allows a lifestyle more in tune with oneself in the midst of so much violence and repression. Therefore, far from accepting these men as the dangerous criminals that the state and other institutions preach that they are, the population's active engagement creates a more just historical order from a problematic postcolonial legacy that has not even begun to be officially addressed (see Dawson 2004; Poniatowska 2001 for useful historical and literary analysis).

If we accept Astorga's (1995) analysis of the *corrido* and *norteño* thug culture in general, all of these cultural markers provide a particular form of social reckoning or catharsis that allows the local population to make sense of an outside world that is far from sensible or fair. In other words, both Juan Soldado and Jesús Malverde, along with narco-dramas and *corridos,* are part of a much larger cultural pantheon which provides a powerful hegemonic articulation in terms of real life-choices. This cultural creation, far from simply and blindly reproducing the social structure, provides singular moments of agency and meaning in a world full of social death and corruption. These particular moments of agency are extremely powerful and have to be hidden to allow actors to escape the powerful censorship of the more normative social institutions; in doing so they provide a twofold production of identity and hegemonic articulation.

It is only by supposedly blindly reproducing the most damning activities of state and other institutions—for example, rape, murder, and theft—that any real subversive, that is, dignified, act is possible. Therefore, far from falling into normative social stereotypes, these nonnormative behaviors manage to escape official recognition by appearing to play into official hands. It is only by succumbing to the official rhetoric that any real freedom, or authentic act, is affected in any socially, politically, or personally meaningful manner. Since the beginning of the twentieth century, a particular colonial legacy has become clear: no form of agency can be secured within the logical and rational ordering of normative institutions' structure; instead, agency derives from a much more dangerous—hidden—reordering of personal desire.

Melodrama has proved to be a powerful tool for producing genuine forms of social identification, precisely because it does not look exclusively to subvert the status quo but merely to reproduce it in old-new ways (see Hall 1997a, 1997b). It is able to do this at a personal level and in socially dead postcolonial settings like Mexico's border region. The quest for human dignity and coherence is, therefore, one of the most subversive forms of revolution. However, this melodramatic element, inherent in the telenovela and the narco-drama, is also an essential part of the population's spiritual quest, not as something external or secondary but intimately related to both cultural identity and daily life.

Thus the belief in saintly icons is not only primed with levels of hegemonic articulation but also essential in the desperate struggle to survive in a setting of postcolonial warfare and emotional desolation. Far from trivializing their memories or melodrama itself, the veneration of Juan Soldado and Jesús Malverde, especially in a recent past burdened by inherent social limitations, intimate frustrations, and a desire for transcendence, escapes the most routine forms of cultural definition and by doing so affords a legitimate way to be who one has always been.

JUAN SOLDADO: THE UNUSUAL LEGACY OF A COMMON NAME

There must be something to him [Juan Soldado] because the people keep coming daily. This is the only cemetery that is open every day, and it's that way because so many people want to see him.
—JESÚS MENDOZA, WWW.ZERMENO.COM

Juan Soldado's folk name is not as generic as his real name, Juan Castillo Morales. He was a soldier in Mexico's border army in Tijuana and, as some narratives state, was wrongfully executed in 1938 for the rape and murder of a young girl, Olga Camacho, daughter of a striking casino worker from Aguas Calientes. One of the more mythical accounts narrates that Juan Soldado was ordered by his superior to bury a large box in the middle of the night, a box that he had no idea contained the body of the young girl. Juan was discovered in the act and with the young girl's blood on his clothes. He was immediately prosecuted and condemned for the brutal murder of the child (Vanderwood 2004).

In keeping with local tradition and an infamous law referred to as the *ley de fuga,* he was given the chance to escape over the Mexican-U.S. border, with the understanding that, if he managed to escape over the border without getting shot, his innocence would be proved. This, of course, did not occur and was highly unlikely under the best of circumstances. Juan Soldado was shot in the back by his military compatriots on the Mexican side of the border and received a mercy shot as he lay dying. His body was buried near where it fell, and to this day thousands flock there every year to ask for favors and to offer their gratitude for his miraculous interventions. His grave site, on the other side of the cemetery from where he was shot (in old Tijuana), is one of the major pilgrimage points in the city, particularly for those with few social resources and who in one way or another have been touched by the migrant dream of crossing to the other side.

As Vanderwood argues (2004), these mythical narratives only show the tip of the complex discourses of urban development, border identity, and union politics that the murder of Olga Camacho seems to have incited in the emerging metropolis of Tijuana. These same discourses also show why it is not hard to envision how a man who led such an unfair life, who held a low military rank, and who suffered a harsh death, even if he was guilty of the horrendous crime, would be ripe for melodramatic identification and provide a means to escape the extreme severity of life in a border city. Tijuana, since its founding less than two centuries ago, has also presented itself, ambiguously, in terms of marking the Mexican border and its troubled relationship with the neighbor to the north. However, particularly in the first decades of the last century, Tijuana saw enormous growth, mainly through internal (and northern tourist) migration due to its new status as a place where every pleasure and diversion seemed to be permitted and actively encouraged. This troubled identity made the city the target of further immigration when many people from other Central and South American countries made it their jumping-off point for illegally entering the United States.

For many, Tijuana is the midpoint of the long journey north, one that is fraught with enormous hardships and great ambivalence. The allure of the north is increased by the fact that the great majority of those who do make it to the other side are able to provide a more dignified economic future for themselves, their kids, and even for family members who have stayed behind. Yet for all of those who survive the border crossing there are many others who face physical violence, including a staggering number of rapes of women migrants, and death (see R. Rodriguez 2002). For these geographical and cultural pioneers, Juan Soldado offers an identity that makes their travails less alienating and that allows them to see themselves as part of a much larger migrant population that has, in one way or another, sought a better life in that swift run across the border.

For all those who run to the other side, as happened to Juan Soldado, the journey is fraught with such enormous perils that even those who do survive are not free of negotiations and negative elements that will condition their lives forever. This is highlighted in the film *Los jornaleros* (The day laborers), where three cousins who make a blood pact must negotiate poverty, violence, and seduction to try to maintain their sacred bond. Thus one can see all these transnational migrants as symbolically "falling" at the border and, in a sense, not making it, as Juan Soldado did not, to the other side. His failure becomes something to identify with easily, providing a plausible scenario in which to understand the difficulty of that imaginary border, now with barbed wire and fascist vigilantism, and, above all, damaged psyches.

Juan Soldado's failure to cross the border is much more complicated than one might think initially. The popular memory provides a perfect borderland metaphor for the millions who know what it is to be "wronged by the system" and to need a "symbol for those failed by justice" (www .zermeno.com). Yet, unlike the journeys of many of those who come to ask for Juan Soldado's intercession, his was not a voluntary attempt but the unfortunate result of military and police "justice." However, even in this profound difference one can see the seductive attraction of identity, since no migrant would ever choose to leave his or her home and language unless pushed to do so by socioeconomic and political circumstances that denied the life that he or she was entitled to as a human being.

What would seem, then, to be a difference is really not and succeeds in marking more deeply the unfair and unjust structure that forces Mexicans and other Latin Americans to abandon their countries and homes to seek a future in the racially ambivalent United States. Juan Soldado is therefore definitely one of the earliest casualties of the imaginary border between the United States and Latin America that has been symbolically constructed to prove innocence if one can make it to the other side. Again, those who are seduced by the idea of innocence are far from naïve, in the sense of believing that the other side provides a blanket social reality from which one can begin to restructure one's life and identity from zero. Rather, the feigned innocence of the other side is in stark contrast to the harsh postcolonial reality of Latin America and the inhuman conditions created by a neocolonial structure of globalization only too enthusiastically supported by powerful national governments and elite interests.

Juan Soldado's failure and death are therefore far from completely true. On the contrary, his failure has become a productive symbol on which thousands, and perhaps even millions at this juncture, base a profound self-identification. There can be no failure when Juan Soldado's life has provided such protective feelings for, and even insight into, generations of migrants and borderland communities that otherwise would feel even more abandoned from trying to make sense of their lives in a schizophrenic existence. Even at the level of the psyche, the knowledge that somebody else has faced and fallen under the weight of such odds makes the decision to pay thousands of dollars, to cross deserts, to wade rivers, and even to hide in the airless backs of trucks a sober one—and all with the knowledge that, however hard this might be, it still pales in contrast to the social misery and emotional death back home. Coming home is more frightening than the journey itself, just as Pedro Páramo found with the ancient shadow of the woman in her son's bedroom (see Rulfo 2003 [1953]).

The other element of failure, and in a profound sense the ultimate one, is death itself. Far from being a testament to the injustice he suffered and the impossibility of his living, Juan Soldado's murder is tailor-made for melodrama. Unlike his sadistic superiors, or generations of unfair agents of the state and the law, it is Juan Soldado, a victim, who is most remembered by the population of Tijuana and who is part of a much more intimate pantheon of folk saints. His victimization, in a Latin American–infused Christian passion, is what provides Juan Soldado with a way out of the death and injustice that Tijuana, and so many of Latin America's other postcolonial cites, provides for the majority of its inhabitants.

It is through this active remembering that Juan Soldado is recaptured daily in people's imagination. However, those doing the remembering are also able to use him to hold onto their own existence and to make it through one more day, or as many painful days as are necessary to make it to the other side. One could also argue that, when the border metaphor is infused with this life-and-death urgency, it starts to lose its explicit geographical, or even psychological, content. The borderland metaphor becomes a testament to that other side of life which is waiting for everyone, on both sides of the political and socioeconomic divide.

It is also in this context that Juan Soldado becomes a pregnant figure not only for those souls infected by borderland dreams but even for those who have come to Tijuana to flee the local nightmare of poverty and desolation. Thus one can also understand the identification, even continental fascination, with Juan Soldado and his life, identification with an icon that, starting as a border signifier, provides an ever greater feeling of power that allows individuals to see in him a reflection of their own dreams and sorrows, as well as hope for an intervention that will make their lives more tolerable. The border imaginary therefore not only transcends the transnational border between Mexico and Latin America and the United States but, significantly, includes the internal migration from Latin America to Europe and the rest of the world *(New York Times,* Feb. 8, 2005).

In one way or another, Juan Soldado's populist canonization marks a general disregard for officializing institutions and normative culture and defines the border elements contained in the postcolonial legacy of *norteño* melodramatic resolution. We are all migrants now, in one way or another, not only with African and European dreams but even with American ones that are transcended by colonial markers from all different times and legacies. It is not an isolated incident that many local narratives refer to Juan Soldado's last words as expressing a belief that somebody will save him ("Alguien me salvará"), a testament to the continuing faith that good and justice will ultimately prevail, even or especially when it is clear that it will not.

Yet, Juan Soldado was wrong and realized it too late. As a response to the crime his death was meant to vindicate, hundreds of people burned down both the police station and the municipal building. Several more people died as a result of these riots, and tens were imprisoned for days (see Vanderwood 2004). But as a testament to Juan Soldado's spirit and his contemporaries who so earnestly expressed their anger, his memory lives on, and with it the hopes that a border region and continent are still riding to get to the other side, wherever that might be.

JESÚS MALVERDE: THE POLITICS OF A BANDIT SAINT

The legacy of Jesús Malverde is wrapped up in a mythical narrative of even greater proportions than that of Juan Soldado; in fact, many historians question whether he actually existed (see Griffith 2003). However, this question has not stopped the veneration of Jesús Malverde from spreading throughout his home state of Sinaloa and from being expressed in border towns like Tijuana and throughout the rest of Mexico and the United States. Because of the circumstances of Jesús Malverde's narrative he has been hailed as the patron saint of drug traffickers and is seen as protecting them in the dangerously violent trade and securing their safe passage over the Mexican-U.S. border. Thus he shares an enormous empathetic relationship with Juan Soldado and his followers, which makes him a key player in the cultural production of narco-drama and *corridos* throughout the region.

Jesús Malverde's official burial site is located in his home city of Culiacán, one of the hot spots for drug trafficking in northern Mexico. As a testament to the pervasiveness of the drug trade and its corresponding violence, many have nicknamed the city Little Chicago, recalling the Al Capone era. El Santo Bandido is thought to offer particular protection to drug traffickers. And since the drug trade is equally embedded along the border, a second shrine on the outskirts of Tijuana attracts drug traffickers on their dangerous but necessary trek to the north.

Jesús Malverde's story places him in Culiacán at the turn of the twentieth century and has him being murdered in 1909 on orders of the then-governor of the state of Sinaloa, Francisco Cañedo. The details are somewhat blurred, but the story always claims a violent and tragic death at the hands of agents of the state, betrayal by his most faithful friend and compadre, and the hanging of his dead body from a mesquite tree. All of these features serve to emphasize key elements of the region's production of a narco-sensibility at the same time that they provide a much-needed emotional outlet for a society marked by high levels of crime and illegal behaviors, especially on the part of the state.

In these narratives, Jesús Malverde is presented as a modern-day Robin Hood who consistently stole from the estate owners of the region and offered many of the stolen goods to the large impoverished community exploited by the rural elite. It is said that the governor singled Malverde out to be murdered and his body put on public display because of the latter's success in stealing from the rich to give to the poor, the enormous following that he developed in his lifetime, and to intimidate other criminals (Griffith 2003). A reward was placed on his head, which in the end motivated his compadre to betray him. Jesús Malverde not only ended up being murdered by the state but also was betrayed by someone he mistakenly thought to be an intimate. Followers have related this double marker of betrayal to express their own fragile regional identification and to provide greater meaning to a dangerous trade, ironically, deemed illegal by an unlawful state.

Malverde's following is in no way limited to drug traffickers but comprises a myriad of loyal subjects who believe in his miraculous response to their petitions. However, it is the drug traffickers who have encouraged recognition of Malverde's life and have significantly contributed to his fame and public recognition. Many Mexican cartels, most of them from Sinaloa, have offered enormous amounts of money to rebuild Malverde's mausoleum, protect his grave site, and provide hours on end of serenades to his memory. All of these acts have increased Malverde's allure in several ways, from creating a greater public awareness of his influence on the drug trade to simply increasing the ideological recognition of comfort for those in danger of being declared unlawful and not belonging.

As discussed above, the similarities between the popular memory of Juan Soldado and Jesús Malverde are clear. Both, in their own manner, reproduce border discourses of illegality, of being wronged by the official structure, and of redemption by the people themselves. However, there are also important differences that sometimes create complements which support each other in a divine narco-pantheon of human dignity. One of these differences concerns the question of the existence of Jesús Malverde. As with other Latin American folk saints, however, the question does little or nothing to decrease his veneration by the people and, in fact, in many ways only seems to fuel the need to recognize him.

The acknowledgment of Malverde's criminal life is also a significant departure from the popular discourse surrounding Juan Soldado. Even his nickname seems to play on the contradictory idea that, although he was clearly a criminal, his behavior is justified because he was helping the poor. This characteristic seems to be a modern-day metaphor for men (and women) who very publicly act violently in the struggle to help their family, friends, and home communities but who appear to be obligated to do so by national and regional conditions.

Therefore, justice and tenderness seem to be important in the narrative and legacy of Jesús Malverde's life, since both deal with and recognize the vulnerable humanity of all those involved. The enormous veneration of Malverde's memory recalls human or divine justice that provides him the recognition he was denied in life by the army and the state. Thus his life did not end with his public execution and betrayal by his friend; rather, it marks the initiation of public redemption and ambiguous hegemonic production. The tropes of official wrongdoing, unjust normative social hierarchies, and betrayal by one's most intimate family and comrades resonate loudly with a regional population that has continued to produce movies and songs that elaborate these themes for melodramatic consumption and hegemonic ordering.

Public recognition thus seems to mean that it is much better to be a bandit for the right reasons than to pretend to be a saint for the wrong ones. This conundrum allows a glimpse at the social fabric that is much less obvious than the melodramatic representation would seem to imply. Things are far less than we might think; therefore, it is much better to be honest about our intentions than to fall into the traps set by normative culture and civilized (nightmarish) dreams. There is no doubt about the kind of person that Malverde was, and this is not something to be taken lightly or for granted in a dangerous postcolonial setting like Sinaloa. The trap is not in becoming a criminal or getting involved in illegal matters. After all, how could one not when every other legal enterprise has been monopolized by the minority elite? Rather, the real trap is to believe that criminal behavior is a trap and therefore to fall for what the state, church, family, and friends tell us even when our gut tells us that these normative scenarios arc not true.

This essential contradiction also provides another marker of Jesús Malverde's legacy—his ultimate honesty both in his life and in how he faced death. The elite had no qualms about Malverde's playing out the last scene of his life, until the melodrama of his inert body hanging from the mesquite tree. Malverde in death became an inspiration to generations to claim loyalty and honesty as the ultimate patriarchal markers not only of machismo but of personhood, which nothing, not even the state, could take. Because of this, honesty cannot be overemphasized in a postcolonial setting where every single shred of history and identity has been ravished over and over again, including in the tainted memorialization and romanticization of the Indian past.

So it might be that this active recapture of human dignity is caught within colonial norms of patriarchal control. But even then it provides a much more transformative element than does the oppressive reproduction of normative culture in its most obfuscating forms. In that scenario Jesús Malverde's life achievement—his heroism in facing death alone, his body hanging from the tree—speaks volumes about the travails involved in encountering an uncertain present with violent colonial undertones throughout.

THE OFFICIALIZING NORMS OF INFORMAL SAINTHOOD

As Roseberry (1994) and others have outlined, nothing escapes hegemonic production. More specifically, hegemonic production is what Roseberry refers to as the "field of force" on which actors embody and contest the different levels of agency that each possesses and vies for. At the same time, this generalized playing field of hegemonic production is constantly advanced by different social moments and forms of transgression;

these consistently and dynamically keep pushing the playing field into other hegemonic arrangements. As Foucault (1998) has succinctly outlined, each transgression pushes the envelope of terrifying liminality precisely because it takes the structural arrangement to a new and still unknown limit of articulation and ultimate hegemonic production. Thus hegemonic articulation is a constant feature of power arrangements and manages to incorporate all counterhegemonic projects without necessarily expressing a complete denial of agency in all its myriad forms.

It is within this changing landscape of hegemonic articulation that I would like to place both these movements that continuously express the sacred production and informal sainthood of both Juan Soldado and Jesús Malverde. On this playing field the production of these two folk saints provokes a constant and disquieting production of what is proper and what is not and serves to contrast the normative production of culturally appropriate norms for the border region of northern Mexico and Latin America. Thus the intimate belief in the divine power of both of these men and the active memorialization of their lives and deaths serve as constant reminders of the ever-agency-filled level of cultural production playing within preset structures and notions of what is culturally viable and understandable. It is also in this manner, I argue, that one must not only contend with the ambivalent hegemonic production of contestatory icons, as in these and other folk sainthoods, but also recognize the complex restructuring of old norms in provocative new-old ways.

The powerful reflection of both discourses on individual lives in particular and narco-culture in general is quite easy to see. The constant tropes of border culture are repetitively reenacted in each man's life and memory to such a degree that they have produced a new ethos of appropriate cultural behavior. At the same time, these tropes challenge the more normative hegemonic representation and steal the sacred allure from these official norms for their own ambivalent reproduction within daily life (see Taussig 1992).

Therefore, both cultural productions of Juan Soldado's and Jesús Malverde's sainthood must play the risky game of hegemonic articulation in dangerous new ways. This also means that they never are able to leave behind the nonblank slate on which their lives, and those of the different generations, were produced. Thus the memory and popular following of both saints produces an almost infinite amount of hegemonic possibility while consistently restabilizing the hegemonic order, because the instability of such hegemonic reordering is only, and always, a mere political hallucination.

It is the pivotal place of agency and resistance, on the one side, and reproduction of the hegemonic order, on the other, that I believe are among the most fruitful areas for this particular melodramatic contribution. In the always powerful iconization of both men, no real social agenda has ever been put in place, at least not in any way that would allow the state to develop its social field of production. Yet it is precisely because of this lack of a strict agenda that popular devotion as a symptom of popular culture can be articulated and, most important, reified in meaningful contemporary terms. It is also in that moment that the reification belies a larger, unconscious moment of hegemonic production that brings with it bigger webs of domination. These are no longer consistently placed outside of the social production of these and other cultural icons but, rather, are expressed where they always have been: in the intimate selection of whom one prays to, believes in, or refuses to follow as socially believable in spiritual terms.

In other words, the active proselytizing associated with these men's memories is always a hegemonic project in the making, ready to be co-opted by the state, the church, or any other cultural structure, because it is already represented in contrasting and reified terms. The wonder is not that these icons are produced without the official recognition of the church or the state but that both these institutions, as well as many others, must pretend to see these iconic productions outside of their field of hegemonic play. Again, this unconscious positioning is essential for any viable genuine popular cultural production not only on an individual level but even for highly stratified social institutions that depend on these ambivalent individual longings for their daily cultural survival.

The wonder therefore lies not so much in the degree of counter-hegemony as in the uneasy relationship between people's lives and self-preserving manners of social identification within the intimate webs of hegemonic production and domination. It is because of this, I would argue, that the memory of both folk saints consistently must reintroduce similar shades of postcolonial abandonment and oppression; otherwise, they would not be translatable in a culturally meaningful way. Therefore, the danger lies not in recognizing their utopian and agency-filled social representativeness but in their necessary alignment with the most intimate forms of the postcolonial legacy of repression. This postcolonial reality is the underlying fabric of their existence, on which their memory and adoration have been consistently maintained and reified.

At the same time, this hegemonic reordering, what I have called hegemonic articulation or structuration, also brings memory production to the order of domination within postcolonial societies. Far from a single or binary process, as represented by official versus authentic memory production, there are a myriad of forms of remembering, which also implies forgetting, in which memories are consistently and contradictorily invented and dynamically changed again and again. Add to this the fact that these memories, for their successful social reification, must continuously shift their production and hide their own process of representation within arguments for objective and accurate historical recuperation. Perhaps this is why heritage is the most easily deconstructable of all memory-related inventions.

If we understand this process of remembering within the iconization of Juan Soldado and Jesús Malverde, it is easy to identify the continuous shifts in their veneration and popular production. Far from being consistent narratives of counterhegemonic articulation, the men embody the contradictory elements of border culture for generations of *norteños*. The structural shifts of these narratives are so profound that it is not only likely but also perhaps necessary for the contemporaries of these two men not to recognize these folk icons in the contemporary embodiment of who they were thought to be or, rather, what they were told these men were. This is also why Jesús Malverde's existence is a minor element in genuine popular cultural production and becomes an asset in reproducing an even more fictive, and therefore more realistic, understanding of his life and, through that, of the undefined period beginning in the twentieth century and continuing to this day.

As Rosaldo (1989), among many others, elegantly notes, border culture, like all cultural production, is dynamic. The same elements form a myriad of interpretations and epistemological viewpoints ranging from the traditional to the resistant to the feminist to the migrant, all of which reflect different solutions to the same puzzle and all of which vie for authenticity and credibility. Yet every proponent of a particular interpretation also knows that she or he is trafficking in cultural- and self-invention, which has an enormous impact on the manner in which people order their lives and see themselves within the restructuring of their own cosmological production. This is possible because there is no single, untainted cultural production, just consistent and unconscious pretense that such a feature exists and that one or the other expression is the rightful representative of such a genuine "thing." At the same time, this viewpoint precludes time itself, forcing one to abandon the idea of before or after and to see active remembering as a symbiotic act of cultural production through which the past is invented and becomes a mere afterthought—even when this past is a major part of a new way of seeing oneself and therefore of inventing one's public persona and contemporary identity in adequate, normative ways.

This, I believe, is where all the different hegemonic actors meet—within the active remembering and forgetting of the hardship of border life as expressed through the recognition of both of these saints' lives and significant spiritual contributions. The story is thus no longer, and never has been, about Juan Soldado and Jesús Malverde, but about a larger field of force in which one's livelihood and identity are readdressed and continuously rearticulated. One sees oneself and does not, finds one's reflection and obfuscates it, all at one and the same time in a culturally ambiguous game of social- and self-representation. Both men, their narratives, and their legacy are authentic markers of cultural identity precisely because they have served that purpose for over a century. And far from being old, they are even more present and productive in the new global landscape of cybernetic capital flow and migrant labor.

These two icons embody everything that the border is about, including patriarchal oppression and postcolonial abandonment; this makes them tragic and has enabled their narratives to become the culturally productive hagiographic history that they are. A century of the effects of power has fixed the nature of narco-culture in the region and created a viable and resistant cultural identity in which there is only lawlessness and murder, as the lives of these two men (and the hundred of thousands of Mexicans at the turn of the century) seem to represent. This feature marks the changing nature of the hegemonic order, including the restructuring of global capitalism and market forces that has increased enthusiasm for Juan Soldado and Jesús Malverde and their dynamic melodramatic resolution. The border continues to have metaphoric value for the understanding of the global cultural divide between Mexico, Latin America, and the United States. *Norteño* culture as embodied in the narrative of these two border saints, is right in the middle, where it has always been and tried to be.

GLOBALIZATION AND ICONS: A MARKET OF CONTESTING VALUES

It is not a coincidence that now more than ever these folk saints and their iconoclastic construction hold such a pivotal place in the lives of a great many migrants and border communities. This in no way minimizes the spiritual value of these two men's lives; rather, it augments the social momentum that allows their lives to be read and appreciated in a particular contestatory manner. In many ways it might seem contradictory that, while capital flows and market expansions are articulated in a provocatively cybernetic and technologically advanced manner, labor concerns and the migration of workers over the U.S.-Mexican border continue their more or less racist historical evolution. Therefore, it is in moments of capital reconfiguration that border concerns and xenophobic practices are even more stressed as important to national security and ideological control.

The pervasiveness of these two icons therefore chronicles a continuous and growing resistance to the ever-present narrative of capital as it is expressed along the border. At this point it is important to note that the migrant metaphor applies not only to the millions of individuals who have decided to take the trip north and to their families, which are affected by the decision, but to all those living in Mexico's northern region who in one way or another are equally affected and rely on dreams of migration. And as these dreams have increased in social standing so have the responses by both the U.S. and the Mexican governments to the increasing control, but not the exclusion, of cheap labor throughout the border region. The increased importance of migration has also fueled the local economy of Mexico's northern region and affected the local production of culture. A complex and dialectical process of cultural production has thus gone hand in hand with the changing needs of capital and the search for meaning in socioeconomic conditions that at times seem hopeless.

Narco-culture in general has been, or can be, seen at a basic level as a local response to the border conundrum in which migrant labor fills a need in the United States' capitalistic evolution but is consistently, and necessarily in terms of human value, denigrated and openly discriminated against. In an essential sense, this neocolonial custom of economic exploitation and social devaluing is a long-standing tradition, and the Mexican border since the beginning of the twentieth century has perhaps seen the latest embodiment of the historical relationship between colonizer and colonized, or the developed north and the developing global south, in contemporary parlance. Therefore, the bandit saints in many ways fill this contestatory void, both personally and socially, to confront an implicit form of racism which is continuously denied in the social negotiations of the north. The official rhetoric of governments, U.S. and Latin American, seems to highlight only what the general population has known all along, that the enemy has never been foreigners or the United States but, rather, something formulated within Latin Americans' postcolonial psyche and political legacy.

It is telling, perhaps, that none of the thousands of migrants killed at the border have become folk saints or icons. It is these two men killed at the hands of the Mexican state who are consistently recalled and to whom people continue to turn and, not surprisingly, respond even after their deaths. The deaths of these two men are no more important than the deaths of those still being inhumanely treated, or even murdered, by the Mexican state or even than the treatment of those migrants who suffer at the hands of the U.S. Border Patrol. Ultimately, all are fighting the same enemy, who is securing the expansion of new forms of capital flow; thus they are united against these forces to create a more humane form of social livelihood, one that will not allow them and future generations to provide a safer space and greater dignity for themselves.

It is also interesting that a full-scale attack of exploitative neocolonial conditions along the border has never been launched. This political failure raises questions about its existence or about whether there are other, more successful, forms of political intervention, such as those that buffer these extraneous conditions while they align new ways of being and identities that rearticulate what being human, and therefore developed, is all about. It is in this sense that narco-culture in general and, more specifically, these two icons provide insight into understanding the new-old ways in which identity can be rearticulated in transgressive ways, beyond the unblinking hegemonic gaze of the state—and all this even though identity production is aided by, or formulated in resistance to, state policies directed at producing indirect ways of rearticulating social life at the border and, as a result, throughout the rest of the continent and in the United States.

Although the racist rhetoric of the nation-states continues unrelentingly, transnational corporate interests have always adapted to the contradictory needs of capital in terms of labor and class in Mexico and the rest of Latin America. This response is clear (and poignant) in the way in which the Americas are presented as a vacation spot for people from the First World who continue to seek things they never seem to have. This is particularly so, of course, not because of any actual geographical or physical elements but because of the larger political constraints on cultural production and, more specifically, cultural representation. In this context, Jesús Malverde and Juan Soldado are burdened signifiers of the kind of cultural objects that the U.S. empire could never have (included in the broad social body of the U.S. empire are Mexico and the rest of Latin America).

I do not mean exclusively folk saints and icons but, rather, richly textured identities devoid of direct political engagement and yet encoded with a political message that transcends the most explicit markers of the time. Che Guevara's legacy probably exemplifies this best, from political leader to a place in the Afro-American pantheon of saints. Our two northern Mexican icons make the trip almost in the opposite direction, from being caught in larger webs of domination beyond their control to obtaining sacred status within the people's understanding of what is socially and personally good and what is not. It is this tenuous connection between daily life and sacredness in which a whole spectrum of cultural production gets expressed, through which new-old manners of expressing oneself and being are politically rearticulated without even taking the explicitly political route. In this way, popular culture seems to beat the state, at least temporarily, at its own game.

The folk icons, far from maintaining a static representation of resistance, symbolize a dynamic new form of identification that is always ready to adapt to and meet new types of social relations embodied at the border. The violence, repression, and other dangerous discourses are restructured in the profoundly meaningful way in which they are lived every day by the local population. It is therefore the challenge of restructuring a different form of being always constrained within the rhetorical reaches of the state that represents the single most important challenge at the border. That challenge, in the sense of not being directly engaged in opposition to the official state rhetoric, which constantly fuels counterhegemony, continues to replenish official and nonofficial hegemonic projects, of which the state is the ultimate embodiment.

Thus the images of both Jesús Malverde and Juan Soldado continue to provide a resistance narrative that has been centuries if not millennia in the making. These men, mythical or not, articulated these discourses during their lifetimes and reached a personal solution that has found relevance with the evolving conditions of border life. Not only has the narrative been created by the border, but in many ways both icons have directly influenced the border imaginary and migrant metaphors that they have been made to represent. There is no separate figurative production, only a consistently influenced manufacture of enormous power that is again used to create a rich local culture that represents the region. It is this same richly textured production that is a beacon for millions of hopeful migrants who envision the violent border life as a form of escape from the catatonic state of the postcolonial nightmare started barely two centuries ago.

At the same time and intertwined with both of these iconic figures are elements of physical torment and sexuality that are less explicit but not any less powerful in their cultural figuration. It is not irrelevant, although quite surprising within the sexist patriarchal structure in which they are embodied, that it is two men who are ritually remembered as ambivalent victims of a racially and sexually defined transnational project. It is these men who in many ways represent the initial policing of young male migrants' bodies, which were the first to transgress the border with the north.

The images of their brutalized bodies and of equally victimized "men with guns" cannot but have enormous homoerotic elements in their popular reification. It is the more vulnerable elements of tenderness and love that are systematically denied to "macho" men even before they cross the border that seem, ambiguously, to be represented by these helpless images of Jesús Malverde and Juan Soldado. It is also telling that this more human and ambiguous homoerotic element is almost immediately, and not surprisingly, coupled with death in the barren region of the north.

This is also perhaps why *norteño* culture is such a culture of death, in which death figures prominently because it is in its most explicit prefiguration that a greater level of agency is afforded to the living. Perhaps this is also why these two men and their productive deaths were able to do something that no other political figure has been able to do: give hope and meaning to numberless people looking to escape their waking nightmare. And at the same time, as in all melodramatic production, *norteño* culture is far from being simply an escape; it is instead an escapist process rich in hegemonic articulation and identity resignification that cannot but produce new ways of being and new effects of power. It is also in this manner that the epistemological explosion of melodrama is afforded. Escaping the censorship of the state cannot but offer new insights and forms of cultural ownership that must be enjoyed and embodied as fast and as long as possible. Nobody owns her or his life, or really knows anything about it. This is a lesson learned over a century ago by Juan Soldado and Jesús Malverde. It is this lesson's being retaught and relearned that can be heralded as one of the most provocative and powerful miracles of these two folk saints.

Eight

LA REINA DEL SUR

Gender, Racial, and National Contestations
of Regional Identity

> *Despertó esa misma noche, estremecida en la oscuridad, porque*
> *acababa de averiguar al fin, en sueños, lo que pasaba en la*
> *novelita mejicana de Juan Rulfo que nunca conseguía com-*
> *prender del todo por más que la agarraba.*
> —ARTURO PÉREZ-REVERTE, *LA REINA DEL SUR*

Pérez-Reverte's impressive novel about a female Mexican drug lord who, after having to flee her country, makes it big in southern Spain sets the stage for a provocative reassessment of the narco-genre in all its gender, racial, and national glory. The fact that Pérez-Reverte is a best-selling Spanish writer only makes more explicit the underlying and enormous tensions of Spain's colonial legacy. These same tensions are further intensified by the provocatively accurate depiction in the novel of the violent narco-culture that characterizes Mexico's northern region.

As part of the writer's ethnographic foray, Pérez-Reverte lived in Sinaloa for almost a year researching the local scene as well as the cultural intricacies of the region. As a result of this experience and the enormous support of local journalists, he was able to create a powerful character in Teresa Mendoza, who, along with the author, has been immortalized in the region's imaginary by a narco-*corrido* created in her honor by Los Tigres del Norte.

Teresa Mendoza stands out as a literary achievement of continental and generational proportions. Her character allows varied elements and discourses to be developed and represented through the narco-genre, in which valuable questions are posed about the nature of national and gender representations. Many of these are already racialized in a disturbing historical form, especially when the recorded, represented, and lived-in history of the novel is one of extreme racial and gender violence.

But the popularity of the book and the *corrido* signal the profound cultural effects released by the antipatriarchal representation of a Mexican woman as the leader of a drug cartel on foreign soil, Spain, the homeland no less. This nonmasculine iconization is quite interesting and powerful, considering the long patriarchal history of Mexico and, more specifically, the patriarchal production of the nation's historical narratives (see Krauze 1997). It is in this manner that Pérez-Reverte seems to utilize the patriarchal narrative structure to give his character life and credibility at the same time that he strives to stand her on her head. And yet, it is this twofold commitment, to use and to subvert the patriarchal retelling of the past, that allows *La reina del sur,* and the melodramatic form of narco-drama, to highlight the same limiting cultural features that make looking toward the north each day such an exercise in futility.

Without wanting to reveal the plot and its rich detective story–like intricacies, let me say that the story mainly revolves around the life of Teresa Mendoza. Teresa is a young woman from Culiacán who must leave the country when her drug-trafficking companion, *el güero* Dávila, is killed. Her second companion, the Galician Santiago Fisterra, is also killed in a drug boat bust, which this time lands Teresa in jail for a couple of years. Her cell mate, Patricia, is the one who reintroduces her to the drug trade when they both are free and provides for her newfound status as drug queen of southern Spain, thus the novel's title.

Patricia dies without seeing her love for Teresa returned, and we are left wondering whether Teresa's inability to love Patricia is less a problem of sexual preference than of the impossibility of love under postcolonial conditions. In the end, Teresa returns to Culiacán to settle old debts and sets up the dénouement of the novel as well as the stage for her enigmatic departure from the public spotlight.

Developed, hidden, and provocatively implied throughout the book are enormous tensions that in many ways highlight the productive contribution of the narco-genre in sorting out not only national but continental and postcolonial legacies that continue to imbue gender, race, and the nation with contradictory meaning. It is these contradictory pronouncements which have contributed enormously to the popularity of the text and not less to the creation of and sustained enthusiasm for the resulting *corrido*. It is mainly these effects of power, translated through the cultural lens of the narco-genre, that I believe are central to exploring the transformative and hegemonic nature of the narco-drama in general.

TERESA MENDOZA AND THE
ESSENTIALIZING NATURE
OF EXILE

A fin de cuentas, el corrido siempre te lo escriben otros.
—ARTURO PÉREZ-REVERTE, *LA REINA DEL SUR*

Perhaps starting at the end will help elucidate some of the characteristics I have hinted at above. One of the major elements that Teresa Mendoza's character has to contend with is exile. Exile in many ways is one of the hidden tropes of the representation of these narco-drama narratives. For Teresa the immediate and most visible exile is geographical, having to leave her home, which in this case, more than Mexico, is Culiacán, the capital of Sinaloa and all that she has known or that has been dear to her. In exile, as is always the case, regional identification grows, as do longings for something she never had. A larger national identification that was never present while she was living in Mexico is also created.

So it is only in Spain that she is referred to as Mexican, and *la mejicana* (the Mexican) becomes one of her nicknames and her identity. Along with this new national identity come broader cultural and social significations, including the meaning of things like tequila, *rancheras, corridos,* and her regional dialect of "Mexican" words, as overdetermined objects that remind her of who she is while remaining forms of obsessive attachments that define who she is (Butler 1997). Perhaps more important is the new status that her national identity provides her within the transnational hierarchy of the drug trade, since in many ways she is now seen as inheritor of the American "glow," or position, attached to Colombians' and Mexicans' knowledge of the drug trade controlling one of the greatest drug markets—the United States. In this regard, why she had to flee Mexico and her companionship with foreigners such as her Galician lover, a Russian Mafia lord, and even her lesbian friend and business partner all mark an outsider status that, through the nostalgia of exile, serves to buttress her social capital in symbolically lucrative ways.

This national exile and transnational element are in many ways secondary, however, or, rather, a more explicit rendering of the subtle exile that she, and all *norteños,* by extension, carry in their hearts. Teresa Mendoza's character is able to reconnect with the essentializing nature of exile in narco-drama and to express the universal element of narco-culture: historically specific human beings caught in violent frameworks not of their making and through it all trying to regain or maintain the most basic human dignity and pride. It is these problematic articulations that Teresa embodies most vividly and that her soliloquies speak to. Her struggle is a universal struggle for love and recognition, but clearly embodied within the context of a *norteño* culture of fierce social competition, rejection, and overarching patriarchy. It is within this regional expression of life's cultural specificity that Teresa's words echo in the hearts of people along the border who live their lives on borrowed time:

> I'll tell you—I'm so afraid, I feel so weak, so indecisive, that I burn up all my energy and my willpower, to the last ounce, in hiding the fact that I'm afraid. You can't imagine the effort. *Because I never chose this, and the* corrido, *somebody else wrote the words to it.* You. Patty. Them. What a *pendeja,* huh? I don't like life in general and mine in particular. I don't even like the parasitic fucking tiny life that's inside me. I'm sick with something that I refused to try to understand a long time ago, and I'm not even honest, because I won't talk about it. I've lived for twelve years like this. All the time pretending and not talking. (Pérez-Reverte 2002a: 385; emphasis mine)

It is the exile trope, an existential element inherent in postcolonial and border life, that Teresa expresses in these words and in her own violent life. Geographical exile is but the manifestation of the pervasive exile that narco-dramas exhibit as one of the major raisons d'être, reasons for being, throughout their narrative.

This is also how the ghost of Pedro Páramo, the protagonist of Juan Rulfo's incredibly accomplished novel, haunts not only Teresa Mendoza but also everyone in *La reina del sur.* What if all the characters in the novel are dead? What if they have always been dead but never knew it? This idea becomes the major breakthrough in a dream Teresa has one evening (see opening epigraph), and it poignantly sets the scene for the personal drama of her life and the social drama of her comrades and region, which have contributed to making her who she is.

This major conundrum slowly creeps into Teresa's subconscious to make her realize that she, along with those from her region, are actually the main characters of Juan Rulfo's novel, that it is they, not the novel's characters, who are caught in a nightmare of violence and death and that they are completely removed from life because they have no awareness of being so. It is this death in life (see Baldwin 1984) that the postcolonial narrative of the narco-drama most succinctly embodies. What if this is not life which narco-dramas explore but, somehow, the physical motions and ultimate denial of life at its most perniciously precious and chaotic. And what if living means not living one's life but doing what Teresa does in the novel, escaping this exile into her own being. It is this essentializing exile that *La reina del sur* captures, and in doing so further clarifies the underlying existential tenets of narco-drama at the same time that it elaborates on the hidden historical norms of race and gender at their most hegemonically productive.

It is this exile that is lived in social terms, and not only along the border, as a liminal existence which is never absolute but always identified by the changing nature of the border and its transgressive effects. It is out of the postcolonial legacy of Latin American exile that the social abandonment of the population by its government and leaders derives. Narco-dramas exhibit the failure of government and explain why a population must engage in dangerous and criminal behavior to ensure human dignity in socioeconomic and social terms. It is the same failure of government which throws Teresa out of her geographical and emotional cocoon into foreign hands, into the country which is most historically responsible for making Mexico what it is today. Therefore, it is disturbing for Teresa to feel so eerily comfortable while in exile in Spain, because every single frustrating social characteristic of her existence in Culiacán, Sinaloa, Mexico, and Latin America, has a terrifying counterpart and a precedent in the homeland.

It is in many ways this failure of Mexico's government (and those of the rest of Latin America) to fully account for its country, in terms not only of personal limitations but also of postcolonial and transnational effects, that marks Teresa's life and the lives of so many who have fled Mexico's borders. International, internal, and emotional migrants have all looked for a way to escape deadening normative existence. As in the narco-drama, national and transnational governments are the bad guys. For Teresa and her faithful bodyguard it is the government that is ultimately to blame for their exile, and for the impossibility for all Mexicans living a meaningful life in Mexico, especially in the exploited northern region: "It's the government, *patrona*. If there wasn't any government, or politicians, or gringos up there north of the Río Bravo, a man could live like a king there . . . There wouldn't be any need for pot or any of that, no? . . . We'd live on pure tomatoes" (Pérez-Reverte 2002a: 331).

The underlying antigovernment discourse and antistate rhetoric continue their development in the novel, as in all narco-genre cultural productions. But in no way is this a democratic proposition for new forms of governance or even more traditional revolutionary alternatives to the reigning political structures; it is a much more radical and chaotic proposition. The narco-genre, as evidenced in the foregoing quotation, strongly indicts the government as merely the current representative of the state. In Mexico this contention has been easier to sustain, since the PRI was in power for most of the twentieth century, but narco-drama contrast a much more intimate and primeval understanding of social life that excludes the state.

Narco-drama's critique of the state does not consider the latter a foreign institution but one that has closely defined and marked the population's life options and therefore defined who people and people's loved ones are. At the same time, the choice presented in the narco-drama is not about reforming the state but about recognizing, as it were, a primeval condition of innocence that has been corrupted and thwarted by the government and its social agents and, ultimately, by every single citizen. The narco-genre borrows from the state's official history a primordial, paradisiacal element to which one could return, at least nostalgically and powerfully. While for the Mexican state this place is filled by a strong Indian and pre-Columbian rhetoric, in narco-genres it is a peasant past connected to the land but, significantly, devoid of any Indian presence.

Through Teresa Mendoza we see the same characteristics—of somebody who had to flee her homeland because it failed to provide the safety, sustenance, and livelihood that it should (and claims to) provide. A young, uneducated woman in Culiacán has no other way than to flee her city to become who she is, and through that to get the respect that she deserves and should have gotten, but never did, in her home country. Therefore, the novel's proposal becomes doubly interesting: first, because Pérez-Reverte makes a woman, and not the man that the patriarchal structure typically demands, the antihero; and second, because it is to Spain, the colonizer, that Teresa Mendoza escapes and where, in a sense, she regains her historical being from the same power that took it away centuries ago.

It is this contradictory postcolonial legacy that Teresa Mendoza's plight embodies as the typical neocolonial power of the narco-drama—the United States—is replaced by the preeminent colonial presence—Spain. It is as if the transnational migrant flow from south to north is but a repetition of a colonial legacy that has been replaced but never interrupted. This is also how Spain enters again into the fray as the ultimate marker of colonial subjugation. Interestingly enough, the decades since the 1960s have also seen a resurgence of South and Central American migration to Spain along with greater repression by Spain of the new American migrants. This might be changing in light of the controversial (for the European Union) migration policy changes championed by José Luis Rodríguez Zapatero's socialist government (*New York Times,* Feb. 8, 2005).

Spain therefore enters the picture in varied ways, activating a postcolonial legacy that has been replaced but never really altered, most of all in the minds of colonizers and colonized alike. One could argue that Spain seems to be depicted in the narco-drama as the original colonial trauma, which has to be healed in order to rid oneself of reoccurring recolonizations (see Duras 1967). Healing implies a reenactment of the original traumatic experience, since only reliving that moment can allow plausible resignification, and thus the liberation of the colonial subject. Perhaps this is what makes Teresa Mendoza's feeling of exile part of a postcolonial legacy that subjects her, and her compatriots, to the effects of power that in the end define her intimate surroundings and who she is and will become. Ultimately, it is this essentializing feeling of exile that gets reproduced, with enormous bouts of nostalgia, in a primeval existence that never was but that is needed if one is to regain the sense of human dignity which has been lost in the violent historical ravaging of the land.

DON QUIJOTE AND THE COMPLICATED TROPE OF WOMANHOOD

One of the most interesting contributions of *La reina del sur* is the central role given to a woman. This female depiction also contains strong national and racial implications. Thus it is not insignificant that the title refers to the colonizer, Spain, and may also imply the American continent. The south in the title is rife with significations of underdevelopment, poverty, and Third World status. It also implies a meaning that is present in the usage of the global south as a new descriptor which unsuccessfully maintains the negative markers contained in the category of Third World. The south is also contradictory in that in the novel the North is northern Mexico contrasted with the South of Mediterranean Spain.

These geographical markers are very strong elements of transnational and postcolonial resignification but are, and could only be, reproduced in people's daily lives, in this case, Teresa Mendoza's and all the other characters'. However, this original geographical structure is even further supported by another literary reversal: providing Teresa Mendoza with a strong companion, Pote Gálvez, as her bodyguard. Since the novel is set in Spain it is impossible not to consider the suggestive and subversive idea of a rewriting of *Don Quijote* in which the gender of the main character, el Quijote, is inverted.

There are very strong colonial implications in the inversion and its being placed in the modern genre of narco-drama. Both gender and continental elements are a complete reversal of Cervantes' original proposal, although it would seem that the inversion stops when it comes to the genre itself. Narco-dramas are in many ways the equivalent of the stories of knighthood (*caballería*), the melodramatic enactment, in culturally meaningful ways, of a moment of contemporaneity. And like *Don Quijote, La reina del sur,* and melodramatic production in general, all narco-dramas take the same elements to their extreme, and in doing so provide a hegemonic positioning that enables a situation to change, or to be constituted in slightly different but similar ways (see Butler 1997).

The unique element in this case is the presence of a woman as the central character of the story. However, the story's patriarchal structure remains unchanged, and has to, in order to make the narrative culturally viable. It is not merely an instance of bringing in a woman to play a role that is usually played by a man, to act out the male part in a much more vengeful way; rather, it is a question of using her (sexual and gender) difference to better express patriarchy's enormous shortcomings. It is in this scenario that Teresa Mendoza must many times work within the patriarchal structure, but always knowing it to be a culturally created scenario that does not respond to her organic understanding of herself or the world.

Her contribution, and that of the novel, is paramount in expressing the notion that, alongside all the other narco-dramas, these different patriarchal elements, including violence but also honesty and loyalty, must be used to re-create oneself in the hope that this re-creation will also construct a more humane world. This more humane world may allow one to become a human being only (or perhaps especially) in death, since being alive was not a possibility while one was merely physically living. In this sense, the structure of narco-drama is very similar to the hegemonic reworking of the telenovela, in which an audience can believe for a couple of hours, or only several minutes, in a meaningful symbol of aliveness, which is normally censored in daily existence.

In this sense, narco-dramas are commercially viable, and their stereotypical representation of the northern border captures something that normally escapes official and alternative media representations. The success of the narco-drama is marked by the reality that violence and drugs are the only mediums of survival along the border or by the majority of the population's being implicated in the drug trade and the violence that surrounds it. In many ways what their success provides is a particularly useful trope of a unique form of cultural livelihood, the drug trade, capturing a social signification of violence, oppression, liminality, border imaginary, and patriarchal structure that people live daily no matter their occupation or social condition. Thus one can also understand *norteños'* criticism of Pérez-Reverte, a Spaniard, describing their region, even though they have been using his novel as their own representation of what it means to be *norteño* and to live in this particular space. However, their criticism belies a much greater weariness of having their story taken away, which is the reason narco-dramas were successful in the region in the first place.

Therefore, the space is marked not only by a vibrant drug trade but also by a borderland existence coupled with a typical postcolonial American government and official disregard for the population. Narco-drama is therefore a viable way to tell the region's story in one's own way, thereby escaping the officializing rhetoric of the local good versus the foreign bad dichotomy. The narrative incorporates the complex and violent surroundings to create a melodramatic story of ultimate dignity and redemption in death. It is this redemption that makes the hours during which one watches a narco-drama a significant representation of a powerful social solution expressed by shoot-outs, bank robberies, and executions by the state.

But it is also at this juncture that the insertion of a woman as the central character provides further insights into the hegemonic articulation of the narco-drama. What happens when it is a female who embodies the sexist and violent stereotypes that are the typical behavior of men in these modern fairy tales of drug and homoerotic competition? The process by which these male narratives have developed seems to be immediately exposed by the performance that a woman, in this case, Teresa Mendoza, is able to carry out. Teresa's articulation of the stereotypical male ideal serves to further ridicule, that is, melodramatize, the genre's subjects' behavior and in doing so to contribute directly to the genre's successful production of impossible ideals mixed in with a problematic and violent postcolonial existence.

In keeping with melodramatic protocol, Teresa must not only survive in a patriarchal world, and act like a man to do so, but she must outdo the men at their own game. This active competition proves in a profound way the artificiality of gendered behavior, like all cultural behavior, while limiting the ridiculing of men (or women) and tipping the social structure to her disadvantage. But this also brings into the fray other issues, including authenticity, thereby begging the question, not only gendered but racialized and transnationalized as well, of what is genuine when one is so clearly aware of one's performance in an effort to survive? The question is particularly apt when performance is no longer clearly expressed in external behavior but makes one dangerously aware of the little difference between the mask and who one thought one was. What occurs when both personas are really only one? The answer leads to the recognition that they have always been one, and that the mask was another performance tool essential to survival in intense and vulnerable situations—personal, familial, and social—that developed out of pure necessity.

It is this particular twofoldness that is expressed by Pérez-Reverte in the development of two Teresas who are in constant battle with each other and who vie to represent the "real" one. The other Teresa, the mask that is an essential part of any genuine character, first appears as a defense against the trauma of being raped and as a prelude to her execution. It is under this incredible duress that the other Teresa first distances herself enough from the experience to be able to survive; in distancing herself she also assumes the coolness and detachment needed to kill the aggressor. It is suggestive that this distancing allows an agency which the real Teresa would have never been capable of and therefore she might have been paralyzed by fear.

This employment of a double persona for Teresa marks a form of survival for postcolonial populations, which, like Teresa's character, have suffered, and continue to suffer, an unbearable amount of rape, murder, and pillage as a matter of course and are unable to escape completely. At the same time, though, this twofoldness also marks the kind of death highlighted by Juan Rulfo decades ago and a reoccurring trope of Baldwin's and other American postcolonial writers: the need to escape a social death worse than the physical one could ever be. In Rhys' (1982a) words, there are two deaths, the real one and the one that afflicts your body. And it is the real one, marked by this entombed or masked other, that is the most deadly one of all, especially or particularly because it is so hard to understand. Thus the ultimate fear is of this intimate other hiding its hermeneutic production, hiding its representational reality to impose itself as the authentic person that one knows must never really exist. Yet, the fundamental denial of the stable existence of such an authentic persona is alluring; otherwise, it would not be so productively seductive that it pushed one to believe something one has always known not to be true.

This is by far the most essential characteristic of all postcolonial melodrama and as such is integral to the narco-drama. In one sense the genre takes upon itself the task of representing reality, in its utter, impossible despair, as a reminder of the extreme harshness of life and the impossibility of escape by pretending to be outside of its hegemonic domain. However, narco-drama is able to represent this melodramatic extreme as a form of supreme irony in which one is not only reminded of one's absolute, ambiguous vulnerability but also of an element of agency in one's acceptance of one's predestined and violent faith. It is only by embracing one's actions that there is actually more hope than in the official pretense of both the state and normative culture of evading them. In this other sense, this double persona is also an essential feature of narco-drama, although, unlike in Pérez-Reverte's text, its twofold nature is always implied in border imagery along with the idealized icon of the antihero in question.

It is this ironic element that makes melodrama and narco-drama most successful. This tongue-in-cheek quality allows for the vivid presentation of the most horrendous scenes of violence, like rape and murder, while providing enough distance, even comic relief, to allow a questioning of those elements that are powerfully displayed and that determine the social life of most of the people, and of all of the oppressed, caught in the grasp of the nation's identity. It is this at which texts like *La reina del sur* and films like *El mariachi* are most successful, adding another layer to the status of the narco-drama and allowing one to laugh at what one was already laughing at, even though there is nothing funny about it.

It is also perhaps because of this added level of irony that the Hollywood remake of *El mariachi, Desperado,* played in nearly empty theaters on both sides of the Rio Grande. The North American melodrama takes on in a seriocomic way something that nobody can see the humor in; a successful Spanish actor, oozing Latin charm and testosterone, pretends to be a Mexican fleeing a drug cartel. The racial and transnational effects of Antonio Banderas' playing this role are no laughing matter, at least not in a *norteño* narrative of regional identification and postcolonial survival, both equally in battle with their Spanish origins.

DON QUIJOTE AND THE ADDED PRESENCE OF RACE, CLASS, AND NATION

Perhaps the two most salient similarities between *La reina del sur* and *Don Quijote* relate to irony and the model of a nonsexual partnership between the main protagonist and her and his companion. In terms of irony one has several elements, including the one discussed above, of ultimate ironic melodramatic representation. Just as *Don Quijote* tackles the knight-errantry of Cervantes' time, so does *La reina del sur* assess the stories of knights of our time and looks to weigh in with its enormous melodramatic contribution. However, there is another ironic contribution which deals directly with the postcolonial nature of transnational relationships, especially those marked by migration and the translocal flow of bodies and their labor. This time it is an American, Teresa Mendoza, who is the central protagonist of the play, which shifts the geographical nature of the story and the racial and national elements that are already in place (see Kaminsky 2001).

Marked within this geographical gender difference is the aftermath of five centuries of colonial and postcolonial processes, which shifts emphasis away from Europe and toward the American colonies, now seen as the producers of exotic and a more authentic culture. America is now hailed as being that which it always was in the European imagination: an exotic space free of the oppressive cultural norms that supposedly were the excuse for "civilization" in the first place. Of course, both pretenses were culturally impossible yet were essential to Europe's historical mask and problematic articulation of its own troubled experience.

This geographical difference also shares similarities with another traditional European imaginary utilized by Americans to express their troubled colonial and postcolonial heritage, William Shakespeare's *The Tempest*. Once again, only the male characters of Prospero, Ariel (who is gender neutral but was traditionally hailed as male until the 1970s), and Caliban are seen as the best interpreters of what being American is all about; the female character of Miranda was ignored for three centuries.

Just like Teresa Mendoza, Miranda embodies many of the characteristics of the male players but does it in a much more troubling fashion. This disturbance is primarily based on how she must pretend obedience and loyalty while questioning her father without affecting the reigning patriarchal structure created by Prospero and obeyed by all the other inhabitants of the island. At the same time, she fears the shadow of Sycorax, the witch ousted by Prospero as he conquers her realm, where he can play out the modern narrative of liberation, absolutely terrifying in its postmodern incarnation three centuries later. Miranda and Teresa both embody a different, more American, manner in which to view the world, one that includes but no longer is limited by Europe. These American shifts, albeit a major distortion both in historical hermeneutic and global cosmology, are, significantly, enabled by the presence of a woman; this allows for a (sexual) difference always to be inscribed. In both cases, the male American characters, such as Caliban and Pote Gálvez, fail to inscribe on their bodies the same geographical difference because both suffer the same inherent limitations of the patriarchal structure that enable them to speak more freely. Both male characters therefore embody the innately limiting frustrations of postcolonial existence, which are enhanced by the possibilities of comparing Miranda and Teresa. Miranda has waited for over three centuries for somebody to fully capture her womanhood, and Teresa is playing on another three centuries of quixotic ironies and chasing of patriarchal political windmills.

It is interesting that in terms of obedience and loyalty both women embody these traits more so than the men, since such behaviors are almost genetically inscribed to secure their popular appeal but also their primal socially gendered identification as women. It is this same quasi-genetic trait of loyalty that has been taken on by narco-drama as an essential, and essentializing, part of the melodramatic narrative. In this case, it is loyalty much more than any other element that marks the antihero's powerful categorization as the good guy of the plot, that defines how he (or she) is defined as the decisively good character. Thus the antihero can kill, even rape, but he must remain indestructibly loyal to a code of honor that provides for the reformulation of an essential human dignity that has been stripped away by the state over centuries, and by his family in his lifetime.

It is therefore not surprising that Pérez-Reverte uses loyalty to infuse the essential melodramatic moment into his story of Teresa Mendoza. He does this by playing up the melodrama in the historical legacy of El Quijote as he makes Teresa's sidekick a Mexican thug who has been sent to Spain to kill her but fails twice. It is in this ironic yet ultimately successful failure, and in the fact that both are less than agile physical specimens, that one can see similarities between Pote Gálvez and San-cho Panza.

More important than the similarities is that what makes Pote Gálvez good is the fact that he sticks by his code of honor, even if it seems like misplaced loyalty, since he has twice attempted to take Teresa's life. Teresa pardons him because he wanted to kill her without raping her, thereby abiding by the established code of honor which she now up-holds. Both meet in a foreign land as equal immigrants from a Mexico (and America) that both know has never existed and mutually hopeful about a recognition of human dignity and companionship that is not completely distorted by notions of race, sex, or even national ideals.

This loyalty is what brings Teresa, and Pote Gálvez, back to the real Mexico, one fueled by national fantasy but nowhere near the Mexico they have nostalgically constructed and used to support their essentializ-ing exile. Once again, loyalty operates as the central marker and explains why Pote Gálvez follows Teresa to Mexico, even though he has given up his agency as a form of reciprocity and gratitude for Teresa's sparing his life. When Teresa attempts to leave him behind comfortably set up in Mediterranean Spain, Pote responds agitatedly: "'Quihubo, mi doña . . . You think you're going to do this alone?'" And when Teresa offers the likelihood that they both will most probably be killed by her enemies he, typically, refers to the promise of a future encounter with death and destiny: "'Well, it's a pretty clear decision, patrona . . . You might as well die in one place as another.' . . . 'And sometimes,' he added, 'it's better to choose how you die, if you can'" (Pérez-Reverte 2002a: 399–400).

Therefore, it is loyalty that serves as an iconic emblem for multiple functions. At one level it reemphasizes the postcolonial reworking of the Quijote-Sancho camaraderie in postmodern, American trappings, enabled by the centrality of a woman's presence. It is also in this nonsex-ual heterosexual coupling that another subversive element is powerfully fixed by the narrative, an element that similarly questions the predation suffered by women at the hands of men throughout the Americas but particularly in postrevolutionary Mexico. This nonsexual hetero rela-tionship reemphasizes Teresa's necessary sexual rejection, first of Patricia and then of her last lover, whom she executes, as a marker of stability which was denied her in her passionate involvement with her first two male lovers, el güero Dávila and Santiago Fisterra. Once again, as seen in the melodramatic reworking of the telenovela, sexual passion brings only instability and tragedy; social and personal stability can be bought only at the price of rejecting one's inborn passion and desires. The narratives of narco-drama also inscribe the most basic melodramatic postcolonial instruction: that passion, desire, and longing can only bring harm to those who admit them and to and all those who surround one.

But, ultimately, loyalty is what defines Teresa's return to Mexico, and on her own terms, something she was never able to do as a young girl abused and overrun by the system. It is also this process as enabled by the code of honor that allows her to put the two Teresas—the real Teresa, a seductively dangerous ideal, and the other Teresa—together and reclaim a psychic unity denied her since birth. This unification marks her death in life, the indicative postcolonial split that the historical subject of the Americas still battles. It is this loyalty that marks her salvation, allowing the space, no longer an exotic America but one filled with corrupt politicians and agents of the state, to unite her two selves into an unendingly enigmatic one.

Teresa returns to Mexico to settle a score with an old foe who pretended to be the protector of her and *el güero* Dávila, a godfather of sorts. She escaped with her life thanks to his misjudgment of her capabilities and unrelentingly sexist belief that a woman could never pose a real threat. It was only after her ascent to power that he was willing to face his patriarchal mistake and look to settle the score by sending thugs to kill her in Spain. But it is Teresa who comes back to Mexico to meet him face to face but on her terms, with no more hidden agendas and the pure irony of their mutual hatred. It is an essential melodramatic moment when they meet in the mausoleum of the folk saint Malverde (see Chap. 7), a meeting that testifies to their shared profession and, more important, to their ascribing to the same code of honor that attempts to limit life's chaos and vulnerability.

Malverde's shadow also seems to highlight Teresa's growth as a returned migrant who is no longer a mere pawn of the state or the drug trade. She is now a migrant who, after copying the state's illegal transnational venture, has achieved a much more authentic, and agency-filled, existence and therefore is a much different person from the one who left Mexico. At the same time it is her growth into a whole person that, ironically, defines her national identity, that is the reason she must return, but that offers a national identity that can no longer sustain her and leaves her exiled for good from the sense of belonging she has at long last found.

Thus it makes absolute sense within the narco-drama that she come back to destroy a man who has violated the code of honor, no matter how revolutionary he might be in helping the poor and the underclass. Ultimately, it is this agency-filled act that destroys the state's revolutionary and officializing rhetoric as Teresa learns its rules and simply decides to live by her own at whatever distance from the nation's geographical boundaries and ideals. It is clear that Teresa returns as Teresa out of loyalty not to the gringos, not for the revolution, not even for *el güero* Dávila, but for herself.

THE RACIALIZED ENDING OF A TRANSNATIONAL *CORRIDO*

Ahí va una morra con güevos—apuntó élmer.
—ARTURO PÉREZ-REVERTE, *LA REINA DEL SUR*

Teresa Mendoza's story is a poignant contribution of the narco-drama genre to the assessment of the troubled normalcy of contemporary postcolonial existence in the Americas. *La reina del sur*'s emphasis on the burdened female is highlighted by the intertwined elements of race, class, and transnational identity. The novel works because it fits perfectly into the rags-to-riches plot basic to melodramatic production, but it adds lower-class and race markers that lead to a more meaningful plot.

Throughout the book, Teresa's racial and national identity is equated to that of a typical lower-class woman living on the margins of Sinaloa's male-dominated society. Her exile to Spain serves to emphasize her alien status by adding "Mexican" as the global marker of an inferior racial and national identity. Her associations with minority Spanish nationalities—Russians and Arabs—confirm her outsider status. This status is also confirmed by her liaison with Santiago Fisterra, a man from Galicia, and her continued involvement with the drug trade. All of these elements, and her brief prison stint, eventually define her as the outsider she has always felt herself to be, both inside and outside of Mexico.

At the same time, it is this outsider status which surrounds her with an aura of exotic foreignness, making her a prime target for hegemonic production. It is as if this figurative, racialized marker represents in Teresa all the ambivalent signifiers both rejected and desired by normative culture within a compulsive schizophrenic impulse. It is this ambivalent identity that Teresa uses to define herself and that she navigates in order to achieve a level of authenticity and coherence for the character that she inhabits in the darkest and most intense moments. Not surprisingly, it is race which significantly advances many of the social resignifications contained in powerfully individual moments of identification.

As in other narco-drama the question of race in *La reina del sur* is an interesting one because it highlights many of the private frustrations of the "national question" in Mexico and the rest of the Americas. Unlike South American telenovelas, which utilize an Afro-American (in the continental sense) population, or the Mexican (and other Central American and Andean) state, which uses the Indian emblem, to contrast their hegemonizing plots, narco-dramas do not utilize either. Without any significant presence of blacks or Indians, narco-drama racializes itself and its national plots in a much more hybrid way, one which in many ways manages both to replicate and to reject the homogeneous production of the nation's identity. Teresa, like all narco-drama characters, is a regionalized *norteño*. It is from regional identification, in contrast to the state's homogeneous production of Mexicanness and the rhetorical and living image of an Indian past and present, that the narco-drama obtains its powerful identification.

As in other parts of the Americas (see Benavides 2002), regional identification becomes a strong racial marker, closely aligning itself with class, national, and status markers to serve discrete and ambiguous hierarchies of differentiation. It is this regional-as-racial identification that narco-drama develops and that the narco-*corrido* also takes on as its own, to produce different levels of regional, national, and transnational identification. It is also this same racial marker that Teresa uses to answer questions about the meaning of her life. But it is this nonblack, non-Indian identity that is the one ready to be marked at the border by U.S. law enforcement as inferior to North American identity. And it is in this border transformation, from categorizations of Hispanic though a range of other, less-generous, epithets that all share the brown and lower-class definition needed by the Unites States' imperialistic domain.

I believe it is essential to resist racializing the characters in narco-drama as simply mestizo or Ladino, and in that way falling into the pitfalls of the wonderfully romantic production of Vasconcelos' cosmic race (1997). *Norteño* identification, like that of most of Latin America, is not a homogeneous blending of ancient ancestries but an unequal production of power in which certain historically racialized traditions relate to and are superimposed on each other. This and other regional identities are related to *mestizaje* and miscegenation in that they are hybrids of their original contributors. But their production is far from a monolithic or equally distributed form of identification or even simply a marker of access to resources. Rather, the slightest shifts in color, gender, sexual preference, surname, accent, dress, and finances are enough to change this hybrid *mestizaje* in provocatively rich and different ways. That is why it would be wrong to blanket everybody with a generic mestizo identity unless it is used as an enormous and ironic provocation.

It is this particular hybrid element that Chicana lesbian border scholars like Gloria Anzaldúa (1990, 1987), Chela Sandoval (2000, 1991), and Cherríe Moraga (1986) emphasize in their work. They use it to mark difference, not homogeneity, since that is what it is used for by the state and society, despite homogenizing, hegemonic rhetoric to the contrary. It is this identity that has had a symbiotic relationship with border crossing from the colonial origins of the Americas to its most modern embodiment in Mexico's loss of land to the United States. But this border mentality, as I discuss above, is far from a recent identity or even simply a geographical marker; rather, it is a much larger discourse of postcoloniality that forever marks the ambivalent identification of a colonial, nostalgic sense of not belonging.

It is this foundational wound of hybridity that narco-drama exploits in its most violent and melodramatic simplicity, and also to which the narco-*corrido* sings in its most desolate moments. This is the same desolation of identity that Teresa revisits through *corridos,* tequila, and other Mexican memorabilia in re-creating a new home on the soil of the original culprit in the colonial debacle, or, as Spain is referred to in official circles, *la madre patria* (the motherland). But it is also this language of identity that Teresa, and all her continental compatriots, must contend with in their long struggle to re-create their identity in honest ways that escape official censors and victims' soliloquies about pseudo-intimate behaviors. It is this process of self-discovery and self-identification that unites both the racial conundrum and the struggle for human dignity, making them the content of *corridos* and America's border life.

In Teresa Mendoza's last scene, she rips up the picture of herself as a young woman which she has carried with her all this time. This picture is already ragged, since she has cut out her first male partner, *el güero* Dávila. Since then the picture in many ways has been a constant reminder of her humble origins and the place she came from. Thus the photograph serves as an anchor for who she was and had always been. Yet, this representational remembering, aided by the picture, in many ways marks the process of valid identification and painful living that allows Teresa to find herself (the person she has always been) and therefore to leave that person behind to become her real self.

This is why, in many ways, the picture, after years of being necessarily overburdened as a symbolic signifier, is no longer an aid but instead an impediment to Teresa's coming to terms with her own identity in all its multiple productions. And again, this is one of the postcolonial conundrums in which it becomes necessary to discriminate between authentic and "real" identities in their ambiguous and problematic plausibilities before they manage to define the subject in the most stringent manner possible. This is not an easy task under any conditions but is even more complicated by the historical legacy of a state that actively produces static identities to secure its own social reproduction.

But even in this automatic hegemonic state reproduction, the effects of power are extremely volatile and unpredictable; in many ways, these counterhegemonic moments secure the state's existence. Thus when Teresa rips the picture and gets into the SUV under the protection of the state's agents and with the enormous respect of her Mexican compatriots, she manages to reproduce and contest her official hegemonic identification as a woman and *norteña* all at once. She no longer needs the picture because she has become a unified person by being who she is.

Her trials and travails have not ended, but they will be of a different nature, another type of melodrama and *corrido* to be written in different ways. The tribulations that brought her to this point have served their purpose; they have finished making her who she always was, and a picture is not needed any longer to keep alive the image that will keep her alive in spite of a legacy of colonial violence and identity repression that will never end. It is also to this legacy of agency and liberation, however limited or coerced by the violent signs of the times, that the audience inside and outside the text looks for inspiration and assurance, even if it can be experienced only in the most alcoholic of silences and private contemplation. The hope is the one that shines in the *corrido*, that all "would listen to, their faces stony, and each with a Pacífico in his hand, nodding in silence. The story of the Queen of the South. The corrido to Teresa Mendoza" (Pérez-Reverte 2002a: 434). These are and will be our own *corridos*, but never to be sung by us or in our own words.

Nine

SEX, DRUGS, AND *CUMBIA*

The Hybrid Nature of Culture

Indeed, [the drug dealer's] greatest protector may be the culture
of Sinaloa, where bandits have always been mythologized,
admired, and even protected by poor people.
—*NEW YORK TIMES* (FEBRUARY 9, 2005)

As a mixed regional narrative of drugs, violence, and mu-
sic, narco-drama expresses discourses essential to the structures of daily
reality in Latin America at the same time that it allows a dynamic manner of assessing, by both accepting and questioning, many of the cultural
norms inscribed in the continent's contemporary existence. In this manner, and as with other cultural products and melodramatic enactments,
such as the telenovela, narco-drama provides a safe and insightful way
in which to engage the terror, both literal and imaginary, of life at the
border.

Studies of the geographical and symbolic space between Mexico and
the United States are as numerous as they are provocatively insightful
(see, e.g., Limón 1998, 1994; Ruiz 1998; Ruiz and Sánchez Korrol 2005;
Vélez-Ibáñez 1996). Perhaps this scholarship is most singularly exemplified by the pioneering work of Américo Paredes (1958) and Gloria
Anzaldúa (1987) and by the fictional explorations of Rudolfo Anaya
(1987) and Ana Castillo (1996, 1994, 1992). All of these scholars look to
assess the historical and symbolic specificity that border living exemplifies and that informs the cultural production of the area as well as the
greater exchange between north and south in the Americas.

Narco-drama is part of this larger border discourse and regional/
transnational dialogue, which opens itself to the rest of the continent. As
such, this chapter (and my whole narco-drama analysis) deals with how
these films contribute to the border discourse.

Narco-drama engages elements such as gender, religion, and colonial discourse (as discussed earlier), but it equally entertains sexuality, music, and parody, elements that are essential to the border problematic. Music, particularly Tex-Mex music such as narco-*corridos* and the Mexican reembodiment of Colombian *cumbias,* has been useful in developing a melodramatic sensibility of what it means to live at the border with its myriad significations and ambivalent desires. As in all melodramas, music plays a pivotal role in the narco-drama in marking key moments and characteristics of the action and characters. This approach is vividly highlighted in Robert Rodriguez' first hit movie, *El mariachi,* in which both music and violence, furiously enabled through the nature of parody, express the ambivalent nature of border life.

Before proceeding with the discussion of music and parody, it seems important to highlight the nature of sexual relationships and interaction in narco-drama, specifically, how sex is melodramatically expressed in the *norteño* regional narrative. Because of the enormous patriarchal inclinations of the continent and the region, narco-drama expresses the ambivalent feelings of women and men toward each other and how their interaction is fraught with violence and hierarchical discrimination. Homosexual or other types of sexual behavior are excluded from normative representation and occur only in subtext, possibly as an imaginary (melodramatic) way to reflect them into daily life. Nonheterosexual interactions are also ignored to place heterosexuality on a pedestal and, perhaps even more important, to address the social angst that is not covered up by macho/patriarchal bravado.

It would be tempting, although unrealistic and misguided, to describe narco-drama as simply playing on the patriarchal stereotype of macho men and defenseless women. Quite the contrary, the patriarchal stereotype provides the rich range of sentiments and social values that is expressed in these melodramas—the same values that are parodied in both Arturo Pérez-Reverte's *La reina del sur* (see Chap. 8) and Robert Rodriguez' *El mariachi.* In both works neither women nor men play the traditional roles assigned to them but, rather, maneuver within the prescribed social rigidity of these roles to express themselves more honestly and thereby to offer themselves in the most truthfully chaotic way possible.

These two cultural products, one a book and the other a film, express sexual parody in the explicit fashion used by all narco-drama; this parodic approach is probably responsible for narco-drama's cultural and commercial success. People in the north do not live the way portrayed in narco-drama, and Hollywood films do not portray anything other than what people wish their lives were like. This melodramatic method is powerful precisely because it allows and sustains an active social imagination, essential for daily survival, and even for the maintenance of the oppressive social status quo. But more important, this social imaginary also captures in a real sense the underlying tropes that define people's lives, even when, as part of the "real," those tropes are underground and shifting in their representative modes.

This melodramatic structure is also clearly visible when it comes to sexual representation. Infused with an enormous gender investment, sex plays an essential role in capturing the social tension of all narco-dramas and narco-culture in general. In keeping with Mexico's (and most of the Spanish-speaking world's) sexual mores, sex, though present, never figures prominently due to the understanding of it as a contaminating, modernizing, and foreign influence. Rather, sex is kept in check, both by the visual distance it is afforded and by its rare positioning at the core of plot development. It therefore provides one of the most important melodramatic differences between the telenovela and the narco-drama.

This in no way means an absence of sexual tension but, rather, a much less explicit way of expressing it, a different way of allowing sex and sexuality to carry the burden of the story. The introduction or not of sex into the narco-drama carries with it a contaminating shadow that signals sex's capacity to change the meaning of everything, even the best understood things. Sex is therefore present, even in its absence, as a marker of modern and foreign ways to escape the moral order and *buenas costumbres* of the region. The fact that drug traffickers, men and women alike, participate in a freer and more hedonistic form of sexual morality is a signifier of their corrupt ways. Sex marks their identity with a corrupted modernity signaled by money, material things, and financial success and co-opts their traditional values with neocolonial ideological manipulation and norms.

This may also be why sexual elements, such as clothing and gender attitudes, tend to figure prominently in narco-drama, almost as a counterpoise to the absence of explicit sex. This also possibly explains why in narco-drama it is the men, not the women, as is typical throughout the Americas, who are burdened with having their clothing signal cultural difference, that is, difference from indigenous identity. Thus the cowboy (not the cowgirl) outfit of tight jeans, tooled belt, exotic-leather boots, and silk square print shirts is an overburdened marker of a tradition expressed in the thirst for material goods, a violent way of life, and, ultimately, hedonistic enjoyment of sex and drugs. Women participate in this costume-burdened traditional representation, but they do so mainly by reifying these same manly clothing markers. In doing so, they carry the responsibility for the outside (i.e., modern and foreign) influence that now distorts what is seen as their original way of life in a pristine, nostalgic place which both the state and the narco-drama, obsessively, are forced to re-create.

This particular use of sex does several things, including re-create a state of natural female purity in opposition to a state of public male agency. This Manichean division has long been debated in academic circles; scholars have claimed that this artificial division is essential to the nature of social representation in different cultural contexts but is never a realistic account of the complex sexual and gender differences that it seeks to explicate. In narco-drama it is the men who are constantly seen as the public, active agents, always the aggressors. Yet, far from this behavior's increasing their status or exonerating their shortcomings, it serves only to put the blame and responsibility for everything that is wrong on their manly shoulders. *Norteño* men (and Latin American men in general) silently accept and carry this blame without question or recourse to anything but music and drugs (even if the drugs are only alcohol and cigarettes), as a way of signaling their being the men they should be.

At the same time, however, men's feelings of sexual responsibility and corrupting influence are tempered by the ambivalent desires of women and men alike to somehow escape their living conditions. These are the same life conditions that have been historically thrust on them and that highlight financial success, access to foreign goods, the possibility of pleasure as a central element. It is these ambivalent desires, in place for melodramatic enactment and resolution, that make possible the resolution of the conundrum posed by the threatening ways in which sex and sexual enjoyment are represented. These ambivalent desires exemplify how these prohibited feelings and longings, far from being contaminated or foreign, are a mainstay of daily life in the region but marked by a colonial legacy of prohibition and nonbelonging that now defines who people are.

Violence is an essential feature of Latin American culture; it existed before the Europeans came and used racist violence as a unique form of governance. The Aztec and Inca states had their own violent political procedures in place to keep their conquered populations in check. Therefore, violence and domination have been American staples since the beginning of the continent's history. They seem, however, to have existed within a pristine sense of exotic innocence. It is this naïveté that Latin Americans use most often to get relief from this horrible way of life by blaming their problems on outside influences. It is this subtle reality of historical violence as a constant that allows Latin Americans to recapture the apparently contradictory feeling of being bad while denying that bad is what they have always wanted to be. Being violent is perhaps the only way, however ambivalently, of limiting the Latin American state's definition of the people as violent, even if it means having to allow violence in one's personal life (see Poole 1994).

One must also take into account that the colonial legacy has left behind the unsavory flavor of an ambivalent relationship with pleasure and what could be called surplus livelihood. On the one hand, while everything in one's surroundings is being destroyed, personal pleasure is the only place to which one can escape; this is the reason why so many people from the north keep crossing the border looking for things in Mexico that they will never find. The north-south pleasure seekers have never been in the oppressed and dominated position that they have so successfully inverted to mean the opposite. But it is also in this construction that one must wonder (and narco-drama succinctly captures this element in its violent portrayal of the region) why is it that pleasure and a good living must be portrayed as foreign forms of being, when this is what everybody really wants. We are enthralled in the midst of a melodramatic enactment that brings together the unresolvable sexual conundrums of a postcolonial legacy and also a legacy ready for successful parody as the most viable manner of resolution. It is also this unfulfilled desire, of which economic exploitation is the most explicit symbol, that best defines what the colonial encounter's melodramatic representation is all about.

EL MARIACHI AND ALL THE VIBRANT SOUNDS IT ENTAILS

The low-budget hit *El mariachi* signals many of the issues central to narco-drama's puzzling popular success. Robert Rodriguez' movie plays on the stereotypical melodramatic representation of male thugs and victimized women in the violent context of the drug and border cultures. As a result, *El mariachi* succeeds at many levels: it can be read as another narco-drama Quijote-like parody that plays on the unending confusion caused by brutish men fighting each other for no real reason. The film, initially a film school project, appeals to intellectuals and hybrid Latinos, who see in it a successful parody of how Latinos in general, and border culture in particular, play within the confines of the melodrama to the absolute disregard of social reality. Contained within the film's ridicule of Mexican machismo lies an essential understanding of the larger discourses of "real" border culture that narcodrama so successfully explores.

El mariachi is also able to express, if more flatly, the senseless violence that the genre exports almost daily. It is in this guise that the movie is advertised on the Spanish-language television channels in the United States and how it has captured an audience of billions of Latinos to its complex dramatic reenactment of the drug culture.

The film was remade by Hollywood in a multimillion-dollar production that flopped. In this Hollywood version Antonio Banderas stars as the mariachi player–Lone Ranger who is erroneously mistaken for a drug trafficker and must escape the cartel's henchman, all the while learning the trade and outplaying the criminals at their own game. The movie and the final outcome play on not knowing who he really is: the naïve young mariachi that he thought he was, or the hardened criminal he becomes and who he must have always been without really knowing it.

The film engages these levels of melodramatic representation without ever having to limit its dramatic resolution. Therefore, it is also able to play all the different elements against each other in an ambiguous manner. By far it is the ambivalent role played by music and machismo that is most immediately parodied and deeply exploited for its hegemonic possibilities throughout the film. The fact that the film takes its title from the most widely known Mexican musical tradition only serves to set the stage for the provocatively commodified negotiation of national identity.

The movie starts off by showing a roaming, out-of-work mariachi player who is as vulnerable as he is burdened with being a representative of the music of the Mexican nation. His being unemployed and unable to get a job in the rural area he is passing through points to the anomie of both Mexico and the rest of Latin America. In this postcolonial anomie things seem not only disjointed but also meaningless, no matter how hard one tries to shift oneself or one's perspective to the outside. But not surprisingly, this anomie is also a façade, since no matter how disheartened the mariachi is, he never abandons the search for a job (or a better life over the border or wherever he can find it), even under the harshest of circumstances.

His constant search is not the only way that anomie is eclipsed in the film. In one of the opening scenes, the supposed deadliness of life-as-usual, that is, the postcolonial legacy that shatters everybody's hopes or any acknowledgment of change, is broken by blasts of machine-gun fire at a bar as one cartel moves in to annihilate a rival group. The scene is telling in many regards, including in its revealing how a naïve ma-riachi is able to outwit the murderous thugs who are out to get him. The film emphasizes that, despite the appearance of normality and bore-dom, a constant undercurrent of violence, both personal and social, defines all those who are trapped within the confines of this national and global identification of Latin American existence and forced global development.

The film also shatters any thoughts that this boredom or placidness is the name or the nature of the game. On the contrary, in many regards, this tranquil existence is what is really happening even as audience mem-bers look for life to be happening somewhere else. In this sense the film embodies Kundera's (2000) acknowledgment that life always seems to be happening elsewhere, because it is going on within and around us but is inescapably impossible to fulfill. This same premise is connected with Latin America's postcolonial structure in the sense that life and promise occurred only in the colonizer's homeland; the nature of the colonial relationship excluded the colonized. In other words, the identity of the colonizer was defined by an absence of hope and pleasure; the coloniz-ers erroneously projected this identity into a past that never existed and onto a geographical landscape that the colonized would never again be able to embody.

Life is always happening somewhere else, in a place that one has never seen; it is, however, constantly infused with a violent predisposition not unrelated to an unwavering feeling that one's life is not being fulfilled to the greatest degree possible. Personal grief results from social policy and economic arrangements (imaginary or not) made centuries ago that continue at the hands of the state and the ruling elite. At the same time, these social and economic arrangements introduce a far more threaten-ing feeling that life never happens elsewhere either and that it never has, that more than anything else this feeling has been the most devastating and destructive colonizing tool because it does not allow each commu-nity's potential to be developed in the most authentic way.

Along these lines, *El mariachi* visually wonders if the most threaten-ing political element of all is happiness, to take pleasure in life. Perhaps even more damning, the film asks whether the colonized were really always in control of themselves and things were not as the colonizers pretended. Did the colonizing folly limit the colonizers' future pleasure and survival?

These questions serve as the dramatic backbone of the movie by allowing the mariachi to realize that he may never have been a mariachi in the first place or exclusively a mariachi. Contained within this national representation might be a much larger, and more violent, possibility of redemption which has always been kept in check by the limiting norms and *buenas costumbres* that were supposedly put into his life for his well-being and not, as it turns out, to exclude him.

Of course, this interpretation fails to consider the most basic one: the mariachi has been corrupted and no longer lives up to *buenas costumbres.* Yet, this basic premise is what allows the melodrama to reach such fabulous heights. The simple, moralistic story is always there to rekindle our belief that one's homeland, territory, and national geography can somehow serve us in both a socially meaningful and a personally satisfying manner, and not as the fodder for larger historical projects, including supposedly egalitarian ones.

This is also why the mariachi's recognition and acceptance of his new, violent fate is nothing but acceptance of the daily reality that he has sought elsewhere, away from the colony itself. The transformation is really his awareness that violence is what life has always been about; not recognizing that has really been a denial of life in its fully chaotic reality. That is why violence does not come from the outside but at first, mistakenly, and later, accurately, is contained within the national black box of his guitar case, out of which he now leads a much more secure life as a Mexican citizen. He is still on the road but this time on his own terms. He shares the road with a turtle, slow-moving like him, but without any false pretenses that he is something bigger and better than an animal in the border project of the Latin American nation-state or of life's postcolonial embodiment at the beginning of the twenty-first century.

El mariachi therefore works because, unlike the more traditional (melodramatically speaking) narco-drama, it carries its parody to the extreme. But in another way it is this embodiment of the mariachi as Mexico's national symbol that burdens the main character and captures another set of elements that otherwise could not express the ambivalence of the national being and escape official censorship. This is the film's contribution to narco-drama's insightful representation of border life and its ambivalently productive and hegemonic effect of power. It is through the use of parody that narco-drama, *El mariachi* included, is able to articulate the problematic of having lived a life elsewhere while expressing it in an exquisitely artistic manner.

PARODY AS A NATIONAL FORM

Parody is an essential feature of narco-drama. As highlighted above, this representative form is expressed through reproduction in sexual and musical symbolism, but by far it is parody, not sex or even music, that is the central metaphor through which melodrama is expressed in narco-films. Just as the telenovela presents over-the-top dramatic acting and constantly pushes the dramatic encounter to its highest point, narco-drama utilizes parody to translate the story's key moments. There is constant interplay of elements and questioning of who really is the good guy (law enforcement, law-abiding citizens, Lone Ranger types, or Robin Hood–type drug lords). The fact that any of these characters can be seen as the hero (or antihero) pinpoints the ambiguity of parody in the plot.

Parody thus stands at center stage of narco-films. Who is really the good guy and who, the bad is immediately in question, since the superficial understanding created by following local laws and cultural norms does not make anything clear in the sense of moral resolution. An even more important question asks who is really who. In other words, if reality is not what it appears to be but, on the contrary, one can be sure only that it is not what it appears to be, then the definition of things is for grabs. Not only are the moral tenets of the characters unclear but even their ontological selves are something we know nothing about. We must be very careful about allowing anything, from the epistemological approach to the social context and our own emotions, to answer these questions for us. Nothing, especially people, is what we think it is.

It is through this parodic game that narco-drama is able to express melodramatically the turbulent world of the border. Far from using parody to paint a realistic picture of the characters' surroundings, what narco-drama manages to do is go back to the central tropes of border life and use them to express the much larger "reality" of what it means to live in an environment marked by centuries of hybrid and conflicted histories. This same parody uses comic relief instead of the more traditional official and pedagogical approach to express hidden truths about an external reality independent of one's daily knowledge of things and emotional circumstances. It is painfully obvious to everyone in a narco-drama that such reified elements as external truth do not really exist, and if they do, they are always maintained outside of the locals' struggle for survival.

Therefore, what slowly gets built in the narco-drama is far from a superficial representation of a realistic description of daily life along the northern border; what the audience sees is the constant renegotiation of everything, including identity, which constructs a place where parody is a matter of life and death. Things are not what they seem, and in a hostile environment like the border it is important to learn this as early as possible, because the quality of life will depend on knowing this. Generations of communities have learned not to accept the status quo blindly, because doing so will never guarantee a good future. But these communities have also learned that questioning the status quo only brings the destruction and rejection of their life. All of this leads to a much more ambiguous and ambivalent way in which to live: acting as if one is following principled normative behavior while one is constantly maneuvering to avoid being backed into a corner.

Narco-drama is in a sense a cultural blueprint for maneuvering the treacherous border. Just as crossing the border is a dangerous business during which no guide should be trusted, living at a border crossing in one's own geographical and personal surroundings takes the utmost concern and care. This is where parody comes in, allowing from a very young age a way of being and behaving that makes sure that true desire and therefore the true self are never publicly expressed, even though they are present in every public and private viewing, and in all cultural interactions. Thus all cultural expressions, such as those concerning gender, racial definition, and religious sentiment, are constantly present within this parodic landscape, which makes the self maneuver through a minefield of differences in which it is hard to separate friend from foe and locate the safe havens.

It is this particularly harsh aspect that narco-drama is able to present with enormous precision, and that contributes to the genre's success in Latin America. Narco-drama destroys the notion of realistic representation but also directly contributes to the constant renegotiation and re-playing of elements and identities in contemporary terms. It, then, is not a mere descriptive or even a symbolic replaying of the same social topic but an active participant in the parodic production of the region. Nothing is what it seems, and for it to be hegemonically successful, neither is narco-drama. This is why it can be rejected and condemned by the state, elites, and intellectuals and still manage to come out unscathed and even more hegemonically productive than it originally was. This ability is inherent in melodramatic production.

Narco-drama pretends to be a stereotypical representation, very much as everybody in the region pretends to accept the status quo for reasons of survival. But behind this façade is a realization that this is merely a parodic game, a cultural game, not that different from the one played by everybody, every day, including while sitting in a theater or in front of the television set and watching thugs shoot at each other while women run around defenseless and the law is under the control of those who always succeed. That this is a game is clear, but pretending that this is all there is, is also a game. This is why censorship and denial have no negative effect on the narco-*corrido* and the narco-drama: all repression does is emphasize that what the audience sees in these cultural dramas is true; the state and the ruling elite are always frightened and intimidated by the genuine and autonomous cultural production of those who are not in control of political power.

Censorship is nothing new, since everybody knows that the superficial reading of the narco-drama is a lie, that shooting and killing to survive is not attractive other than as a way to dramatize a desperate situation. Censoring these images only makes it evident that there is something even more disturbing, and therefore genuine, behind these cultural expressions. And since the dramatized violence of the drug wars is not real, there must be even greater forms of social agency and personal fulfillment inscribed within these images than immediately catches the eye. Narco-drama thus contributes to the national configuration of parody as a way of life by both representing and rearticulating a way of being which is central to normative behavior precisely because it is never explicitly defined as such.

Self-representing parody in many ways is what defines the popular appeal of narco-drama. It allows a reprieve from daily situations that are clearly unfathomable in absolute terms. Narco-drama in other ways allows for a reworking of these situations in, hopefully, more productive ways. This is also how such a regionally specific production can serve as a symbol beyond its locale and relate to the general theme of parody as a postcolonial style throughout Mexico and the continent. Neither narco-drama nor *norteños* are the only ones that rely on parody as a way life; on the contrary, parody is a way of life for everyone in a country where revolution has been institutionalized and seventy years of democratic rule did not allow a single opposing party to hold (or even run for, except rarely) executive office. After all, Mexico has a national television variety show called *La parodia* (The parody), which is exported to the United States as well.

Parody, therefore, is very appealing in allowing the most mundane and subtle problems to be articulated in a public way. Nothing is expressed in only one way, just as in real life, and dramatic portrayals and resolutions are equally ambivalent and are interpreted by the beholder, just as actions are. Dramatic action therefore allows everyone, both young and old, to learn not to be single-minded or superficial about the pitfalls of simply going about one's life. The lessons are there, and they have been learned the hard way, with constant reshuffling of intentions and hiding of the most intimate desires. Because these hidden elements and, ultimately, the true self cannot be hidden forever, there is a constant push for dramatic representation. This drive makes it that much more urgent to understand what is going on and to get some pleasure in the process. And since pleasure and joy come only rarely, there is no problem with enjoying them wherever they are found.

Narco-drama participates in this way in the grander scheme of parody as a national, and even continental, form of cultural expression. It uses this trope to express things as they are, even though they will always be different from how they look or are described. Everybody knows that beneath the macho swagger, fragile women, and irrelevant law enforcement officers of narco-drama are hidden much more dangerous and frightening pictures of what daily life is really like. This is the lesson that cannot be missed, especially when one's future depends on that limited space of dramatic and social agency. Narco-drama is filled with exaggerated and ambivalent figures, and they maneuver their social world with parody as their only distancing tool in the search for emotional survival. It is these dramatic, succulent lessons—so essential to hegemonic enculturation—that are consistently devoured with pleasure, especially by those on which the border has made a significant imprint.

THE HYBRID NATURE OF CULTURE

Narco-drama is by its very nature a provocative object of cultural production that entertains more than one area of society in its successful representation of thugs and antiheroes. As such it provides a very useful window into the production of popular culture, particularly as it moves away from state censorship or examination by progressive academics and intellectuals. Rather than seeking the approval of two of the most overt cultural structures in the country, narco-drama has been able to develop independently, independently, that is, of state and academic agendas but not of its own popular and daily ideals.

It is in this milieu that narco-drama is able to provide answers to questions about how popular culture is articulated and about its corresponding political, hegemonic, and authenticity conundrums. As a cultural vehicle it clearly exemplifies the difficulties of relating cultural life to cultural representation, as that relationship is always mediated by some form of emotional and social distancing. Again the trap is to believe that somehow narco-drama provides complete and accurate descriptions of cultural phenomena involved when, on the contrary, what it does is give the audience a sense of what cultural life really feels like. It is the genre's always-disturbing presentation of sentiment and emotion that provokes the most authentic production as well as the one that allows for the least amount of official co-option.

Sentiments and feelings are by nature impossible to control or predict, which is why the colonial and postcolonial authorities in the Americas made them one of the areas most closely guarded by the state. It is feelings, however, which provide the greatest sense of freedom and agency, because they can escape official supervision. It has always been very clear that these same feelings and emotions are what make a sense of liberation from the oppressive status quo possible and, in many regards, what garnered the popularity of the golden age of cinema in Mexico and of the great *ranchera* and *bolero* singers of the twentieth century. They account for the success of the narco-drama as well.

Feelings validate what is being expressed in the sense that they clearly are not being dictated by the forces in power and are able to escape their hegemonic vision, all the while being able to rearticulate their own problematic cultural agenda. Ultimately, melodrama shares the capacity for being able to escape censorship, articulate criticism, and provide for a more realistic agenda under the guise of doing the opposite. Narco-drama, as a successful Latin American melodramatic contribution, has provided a discrete way of keeping the contending cultural forces at bay and navigating closely enough to the shore of cultural continuity not to founder on its reefs.

The biggest conundrum in the narco-drama is the stereotypical reproduction of the most violent and harshest realities of border life. This feature, topped off as it is by patriarchal absolutes, is enough to send the censors away, satisfied with the genre's paean to the inequalities of modern life. Yet this feature does not fool anyone who knows that life is always much more complicated than can be presented in art. Because of this, narco-drama continues to produce powerful sentiments that are implicitly understood by everyone in the theater except the nationalizing forces that look to reinscribe their own limited tropes in this cultural production.

Other contesting forms of cultural articulation exist and provide for a problematic resolution (if any resolution at all) to the conundrum of culture: the regional development and representation that narco-drama portrays are always indebted to implicit national tropes no matter how much they appear to avoid censorship. Even more problematic is that, in many ways, official and academic censors do a disservice to the state and its corresponding image of the nation because both—state and nation—are always in need of counterhegemonic devices and cultural articulation to inform their new adaptations to the changing times. Therefore, escaping censorship is in itself an essential element of the production of popular culture but it also signifies a reinscription, perhaps subtle but no less stringent, of the indispensable marker of the state and the nation.

The state and the nation serve as independent signifiers that are burdened with both practical and symbolic significations. Although they are independent of one another they are intertwined in profound and symbolically meaningful ways. The narco-drama is, because of its success, implicated in the future well-being of the nation and the state, the same entities whose censorship it is able to escape and critique in such colorful and provocative ways. It is as if its being able to escape a basic level of complicity assures its involvement at an even deeper level. The narco-drama cannot succeed without a nation and a politics against which to contrast itself. This is the perplexing difficulty all melodramatic endeavors face, that somehow they are implicated in the critique they are expounding; otherwise, they would have no context or political medium through which to express themselves and popular discontent.

Therefore, it is in this double production of agency and structure that the narco-drama is able to successfully express a new cultural conundrum: how to be *norteño,* to belong to the new millennium, all without leaving behind (as if it were possible) the historical legacy that has contributed to the *norteño* identity. In this sense, the narco-drama is about remaking the *norteño* identity into what one thinks it should be, not about sidelining its essential features. At the same time, the narco-drama is not the exclusive definer of that identity. The nature of capital, particularly border capital in all its guises, is also an essential part of the production of authentic culture.

None of these issues are posed in the narco-drama as questions or even obstacles, because, if they were, no narco-drama would ever be successful. On the contrary, these issues are unconsciously presented and, most important, resolved in profoundly personal ways within the national trope, as part of somebody's desire to be represented, as he or she is defined by national cultural norms, in film or music.

The narco-drama has thus created one of the most original and authentic forms of Mexican cultural life at the turn of the twenty-first century. In its regional bravado and opposition to the state it presents a double co-option, of and by the Mexican state, all while the nation's cinematic and musical images appear to be safe. However, it is in this problematic representation that one immediately senses the genre's unique cultural contribution, not only in Mexico but also on the continent.

I am not arguing that there are no other culturally authentic social movements in Mexico or the rest of the continent—Chiapas and Mexican wrestling spring to mind—but that in its portrayal of the northern border region the narco-drama is one of the movements that has most successfully effected a transnational image within a greater landscape of global capital and immigrants on both sides of the border with the United States. It is therefore in this new, and by that I mean recycled (or reconverted, as García Canclini [1992] would have it), form that new-old types of regional being are taken to their natural and logical national outlet. Old ways of being are not, and can never truly be, abandoned but are reinterpreted to reflect the difficulties of contemporary life. Life along the border has changed over the last century, and the narco-drama in many ways represents that shift and, above all, adaptation to the changing nature of capital, both national and foreign, since those two are never independent of one other. Thus, from the first *corridos* through the ever-evolving and frequently exported *rancheras,* the region has experienced profound changes, and the narco-drama as buffer registers those changes in the most personal and social ways possible. This does not mean that this is the best way, but it is the only way under the hegemonic circumstance of state control and contemporary cybernetic capital.

The images afforded by the narco-drama have in many ways overshadowed the traditional indigenous representations of Mexico's south and the intellectual production of central Mexico; even the revolutionary images have been in some ways replaced by the more fun-loving and gun-toting images of hedonistic thugs. For some, particularly the elite intelligentsia and those associated with the older, more romantic images of the revolutionary state, these romanticized pictures of today's *norteño* identity are a betrayal of the most sacred national ideals. What they do not realize, of course, is that these depictions, like the ones they defend, also embody the undying ideal of the Mexican nation-state as a beacon for Latin America's way of dealing with its powerful northern neighbor. They all share a hegemonic resilience and determination to continue to provide a cultural icon, even under the most violent and terrifying circumstances; after all, violence and terror are nothing new but, rather, old forms of being Mexican, Latin American, and a postcolonial being on the continent.

What is expressed in the narco-drama is an new-old way of existing that necessarily interprets new tropes of representation within historically burdened forms of cultural production. There is nothing novel here except the elimination of any pretense that there is something different happening, and this, like many other elements that catch the attention of the population, is what makes the production of popular culture successful in the first place. This more than anything else allows for hope for the future and continuing engagement with a life that is as harsh as it is unalterable. But at the same it is the distancing mechanism afforded by the narco-drama and other melodramatic approaches that works for a more honest understanding of the ways in which personal life is intimately intertwined with and constrained by both nation and state. And this relationship becomes even more problematic in light of the corrupted figure of the benevolent state and caring nation afforded by the Mexican icons of long ago, resurrected once again to the enduring discomfort of all.

QUESTIONS AND CONUNDRUMS

This work addresses the central question of melodrama and politics: What is the nature of hegemonic articulation in the production of popular cultural media such as the narco-drama? Possibly the most serious quandary involves the relationship of melodrama to the development and evolution of hegemonic constraints within the regional, national, and transnational context within which narco-drama operates. As outlined above, this answer to this question misses the point if it considers only a binary opposition between reified categories of social exclusion and liberating agents of social control. It would also be a disservice to claim simply that hegemonic articulation is a mixture of both categories without spelling out what that means and what the full implications are in terms of hegemony and cultural production.

I believe it is essential to leave by the wayside the idea of contrasting hegemonic and resistant forces and melodrama as free of these influences. On the contrary, melodrama as a cultural tool of political rearticulation is always constrained by these contrasting forces, and many times unequally so. At the same time, melodrama's embeddedness in the social fabric allows it to carry and be burdened with the numerous and ambiguous significations which allow it to be heralded as a medium of popular culture. This is one way in which it can escape the Manichean division that has cursed Latin American social science research over the last century and instead find in that division an insight into the national imaginary in which all cultural products and social lives exist.

Of course, I am resorting to a poststructural approach, as outlined particularly in the work of Michel Foucault, in which domination and resistance cannot be seen as opposite elements in any social phenomena but are intricately woven together in support of each other. Starting from this stance, one is able to understand much of the complexity of cultural institutions such as hospitals and prisons, which, although serving a progressive and liberal agenda, have somehow always been able to align themselves with the most dominant segments of society. But if domination and resistance are not really opposites, just different sides of the same coin, then it is much easier to understand the impossibility of clearly separating one from the other. Perhaps even more important within the Mexican landscape is that this understanding would also explain why revolution could never eradicate domination and repression, merely readapt them to the newly powerful social conditions that fueled the revolution in the first place.

It is in this context that I maintain that we can better assess the powerful political implications of melodrama in general and narco-drama in particular. Narco-drama has never claimed to be neutral or free of the dominating forces of *norteño* society; quite the contrary, it has very proudly heralded a claim to long-standing regional traditions, all of which are intricately implicated in the unequal and hierarchical distribution of social resources. If anything, this unrelenting claim to a much more complex understanding of society has been the primary critique of the narco-drama from progressive groups, intellectuals, and academics, all of which are still implicated in the search for a rapid solution to the continent's undeniable problems of inequality and exploitation. However, this has never been the narco-drama's objective. Far from it, the genre has made a career, and a financially successful one, at that, of restating many of the traditional patriarchal stereotypes. Like the news, it looks to report social reality, not apologize for it.

The narco-drama therefore has not escaped into some sort of political denial and made-up progressive fairy tale that would serve only to erase any contribution and further confuse the political conundrums of the new century. By engaging the tortuous and tormented political landscape, the narco-drama has been able to contribute to the changing face of that same landscape. In Zen terms, things seem to respond most effectively when one is looking the other way, what Foucault (1980) calls the secondary effects of power. The narco-drama has thus been able to open a window to the dramatic structure of the nation by appearing believable to hundreds of thousands, if not millions, of viewers who are more used to being fooled and lied to than entertained and challenged by the media.

It is not a coincidence that, with the popularity of melodrama and narco-drama, actors who are less upper and middle class and more rural and Indian have made their way onto movie and television screens. It is also not a coincidence that the introduction of this more democratic form of national representation has supposedly led to the genres' fall from international tastes. The elite no longer heralds Mexican films as the latest cinematic sensation, and yet more Mexicans than ever are seeing themselves in these films. The narco-drama is just one of the many genres that has been able to take advantage of this epistemological explosion and provide for a much more representative presentation than has been supported by the Hollywoodian melodrama of the (intended) silver screen.

It is also no coincidence that narco-drama has gained a foothold in the media when we remember the large migrant Mexican influx toward the north in search of a better life in the United States or at least along the border in cities like Tijuana, Chihuahua, Juárez, Nuevo Laredo, and Culiacán. More and more, these communities are articulating a new way of being *norteño,* one that is inscribed in border traditions but that has exploded with new, independent ways of being that have left the romantic, revolutionary state with a bitter taste in its mouth. A new metropolitan border mentality, and the influx of new money through the transnational Andean connection, has led to a another way of seeing oneself regionally that has made its way to a growing market of people willing to pay to see themselves on the screen—to have their own dreams and lives immortalized on the screen, just as divas and charros did only a couple of decades ago.

The narco-drama has contributed to creating a different historical subject still perplexed by the conundrums of border life. Left behind were all of the exclusive elite representations that had held the national and continental audience's attention to the quality and tenor of Mexican cinema, a film industry that, not coincidentally, was avidly supported by Hollywood producers (see Fein 2002). The new subject of the narco-drama was the common man (with all his terribly frightening gender inequality) living an imbalanced life against oppressive odds represented by the state and its bureaucratic and repressive agents. It was this image that finally allowed millions of *norteños* to see their struggle represented on screen and in that fashion regain faith in themselves.

This trend cannot be separated from the political control of the ruling party, the PRI, which would finally end after more than seven decades of autocratic rule to fall into the hands of an even more reactionary political party, the Partido Acción Nacional (National Action Party, PAN). However, even this newfound victory had to be claimed by a *norteño*-conscious governor, as Vicente Fox sold himself to be. Perhaps even more important, PAN candidates had to run on an impressive migration platform plank that looked to create a progressive agenda in the party's interaction with the United States in the struggle for recognitions of the Mexicans who had been consistently forgotten by the revolutionary state for decades. This plank was the central element of the agenda of Fox's secretary of state, Jorge Castañeda, who resigned after it became clear post–September 11 that the United States was not going to agree to more progressive immigration policy.

All in all, the narco-drama has been essential to the reconstitution of a *norteño* focus that has slowly been able to claim to be the most viable transnational symbol of Mexico. It is both a result of changing conditions in the north and a key player in enabling this change in the face of trying factors of a transnational magnitude like the drug trade, NAFTA, and, even more recently, the influx of maquiladoras and a recognition of the culture of feminicide at the border. In these films, aided by the musical tradition of the *corrido,* the outsider, the criminal, has slowly been heralded as the true hero, the one who has maintained the valid moral order beyond the superficial norms that only further the exploitation of migrants and rural populations. This recent historical subject is fed by old tales of Lone Rangers and macho men but also by new forms of subjection and livelihood that look beyond revolutions as a form of salvation.

One cannot but help, then, make the serious, romantic, mistake of claiming narco-drama's enduring contribution to a more liberated state of being than has been historically allowed by the postcolonial state in Mexico and the rest of the Americas. Since the 1960s, the narco-drama has infused Mexicans with a different way of being and an independent way of seeing themselves represented on the screen and in real life. This is no small contribution but, in the political game of the nation, is being rearticulated into more dramatic forms of hegemonic constraint. One can only hope for even more new ways of looking at the subject, if not via melodrama at least through popular cultural production that corrects the move toward even greater social constraints and historical subjection.

Ten

CONCLUSION

The Postcolonial Politics of Melodrama

MISTERIO ESTUDIO Q:
THE STUDIES OF MELODRAMA

El problema, señora, es que usted ha confundido el
matrimonio con el amor.
—*EL PARAÍSO NO TIENE PREFERIDOS*, 2005

In the mid-1980s, an interesting melodramatic scenario was expressed in the movie *Misterio Estudio Q* (Mystery Studio Q). Unlike other melodramas, it plays on the medium itself, questioning reality from the viewpoint of fantasy and the nature of melodramatic fantasy and social reality. The film opens when a second-rate telenovela actor finds himself unable to turn down the latest soap opera script when he realizes that it is based on his life. He finds himself repeating the same lines that he is saying on a video so that he and his image are saying the same things at the same time. The problem, of course, is that he has never performed this scene, said these words, or read the script. The mystery is made more apparent when he realizes that the script contains all his dialogue, which he did not even know he was thinking or, odder still, was about to say.

He is intrigued and rushes home to tell his wife that once again they must postpone their vacation because he has finally found "the telenovela," one that has been custom made for him. His decision throws his wife into a rage, which concludes with her threatening to leave him and telling him how little she thinks of him and of his manliness. He agrees with her and offers to start over now that both of them have finally been able to be open and honest with one another.

But as the fight seems to be reaching its melodramatic conclusion, the director/producer interrupts and tells them that it is all wrong. And that is when the audience (through the male lead) learns that something is awry. All along, the male lead thought he was having a fight with his wife in their home, only to realize that they are on a set and that his wife is an actor, just like him, and the fight just another scene in a telenovela. His discomfort is reconfirmed when he drives quickly away from the set to his apartment building only to find himself once again in the studio.

The conundrum elaborated by this film serves as an instructive, albeit concealed, lesson about the ambiguous role that melodrama plays in the contemporary landscape of Latin America. The movie places in dead center a frightening question: What if we are not really alive but, rather, merely players in a prefigured and generalized telenovela with stock characters and stereotypical dialogue? What if, far from being agents of our own fate, we are all constrained by a larger "field of force" in which the decisions we make, the thoughts we think, and even the doubts we have, have all been decided for us beforehand? In many ways this movie serves to frame these questions within the angst-ridden context of the power of performance in our daily lives. It is to this age-old enigma that Shakespeare speaks when he has Jaques say in *As You Like It,* "All the world's a stage, and all the men and women merely players." And this is the same mystery that Oscar Wilde (1964) elaborates to assess the complexity of a postcolonial and gendered subjection.

It is this particular query that I wish to emphasize in the final chapter of this book with regard to the function that melodrama serves in contextualizing a particular postcolonial identity within the changing nature of Latin American society. The stereotypical melodrama of life in Latin America is not a matter of great controversy. In a hierarchical society of heightened social differences, stock roles and responses to difficult life situations could only be molded into specific melodramatic resolutions. That melodrama, defined by excessive sentiment and constrained resolutions, is an active element of life in Latin America is a given and demands little analytical explanation. However, the artistic proposal of elevating melodrama to dizzying representative heights for Latin America, in telenovelas and narco-dramas, is prime for political production.

Thus *Misterio Estudio Q* plays on the knowledge that all Latin Americans inhabit a telenovela or melodrama of one kind or another. That they are constrained by such powerful forms of discursive control is nothing to cry about, no matter how terrifying that limitation might prove to be. However, what *Misterio Estudio Q* does provide is a significant way in which to understand the role of melodrama in outlining an identity that, although transfixed by the postcolonial gaze, is able to rearticulate itself within dynamic moments of unique transformations. The characters in *Misterio Estudio Q* might be caught in an unending melodrama of intrigue and seduction, but this is never an excuse not to struggle against the discourse of desire. On the contrary, these hidden discourses serve to structure the emotional response and intensity with which one must be ready to defend one's life and the people who are most endangered by one's love and attention.

Melodrama is therefore used, after a fashion, to further mediate between the lived-in reality and the deeper notions of the "Real" that must, by their very nature, remain unheeded and unreachable. The telenovela and the narco-drama provide a distorted mirror in front of which to play out one's most hidden desires without interrupting one's own melodramatic livelihood. This form of mediation is essential in a postcolonial setting in which stating a desire or questioning the emperor's new clothes (Sayer 1994) is problematic and comes at a costly personal price. Melodrama, in a way, allows for distancing while maneuvering the troubled waters and permits the Real to continue its unfathomable existence.

Thus the lived-in melodramatic reality is never static; its configuration shifts as a result of the productive effects of the Real and melodramatic distancing mechanisms. It therefore does not matter which side of the camera one is on, or where the melodrama is set. Audience members are united by the melodramatic enterprise as, hidden by the constrained responses of the telenovela and the narco-drama alike, they reposition their lives and desires. Of course, as I have discussed throughout the book, both genres are far from stereotypical but are afforded enormous hegemonic possibilities through the disguise offered by the social constraints of stock characters, plots, and responses.

Far from being an emblem of backwardness or static cultural reproduction, melodrama is a dynamic component in social change. The telenovela and the narco-drama are able to integrate a wide range of cultural situations as they rearticulate and reconfigure melodramatic possibilities. Both genres are able to fulfill their popular-culture ideals, since they entertain an audience that is now capable of recognizing itself in those visual settings that only the upper class and regional elites once inhabited. Even this new democratic representation escapes normative control in the sense that everybody, through the new melodramas or regional tastes, is now able to embody herself or himself as a main protagonist in made-up (and unbelievable) plots, just as happens in real life.

After all, as one of the secondary characters in *Misterio Estudio Q* expounds to the male lead, "You can't take all this melodrama seriously; it is just a telenovela, done for the sheer entertainment of it." All the while he is plotting and conniving to have his character become more important in the story, which suggests what the telenovela and the narco-drama have been able to accomplish for the lower classes. Melodrama has converted dramatic representation from merely an elite form of reproduction and provided for a much more popular form of visual representation, one that allows for powerful identification, and with it many forms of political resolution. As Lévi-Strauss (1973) pointed out decades ago, culture is good to think and eat, but it is also good to see. And in this framework, it is the melodramatic genres that allow the continent's population to visualize itself differently from how it has typically been caught within the official vision, as well as the roles that it has been forced to play out regionally.

Therefore, both genres provide a visual political economy that enables and empowers two of the communities that have been most disenfranchised: women and thugs (criminals). Both groups have been able to accumulate a form of social capital that has escaped its conscious potential, empowering them more than is warranted and producing a revolution (see Martín-Barbero 1987) that has escaped official paradigmatic portrayal. In a profound way, women and thugs are the "creatures of the night" (see Dávila Vásquez 1985), who inhabit patriarchy's repressed world. It is not surprising that both women and thugs, forced to the margins of an official Latin American reality, have been so valuable in melodramatic representation.

Government, the armed forces, and the Catholic Church have been slow to integrate melodrama into their proselytizing, making their disdain for the medium obvious. The fact that the official forms of control have been content to call the telenovela and the narco-drama bad theater allows for a much more convincing form of popular identification, which the genres' enormous revenues serve to further legitimize.

In many ways, *Misterio Estudio Q* serves as well to seal the enduring differences between the telenovela and the narco-drama. The male lead is able to use a prop gun to kill the director/producer, which emphasizes several key political elements in both genres. At a basic level, the murder, if one could call it such, is, tellingly, a defensive act of survival, since the actor is called to play Russian roulette in the scene and shoot a lamp as he toys with the idea of ending his life. However, he makes sure the gun is loaded with real bullets, as he is clearly conscious of his desire to kill the director/producer and end the melodramatic farce once and for all. (It should be noted that at least one real actor has been accidentally shot to death in a narco-film.) His conscious decision escapes the predetermined script, and the fact that the stage manager sees him loading the gun with real bullets but does not stop him speaks volumes to the transformative role of the act.

We are left wondering if this unscripted act, the only agency-filled one in the film, is itself a scripted performance within the larger field of force, therefore making the end of the film mean nothing, since there will be other director/producers in the new configuration of the playing field. The end of the film, like that of all telenovelas and narco-dramas, is not really the end, merely a break until the next melodrama begins, both within and outside of our lives. Therefore, the viewer is never really able to escape the melodrama, since as part of life it has no beginning or end or, more important, outside or inside. *Misterio Estudio Q's* ending also brings into question the hegemonic nature of melodramatic production as a whole and its inevitable role in the political production of cultural identity.

As an essential part of the hegemonic enterprise, melodrama is a continuous cultural project that escapes any particular, narrow, or completely definable agenda. In this sense, the director/producer in *Misterio Estudio Q* is but a symbol of something broader as well as permanent. It is the officiating role of director/producer which looms large and socially essential, not the forces or players that occupy the role at any given time. This is also why the death of the director/producer is not only possible but, ultimately, irrelevant to the development of the melodrama, no matter how defining it might be for the male lead or anyone else who is part of the telenovela in the film. What does matter is the belief that there is always somebody or something beyond the conscious structure in the melodrama and that, as long as this political process is organically in place, the evolution of the melodrama will be secured and made socially relevant.

It is this discursive power, iconoclastically represented by the director/producer, that highlights the key element of hegemonic devices in melodramatic production and its cultural stronghold. Nobody can escape melodrama, either in real life or life as portrayed in the media. In an essential way, the telenovela and narco-drama are merely emblematic of the larger condition of life as a melodramatic farce, lived throughout the continent. It is the pervasiveness of melodrama that also assures and explains its cultural and political success. There is something quite powerful and revolutionary about being presented a picture of one's life under the guise that it is not, and cannot be, one's life. It is a guessing game that enthralls audiences and satisfies seductive, unaddressed desires even though the same plot repeats itself ad infinitum, always with a romantic happy ending and violent shootings.

The repetition does not limit the audience's enjoyment but highlights the very things in melodrama that cannot be mentioned in polite (or academic) conversation. It is precisely because nothing works as it should that the phantasmagorical melodrama of lies and deceit as well as cheap sentiment must be put forward as the only viable form of cultural representation. Melodrama buffers the unreality of experience in both life and representation and in doing so distances us from ourselves (or from those things impossible to digest) while, most important, outlines the complicated form in which the hegemonic enterprise is continuously reformulated.

Hegemony, as a cohesive form of political power and control, works because nobody is able to define its inner workings. Put more specifically, it works because there is really nobody standing outside of its realm of influence or secretly directing it. The secret agenda is that there are no secret agendas (Abrams 1988) and that culture, far from being separate from political process, is its product, birthed at the very center of power and knowledge. There is no "outside" to hegemony. Melodrama, therefore, as one of the most successful contemporary forms of popular culture, is enormously invested in the hegemonic reformulation of Latin American society. The success of melodrama, like that of hegemony, is secured in its social reproduction and in its being able to state similar forms of political domination in differently oppressive ways.

Melodrama's hegemonic success is afforded by the creative manner in which it is able to offer visual representation to the people who are caught in its grasp. However, this Foucauldian understanding of hegemony (and melodrama) does not necessarily preclude agency. Quite the contrary, hegemony is defined by an enormous amount of social agency, as the social actors tend to be represented by the full realm of counterhegemonic possibilities. The official voice of the state and the nation is but one of the many voices in all the forms of social organization. It is in this hegemonic scenario that culture plays its most important role, as regulator of content. Social voices are taken seriously, but the official voice is the loudest, that is, the most normative, and is the one against which the rest are measured.

Melodrama, in Zen fashion, works because it does not look to do so. It is offered (and created) as entertainment that allows audience members to escape the official lies that they hear daily in Latin America. However, it offers a means of reformulating identity beyond the control of the censor and incorporating underlying attitudes that can be taken into consideration only because they are deemed unimportant. Melodrama is part of the larger hegemonic endeavor that ties the Latin American population to a form of social control and culturally normative behavior inherited from colonial times. However, in doing such a good job on the hegemonic front melodrama also provides agency-filled landscapes that have secured its cultural success and provided millions of Latin Americans the possibility of a more humane and viable lifestyle.

Melodrama is far from a static or merely escapist cultural practice. If anything, it escapes censorship as well as the watchful eye of its own markets and producers. It is this ability that is perhaps the most hopeful result of the decades in which melodrama has been produced in Latin America. It has allowed not only a more democratic form of visual representation but also a particular, distinct Latin American way in which to represent oneself on the continent and to the world. It is, in a manner of speaking, the cultural identity offered by both melodramatic genres that is always looking to escape the single-minded cultural environment in which the genres, by necessity, are being produced and recycled.

Cultural identity does not, and cannot, escape hegemony; on the contrary, it is capable of dynamically reformulating hegemonic controls on its own terms. It is precisely because melodrama does not look to revolutionize the cultural landscape that it has been so successful over the last half century and has slowly been able to escape the official discourse it so vividly embodies. Melodramas are not self-contained, despite their having been successfully marketed to deceive everyone, including their own directors/ producers; they have captured Latin American audiences, which have, provocatively, used them as vehicles of self-representation.

THE POSTCOLONIAL CONUNDRUM OF MELODRAMA

Así aprendí que hay que fingir
para vivir decentemente
que amor y fe mentira son
y del dolor se ríe la gente.
—"MADRESELVA"

As I have argued throughout the book, the telenovela and the narco-drama are heavily laden vehicles of cultural identification within the postcolonial context of Latin America. They mark two discrete moments of revolutionary fervor in which Latin America on the whole has looked to envision a way of being different from its postcolonial heritage. The telenovela came of age when both leftist revolutions and guerrillas were springing up throughout the continent alongside the paradigmatic moment in which television entered tens of thousands of households. To an important degree, both revolution and telenovela mark a way of making globalism essential within the local landscape of Latin America and of representing the local to a global audience (and market).

Since the 1960s, both armed revolutionary groups and telenovelas have presented contrasting identities of Latin Americans for continental and global consumption. Both the fiery images of Cuba's Fidel Castro and the rosy ones of the telenovela have seduced audiences into accepting a particular form of Latin American exoticness. Perhaps in many ways, the evolution of the romantic image of Che Guevara since the 1950s has united violent and melodramatic images into one seductive scenario of a desired and democratic future (see Guillermoprieto 2001). This may explain putting Che Guevara's (supposedly) nonpolitical youth on film in *The Motorcycle Diaries*. And the fact that one of the best-known Mexican actors (Gael García Bernal) portrays Che is a testament to the continued blurring of national boundaries, to the marriage of melodrama and revolution, and to culture's political potential. These factors are confirmed by Che's entrance, alongside María Sabina and el Hermano Gregorio, into the pantheon of deities in Venezuela's syncretic African religious tradition.

The narco-drama is laden with a different set of postcolonial parameters. Unlike the telenovela it has never been responsible for creating romantic Latin American images. Quite the contrary, it has been consistently committed to showing a particular *norteño* regional identity at its grittiest, most sexist, most violent. It could easily be argued that, as one of the earliest revolutions of the twentieth century, Mexico's, more than that of any other Latin American nation-state's, demonstrated a disillusioned fervor decades before the rest of the continent. It is this particular form of revolutionary failure that the narco-drama not only inherited and vividly embodies but that has fueled the genre's cultural enterprise. Far from providing a form of utopian liberation, the narco-drama has adapted to the impossibility of liberation and provides a hardened view of the best way to adjust to consistently negative personal and social situations.

In its own way, the narco-drama has been able consistently to reap the benefits of a population no longer able to believe in the ideals of the continent because one-party government institutionalized the Mexican Revolution for over seventy years and killed it and its democratic ideals in the process. The narco-drama therefore learned from the melodramatic trope offered by the telenovela and its utopian ideals (even though those ideals were mainly limited to the romantic arena) but adapted that trope to the changing historical context of Mexico (and the changing political scene of the continent). Border life and the central place of the underground drug economy became the main ingredients of a new melodramatic project that looked to channel the desperate hopes of the struggling Latin American nations.

Therefore, in their own ways, and programmatically separated from each other, both the telenovela and the narco-drama position themselves within the postcolonial legacy of having to deal with the death of the utopian possibilities of revolution in a changing landscape of transformed globalized, capitalistic existence. Both genres have managed to make it to the beginning of the twenty-first century as two of the most popular forms of entertainment. An enormous component of their success is their being able to secure a financial stronghold in those same capitalist relationships that fuel, constrain, and assure their reproduction. Both genres have survived and revived the seductive image of hope and change that was destroyed along with the revolutionary utopia at the end of the twentieth century.

David Scott's (2004, 1999) work is quite instructive in explaining the failures of the postcolonial project and its current embodiment. No one currently living in Latin America, including most Caribbean nation-states, has lived through colonial occupation. The postcolonial project embodied in the struggle against occupying European forces has ended. Gone are the British, Spanish, and most other European armies and agents of control, only to be replaced by an equally violent form of internalized colonialism. The colonizers might be gone but they still define Latin America's form of governance. Therefore, new native forms of subjection have been developed and locked into place; foreign colonizers are no longer needed to do to the formerly colonized population what they now can do to themselves.

This internal form of colonialism was already outlined at the moment of national liberation in the mid-1950s. This early postcolonial project envisioned a continuum between the struggle against occupying forces and the legacy of those forces in the minds and psyches of the colonized populations. Césaire's (1969, 1966) and others' social legacies, including that of the Cuban Revolution, entails a commitment to rethinking and reformulating the most intense and innate forms of struggle to create a new, more humane, form of identify formation. Yet, it is precisely this postcolonial project that has failed or, rather, was never a linear project as was previously thought (see Guillermoprieto 2004).

The ideal of a utopian revolution is moribund in Latin America, but this does not necessarily mean it is dead. A completely new scenario of both domination and social transformation has pervaded the new post-colonial projects in the changing landscape of the continent. The figure of an occupying foreign army is from these contemporary embodiments, replaced by a new socioeconomic empire represented by the north. The United States has represented since the early twentieth century internal-ized foreign occupation and has established a neocolonial form of domi-nation that is only one of the many links between the colonial past and the internalized postcolonial present.

If, however, the specter of neocolonialism has infused the current post-revolutionary fervor in Latin America, the new ethnoscapes (Appadurai 1996) created by global capital and postmodern identities only complicate and pluralize a postcolonial project that had been forcefully represented and pursued. It is here perhaps that the first fracture—recognizing the plurality of a postcolonial project that could never have been homoge-neous even when it needed to be presented as such to ensure short-term political success—must be confronted. It is this plurality of effects, a par-ticular form of the vengeance of the plural, that seems to be clearer now than ever before and that perhaps only now can be incorporated into the postcolonial projects that have always been in place but have never been presented as such.

It is in this plurality of the postcolonial that both the telenovela and the narco-drama are at their most politically meaningful and most sig-nificant in personally social terms. Both genres are responsible in many ways for infusing a new and plausible awareness of the plurality of the social, which in the Latin American landscape means the postcolonial project. The telenovela and the narco-drama make explicit Latin Amer-ica's disunity in every sense but political fantasy and rhetorical ideal. Rather, the continental landscape is filled with national divides, trans-national influences and links, and smaller regional affiliations even cut across national borders. It is in some ways this benefiting of the regional that has been most explicitly expressed in both genres.

The most successful telenovelas, therefore, have always been those that have been most identifiable with the nation or the region and that, almost contradictorily, allow for greater continental identification within a regional representation. Narco-dramas are similar in that these violent visual narratives of the border have been successful in successfully exporting an extremely well defined (even stereotypically so) *norteño* identity to the rest of the continent.

But the popular identity of the narco-drama throughout the continent also points to its violent border narratives, which speak volumes about the homogeneous fantasy implicit in a context constrained within a set of powerful regional markers. This particular form—the violent return of the local—is not unique to Latin America but can be distinguished globally, even when its American configuration has its own features, with melodrama being one of the most visible.

Having been both influenced by and influential in the reworking of a plurality of postcolonial projects, melodrama can be placed within the understanding of new forms of postmodern identity formation as well as the ways in which these new projects are infused with relevant forms of resistance. These two melodramatic genres have been able to present a much more complicated social and political picture than the one embodied in the initial revolutionary postcolonial project, precisely because this was never a concern. Far from being imbued with clear political demarcations, melodrama has looked to efface these gnawing/knowing forms of political mishandling, to make it possible to forget them for a moment.

Therefore, it is out of this need to shift the focus of the social that a whole new form of popular entertainment has succeeded in making a significant part of the continent forget its own existence. This kind of forgetfulness (which was very early on defined, conveniently, as escapist) has been, significantly, productive in several ways. On the one hand, it has reinserted itself in the political landscape, which it had really never left, in the form of a resurgence of popular identity formation that had been limited to key political figures and moments in the preceding decades. In affording this kind of political identification, melodrama has been able to have a voice in places that repressive governments, including Mexico's and Argentina's, have excluded from public discourse. At the same time, these genres have been able to infuse programming with critical awareness, a strategy successful because of the invisibility of the protest. And that protest was already contained in the need for an escapist genre because social conditions were so chaotic that escape was warranted. The mere existence of an escapist form of social melodrama demonstrates the trying conditions of nation-states caught within the webs of their own repression.

On the other hand, we have the burden of the social in full-blown heterogeneous struggle for visual reification, since these social discourses' burgeoning existence has been so utterly (and historically) denied. We could therefore envision melodrama's success as springing equally from the revenge of the repressed and the vengeance of the local, both infused by a heterogeneous social constrained by its own forms of self-definition in the postcolonial liberation project. It is this ideological push that has been enabled and enriched only by the timely insertion of daily melodrama. Thus it has been not only a matter of a greater democratization of identity formation but also of the incorporation of a more intimate form of the personal, in which life and decision making can be seen in the mirror of the television or movie screen without needing translation into divaesque or heroic behavior.

MELODRAMA'S POLITICAL CONTRIBUTION: RESISTANCE (AND HELL) REVISITED

It is these two elements of melodramatic production—infusing a political landscape with its own political absence, and defining the personal as the new visual recognition of the political—that have allowed melodrama to embody the plurality of postcolonial projects. Melodrama is able to hide its initial meaning of escapism or limited personal scope to create a new way of envisioning those same old colonial and neocolonial relationships that fuel contemporary postcolonialism. Therefore, far from representing the old kind of retelling the Latin American social narrative, melodrama is able to project itself into new ways of envisioning nonutopian survival. And in doing so, it has been able to rekindle hope in a way that seems to have been out of the reach of postcolonialism and to define life in a way that is closer to its regional and tragic local (and lived-in) scenario.

We can therefore also envision a kind of resistance in the melodrama's continentwide success. It is able to articulate a kind of being different from the official scripts used by both the nation's and the state's hegemonic enterprises. However, I would distinguish this form of resistance from the utopian form in the revolutionary ideal. The resistance we can discern in melodrama does not propose explicit or even direct counterhegemonic projects; rather, melodramatic resistance comprises multiple strands that, at least on the outside, seem to reconfirm the most unbending limitations and oppressive qualities of daily life. Of course, behind this façade of repressive behavior the unconscious repetition of the most arbitrary cultural practices is exposed in the parodic contribution of melodrama.

Melodrama, more explicitly, proposes an even greater revolutionary ideal by denying that such an ideal exists. Again, it is not from the opposition to mainstream cultural norms that it obtains its power; instead, its influence derives from its apparent contribution to the hegemonic stranglehold. Thus the absence of traditional forms of active resistance cannot but dissipate the nation-state's most explicit political power. After all, power and resistance are never really separate or even abstractly different from one another. Therefore, if power and resistance both are essential to the hegemonic reproduction of the nation-state, the absence of (or even a decrease in) one must have a potentially destabilizing, that is, revolutionary, impact on the whole enterprise of domination and control.

That is why we could argue for melodrama's potential for resistance, not as coming from traditional ideas of resistance or even from contemporary ones, but, rather, as coming from an entirely different set of conditions that up to now have not been defined. Its potential for resistance does not even stem from feigned collusion because, as discussed above, such complicity would be the same as revolutionary fervor within a Zen mind-set. Melodrama's contribution is more along the lines of realizing that there is no way out of the social maelstrom, that there never has been, that the utopian fantasy of liberation and a homogeneous postcolonial project were themselves part of the secret agenda, if one existed. However, far from the control of the agents of the state, a chaotic and socially painful existence continues to shatter the state's complacency on both the conservative and the progressive sides of the argument.

It is this newfound knowledge that hell cannot be escaped so it might as well be enjoyed that calls forth new forms of social rearticulation. These destabilize and restructure the hegemonic enterprise at one and the same time. These contrasting forms of political participation and daily survival are portrayed in melodrama for many of the reasons I have discussed. Yet, perhaps most significant is the fact that there is, finally, a sense of liberation when one realizes one is in hell, in an unhappy marriage, in a dysfunctional family, or living under the thumb of a repressive state. There is a kind of awareness, even when it points only to the untenability of liberation, that looking for escape routes only tightens the knot of identity. Searching for an escape also provides for the knowledge that at least there is one level less of delusion. Further, although one is in hell, at least one finally understands how bizarrely toxic home is, but it is identifiable at last (see Salinger 1978). This is also how melodrama seems to better embody the plurality of postcolonial projects that started two centuries ago and continue to affect the imaginary of what Latin America is and should supposedly aspire to be.

THE MELODRAMATIC
PAINS OF THE NATION

Patria, a veces quisiera ser estatua,
para no sentir tanto dolor.
—"FINAL FELIZ"

My exploration of melodrama's contribution to the social and political landscape of Latin America has been particularly interesting and provocative to me. It has allowed me to assess the changing nature of the postcolonial project from a supposedly singular enterprise to more than one endeavor requiring enormous effort and unconscious resolution. At the same time, it has allowed me to ponder the postmodern identity of Latin America in the twenty-first century and the role that popular culture plays in sustaining, resisting, and reinserting discourses of power in ambivalently hegemonic ways. My research has also contributed to relating melodrama to politics in a way that, while doing justice to the former's contribution to the social, also captures the tensions created by the changing nature of capital and globalization in their new local configuration.

Of course, contained within these new melodramatic forms of postmodern Latin American identity are the pervasive legacies of a postcolonial past that is gone only in its narrative construction. Both the telenovela and the narco-drama embody and project into the future a colonial past defined within a very strict hierarchy not only of class and status but also of race, sex, and gender; all the while they utilize this hierarchy to express and produce subversive elements of popular culture. Thus the violence of guns and murder in the narco-drama speaks volumes about a past in which human lives were less than "bales of capital" (see Kincaid 1997) and inhabiting the correct social mores was marked by strict racial and gendered codes. Therefore, just as is the telenovela, narco-drama is indebted to a postcolonial project that is marked by (and for) a failure to continue the abundant reification of inadequate ways of being a woman or a man and never meeting the European ideal that, because of the very nature of the colonial enterprise, even eluded Europe.

In the final pages, therefore, I would like to address in particular the national melodramatization of the "Real" (in the Lacanian sense). In other words, how closely do these stereotypical dramatizations capture the national discourses that define people's real lives in daily interaction. What are the personal and national emblems that get reutilized to mark melodrama's ability to take to the public sphere the most intimate of desires and doubts, to resignify a public/private split that is as nonexistent as it is socially productive.

The recent Colombian hit *Bolívar soy yo* (I am Bolívar) might help elucidate these points. The movie parodies telenovelas much like *El mariachi* (see Chap. 9) parodies narco-dramas. Both films assess the full implications of a melodramatic turn of events that catapulted Latin America's new identity, translatable in globalized and postmodern terms, into the limelight.

Bolívar soy yo follows a troubled actor (Santiago) who, while portraying Simón Bolívar (the liberator of five South American nations), has a nervous breakdown as a result of his identification with the character. All of the other characters in the movie, from other actors and producers to the president of the country (who is taken hostage by the actor playing Bolívar), are under the impression that Santiago wrongly believes himself to be Simón Bolívar. This assumption is warranted by their refusal to see the actor clearly, since that would mean agreeing that a thorough examination of Bolívar's life is defensible. Even more problematically, they would have to question the value of his melodramatic representation and the failure of the Colombian nation-state (and that of all the other South American nation-states) to fulfill even the most basic of the liberator's dreams.

This anxiety reflects the lack of recognition of most communities at the hands of the state and also from themselves. As part of the postcolonial legacy of violence, it is impossible to recognize the nakedness of the emperor without looking to suffer death; even the image of Bolívar is a vivid reminder of this. This obvious denial (as all denials do) is what makes the dramatization of Bolívar's life a telenovela and what contributes to the character's crisis-driven identification with the historical figure. As Santiago states throughout the film, there is no question in anybody's mind that "of Bolívar's dream the only things left behind were nightmares." Therefore, the liberator must be remembered in official ways by the head of state and even in a melodramatic representation but not in any acknowledgment of the historical denial (as part of its historical hermeneutic) being effected. It is this same postcolonial condition that makes the actor state to the actor portraying the liberator's companion, Manuela Sáenz, "You have grown so used to 170 years of lies that one more does not even matter."

The movie also tackles the essence of melodramatic representation within one's own life. In a telling scene in which Santiago is sleeping with a prostitute whom he visits regularly, he complains about the artificiality and phoniness of his trade and prohibits her from watching his telenovela when it comes on. The prostitute's reaction is equally powerful, as she declares the importance of the telenovela in her life and how she watches it religiously, even interrupting her sex work, because it fills a void that she on her own is unable to fill. But she also adds that it is precisely the phoniness of telenovelas that makes them as effective as they are; after all, "they pay you to feel while I just get paid for pretending with each client."

The prostitute's words are dramatic because they immediately clarify two larger problems. If, as she says, her job is to pretend, then what proof does Santiago have that her feelings toward him are any different? But however traumatic this scenario is, it is only the tip of the iceberg. What if pretense is all there is all the time? And if that is the case, what if it is only in that game that any authenticity and truthfulness can be afforded? Centuries of postcolonial embodiment have left a desert of life and allowed the melodramatic representation of it to be the most worthwhile way in which to efface the void. This is a terrifying possibility.

It is this particular lesson, of melodrama as an authentic lifestyle, that the film, through Santiago, most successfully teaches. The prostitute's words resonate in Santiago's understanding of his identity crisis and allow him to blurt out in front of the Andean region's five presidents: "What they do is not politics but merely theater." The lie is their meeting to publicly commemorate Bolívar's image but not his true legacy. In many respects, it is this secret recognition that Santiago may never have been more alive than when portraying Bolívar that is demonstrated in his identification with the character he is playing. And his difficulties with life before this new shattering identity are clear in his choice of an uncommitted affair with a prostitute, in his still living with his mother, and in his working in a telenovela (the least respected branch of the acting profession) being the most significant achievement of his life and career.

Yet none of this makes him think he is Bolívar; that occurs only when something about the honesty of the character he is portraying makes him aware of a legacy of change, revolution, and truth of which he was unaware. It is precisely because of the fact that, in "acting out" Bolívar, he feels a wealth of emotions that we must wonder about the authenticity of melodrama and the desert of social life. It is this same feverish national identity that is expressed by all the viewers of the telenovela (both in the film and outside it) as they come to realize that they have been denied, and have denied themselves, the opportunity to be faithful to an ideal, national or not, and to live their lives how they would like to and admit to doing so.

Santiago's struggle represents that of any citizen who for one reason or another is confronted by the deception of his or her life and the ongoing difficulties that he or she faces, both internally and externally, when trying to meet the contradiction head on. Melodramatic identification is not just something that could happen to a telenovela actor; it could happen to anyone who watches the telenovela as well. It is the safety present in this overburdened identification which melodrama provides in all its forms along the border and throughout the continent during an hour or two. That identification, however, sees its most dangerous elements expressed when it looks to escape its social containment and begins to represent and question life's inauthenticity every hour of the day.

This is really Santiago's (and everyone's) problem, as the actress playing Manuelita states: "He has stopped being Santiago, and we did not understand that." What is effected by this transformation is not the character's believing he is Bolívar but what the melodramatic confrontation with the feelings expressed in the program provoke. He, the character, and we, through him, are made acutely aware that he has not been truly alive heretofore, even though he had assumed he was and acted as if he were. It is while acting, or role-playing, that he realizes that life is much more open and broader than anything he ever experienced or could have imagined.

This is the same feeling that melodrama provides for a continent, the commitment to a postcolonial project that is as doomed to failure as it is expressed in the neocolonial relationships that have fueled and sustained it over the last century. This is the feeling that has catapulted Latin

Americans into dangerous areas of overburdened identification and the productive effects of life's passionate seduction.

One must always make a choice, but sometimes the "drug chooses you." And melodrama as a drug of choice causes paradigmatic breaks with the postcolonial past and the neocolonial present which cannot but provoke a terrifying trip into the violent destruction of the identity one has always believed in, an identity recovered in a new historic constitution of the Latin American subject. This is the trauma that Santiago senses as he realizes that "the more that he attempts to break out and escape, the deeper the abyss he seems to condemn himself to" (see also Stevens 2003). The conflict of reemphasizing one's identity as one tries to escape its condemnatory features as is at the heart of the postcolonial struggle and that melodrama thrives on. Melodrama is nothing more than the most unambiguous cultural vehicle through which to express the conundrum of the continent's postcolonial existence, which has refused to die but also refuses to be reincarnated in more liberating forms of self-identification and social interaction.

In the meantime, nationalism or national identification and history play particularly privileged roles in defining this postcolonial project's ambivalent plurality. As Baldwin (1990: 480) notes, "power is history's most seductively attired witness." And *Bolívar soy yo* handily expresses these passionate national and historical attachments. Bolívar's historical character provides a chance to look in a historical mirror and try to create a different past, one that will give life to a different present from the one that seems to have entombed us. It is because of this that Spivak (1999) sees the historical enterprise as always about the vanishing present. It is contemporary constitution that allows us to reflect on our lives but also to imagine a different past that would allow the present to be constituted in a different way. It is because of this that both the past and the present change every single day (see Kincaid 1997).

In the case of the film, but also most of the time in Latin America, it is historical recovery, heritage as a daily activity, and national identification that create the most powerful social effects. The characters in *Bolívar soy yo* wish for a different and better Colombia. Santiago wants to rekindle the failed nationalist project of Gran Colombia (which for several shining months in 1830 united Colombia, Ecuador, Venezuela, and Panama into a single nation); he envisions a different difference, socially, economically, and culturally speaking, from the one that has been inherited and that the characters seem destined to play out with boring regularity. What is lost in these national and historical identifications is the understanding that the rhetorical wishes of the past reflect national and historical failures; revisiting similar sites of contention and contradiction would again lead to failure. What is also lost is how these social failures are enterprises that successfully capture people's painful lives and subsequent identities in multiple ways.

History's failure is really what secures a national identity (Renan 1990). The future of a nation depends on the memory of historical failures remaining hidden in a legacy of denial; that denial resides either in successful historical memory (as in the United States) or memory cloaked in misery and victimization (as in Latin America). Either way, historical failure or the failure of history is never, and could not be, without quite powerful and acknowledged effects. But what is also not recognized is the success of this historical failure in fueling a nationalist project that surpasses what the inversion of this failure would look like. The nation demands these sacrifices of conscience as much as it demands physical sacrifice during war and citizenship status. The nation, more accurately, depends on a citizen's reinscription in these historical failures to signify his or her most intimate personal and national identification.

Therefore, revolutions have been doomed to failure in the postcolonial landscape of Latin America. Their empirical failure, backed by historical failure, is what serves as the benchmark of each Latin American nation-state's existence. What has been lost is the ability of these failures to expose national and personal existence as one and the same thing and to hide their own hermeneutical process. It is not only never or exclusively about the nation, or only about history's legitimizing role as a narrative of denial in the construction of the nation; the people of Latin America are the only ones who can create themselves, and the nation in the process. They, and no one or nothing else—no secret agendas, no army officers, no hidden cameras—do better what they have learned to do themselves: subject themselves to the postcolonial process and its multiple social identities.

At the same time, of course, revolutionary fervor is marked by the obsessive insistence on believing that something or somebody is standing outside of the hegemonic enterprise of the nation-state. The narrative of historical denial has been elaborated over the last century as if there is always somebody, the enemy or oneself, standing outside of history and time, who can rearrange the elements of history, hopefully, in a more humane way. But the fact is that reality is far from formulated from the outside. In actuality, there is and always has been only "inside": "The struggle has always been inner, and is played out in the outer terrains. . . . Nothing happens in the 'real' world unless it first happens in the images in our heads" (Anzaldúa 1987: 87). Nothing ever stands outside of the hegemonic enterprise but the need to believe in this possibility. This need to believe has fueled the failed national projects that have kept the Latin American nation-states in healthy competition over the last century. This is also why Santiago spends the last half of the film rewriting the history of Colombia but finally has to state that "he cannot find the ending that this history deserves." Of course, the ending will be his and Manuelita's death, with his voice, contradictorily, signaling the final cut of the film's final scene.

That is also why, over and over again, death is seen as the only way out and why melodrama, as a stereotypical form of death, is heightened by the powerful effects of social contribution and difference. The narco-drama always has somebody dying, and the telenovela kills any belief that the life it portrays could ever be ours. All there is, is death, all the time. It is through death that these melodramatic projects have enlightened Latin America's entry into the twenty-first century, with their lasting impression of the life the continent has never had and never will have. But far from this being a sign of the ever-present "modern," it helps us resignify yet another way of being different and constituting Latin America's historical failure in slightly different ways.

A song by the Argentinean Piero ("Lo que pasa" [What passes by]) speaks to a generation of people being killed and disappeared by the brutal military regimes supported by the United States in the 1970s: "Pasa la historia de nuestra nación, siglo tras siglo sin solución" (The history of the nation passes by, century after century without solution). That failure, that deadly invitation, is chosen for melodramatic representation and, hopefully, more enlightened forms of personal and social subjection as well.

*I never feel more beautiful than when I am playing
the role of Betty.*
—AMERICA FERRERA

As I was writing this book, ABC began airing a new television series, *Ugly Betty*. The series is based on the Colombian telenovela
Betty la fea and looks to further capitalize on the U.S. market that the
original telenovela opened up. *Ugly Betty* thus joins other remakes of the
melodrama, such as Mexico's *La fea más bella* and European versions that
have been produced in recent years, to emphasize the success of Latin
American telenovelas in capturing viewers' imaginations worldwide and
how melodrama serves as an unconscious catalyst for many of the social conundrums that a globalized world has brought into focus in the
twenty-first century.

This North American remake of a Latin America telenovela, however, is fraught with tensions that are worth at least acknowledging.
Without a doubt, shows like *Ugly Betty, Dallas, Falcon Crest,* and *Dynasty* deserve study in terms of the social and political issues that they
seem to channel in their unique way. All of these shows represent, I
would argue, a distinct genre that is a hybrid of soap opera and sitcom,
which contributes to their popularity. It is perhaps this hybridity that
makes *Ugly Betty* such an interesting production, one in which the
melodramatic trope of the telenovela is reused ("reconverted" in García
Canclini's [1992] terminology) to develop insights into the new social
makeup that surrounds it.

The success of *Ugly Betty,* marked by both its ratings and Golden
Globe nominations, is particularly striking considering how critical
Latinos were of the idea at first. This is not an insignificant factor when
one realizes that it was this same Latino market in the United States

that was the original targeted audience for the program. Initial criticism came from a very savvy assessment that the program was geared to the Latino market because Latinos have surpassed all other groups, including African Americans, to become the largest minority population in the United States. Their sheer numbers and concomitant financial power have made Latinos (and the gay male population as well) central targets of many new commercial enterprises (see Dávila 2001).

As I argue throughout the book, however, market is not anything to be squeamish about when it comes to melodrama. It is precisely the market and, inscribed within it, the new postmodern narrative of capital that fuel these new melodramatic enterprises. *Ugly Betty,* like all products, sells as part of a greater phenomenon in the new global market that makes difference, in this case, *latinidad,* a new version of the global other. But it is precisely in melodrama where these supposedly reified categories—of otherness, the local, and the global—are meshed in a more interrelational setting than we are usually able to understand. But for North Americans, particularly Latinos, this integrated reality of the local as the global (as I discuss in Chap. 3) is not an academic matter but a daily reality.

If the market is one of the central concerns of melodramatic success, the cultural layers that the medium assesses also have a primary place in the configuration. *Ugly Betty* thus speaks to a large hybrid audience beyond Latinos, who see themselves enmeshed in a postmodern world where difference is being articulated in new ways. *Latinidad* as a newfound identity embodies a signification which is central to the contemporary structure of the U.S. nation-state, in ways which are being articulated in both explicit and subtle ways. Within the popular success of icons such as Jennifer López and Ricky Martin, *Ugly Betty* is but one more element for cultural resignification in a much greater cultural field of force than can be readily understood in explicitly economic terms.

It is also in this respect that the presence of talented artists such as America Ferrera, Salma Hayek, and Vanessa L. Williams highlights the important contribution of minority actors to the show (and the nation-state). In no way does this mean that minority actors are a new phenomenon, or are even rare; rather, the cultural setting and market structure of the United States in this contemporary period allow such success to be read in a more nationally popular way. There is no reason, other than racism, why an African American had not received an Oscar for best actress until the 1990s, or why the market was previously unable to integrate such changing cultural dynamics.

It is this same reality that makes the two female Latina leads in *Ugly Betty* such an interesting political device in the popularity of the program. On one side, America Ferrera's presence carries with it enormous social capital stemming from her own artistic trajectory, particularly in her breakout role as the young Latina in *Real Women Have Curves.* That film translates the enormous conflict of Latino immigrants who are coming of age despite continuously being caught within the shifting old Latin American and new North American cultural mores precisely when the U.S. market is reinscribing in Latino bodies a new way of signifying the same difference. It is also in this manner that the specter of previous Latino actors from Raúl Julia to Lupe Ontiveros (who plays America's mother in *Real Women Have Curves*) roams *Ugly Betty* in powerfully unpredictable ways.

It is perhaps Lupe Ontiveros more than other Latino actors who today embodies previous struggles to have our histories be told on the stage, in film, and on television in a realistic way. From the maid role (played by Shelley Morrison) in the hit sitcom *Will and Grace* to the almost one hundred maid roles (including in *Something's Gotta Give*) played by Lupe Ontiveros, there is a coming-of-age for Latino cultural production that is not separate from the historical struggle of Latin Americans on the whole or from the new global conditions being rearticulated in the United States and even worldwide. It is this complex tension that Ontiveros seemed to hint at when, in a recent interview, she remarked how proud she was of having played a maid so many times and quickly emphasized that she had made a point never to have employed one herself.

Therefore, both America Ferrera and Salma Hayek embody (and there is no way they could not) differing manners in which the local global is being reinscribed by a productive Latino identity in the United States today. Both actors symbolize in a different way new ways of being Latin American in the novel transnational marker of Latino production. In this regard, Salma Hayek, both as actor and producer, makes use of powerful Mexican transnational cultural capital that was central in making the program a reality. However, in line with this transnational way of being, it is also not surprising that *Ugly Betty* is popular not only among Latinos but also among a wider American audience that is enthralled equally by the social and political constraints of postmodernity.

It is perhaps the program's orthodox approach to melodrama that has made it so popular. Just as the program has been willing to differentiate itself from a strict telenovela format, it also has been truthful to the most stereotypical tropes that the genre allows for exploration, from the blatantly racist structure of having the white man placed at the center of all the women (and men) to re-creating the happy and loving Latino family that movies like *Real Women Have Curves* so painfully look to disarticulate.

Yet it is precisely the mining of these stereotypes that makes melodrama, including *Ugly Betty,* useful in terms of exploring the complex manner in which sexual and social desires have been central in constituting personal identity. At the same time, melodrama permits an understanding of how that identity is far from being merely personal but, rather, has long-standing and subconscious constitutive structures that speak to the greater spectral production of the social (see Anzaldúa 1987; Butler 1997; Lacan 1977).

Yet again, in keeping with melodramatic production, *Ugly Betty* has successfully placed queer elements within the very structure of the plot to enable its telling. Perhaps the two most significant queer elements in this regard, other than the central one of Betty's own stereotypical behavior and wardrobe, is Betty's younger brother's "queer/gay" identity and her father's immigration problems. Again, in keeping with the melodramatic format, these queer elements are actually what keeps the story honest and allows taking in the structure on a whole with the grain of salt needed to digest such initially racist provocations. The timing of both cultural elements—a modern gay identity and the recurring questioning of one's migrant status—is part of a larger cultural war that, although involving Latinos, is part of the much broader North American ideological and political conundrum.

All in all, *Ugly Betty* is a "terrible" success in the same way that Latin Americans are constantly caught in the "terrible nostalgia" (as highlighted in the famous bolero "En mi viejo San Juan" [In Old San Juan]) that a hybrid identity entails. As Pérez Firmat (1995) expresses in his poetry collection, *Bilingual Blues,* "how to explain to you that I; don't belong to English; though I belong nowhere else." Thus the program marks a coming-of-age of multiple identities (beyond that of *latinidad* or Americanness), market configurations, and ideological conundrums that has made its success such a ready possibility. And as good melodrama it keeps all these greater social discourses in check while we are riveted by one episode after the other, even though we have to wait a week for the next installment, rather than only a day.

Ultimately, it will be interesting to see if *Ugly Betty* marks the continuous production of a similar genre in a way that *Dynasty* and *Dallas* were unable to maintain. Either way, there is no doubt that melodrama is changing along with us as we populate a twenty-first century plagued with warfare, exploitation, and social discrimination. And although melodrama has never promised to address, or solve, these repeating social maladies, there is no doubt that each melodramatic program embodies such reflective concerns on the part of all the artists and viewers who are central to its success.

REFERENCES

Abrams, Phillip. 1988. "Notes on the Difficulty of Studying the State (1977)." *Journal of Historical Sociology* 1(1): 58–89.

Agrasánchez Jr., Rogelio. 2001. *Cine Mexicano: Poster Art from the Golden Age, 1936–1956*. San Francisco: Chronicle Books.

Allen, Catherine J. 1988. *The Hold Life Has: Coca and Cultural Identity in an Andean Community*. Washington, D.C.: Smithsonian Institution Press.

Amado, Jorge. 1967. *Tieta de Agreste, pastora de cabras*. Buenos Aires: Editorial Losada.

Anaya, Rudolfo A. 1987. *Lord of the Dawn: The Legend of Quetzalcóatl*. Albuquerque: University of New Mexico Press.

Anderson, Benedict. 1991. *Imagined Communities: Reflection on the Origin and Spread of Nationalism* (rev. and exp. ed.). London: Verso.

Angelou, Maya. 1986. *All God's Children Need Traveling Shoes*. New York: Random House.

Anzaldúa, Gloria (editor). 1990. *Making Face, Making Soul: Haciendo Caras: Creative and Critical Perspectives by Feminists of Color*. San Francisco: Aunt Lute Foundation Books.

Anzaldúa, Gloria. 1987. *Borderlands/La Frontera: The New Mestiza*. San Francisco: Aunt Lute Books.

Appadurai, Arjun. 1996. *Modernity at Large: Cultural Dimensions of Globalization*. Minneapolis: University of Minnesota Press.

Astorga, Luis Alejandro. 2003. *Drogas sin fronteras*. Mexico City: Grijalbo.

———. 1996. *El siglo de las drogas*. Mexico City: Espasa-Calpe Mexicana.

———. 1995. *Mitología del narcotraficante en México*. Mexico City: Universidad Nacional Autónoma de México.

Baldwin, James. 1998. *Nobody Knows My Name*. In *Baldwin: Collected Essays*. New York: Library of America.

———. 1990. *Just Above My Head*. New York: Laurel.

———. 1988. *The Fire Next Time*. New York: Laurel.

———. 1984. *Notes of a Native Son*. Boston: Beacon Press.

Bartra, Roger. 1987. *La jaula de la melancolía: Identidad y metamorfosis del mexicano*. Mexico City: Editorial Grijalbo.

Bastide, Roger. 1971. *African Civilisations in the New World*. London: C. Hurst and Company.

Bataille, Georges. 2000. *My Mother; Edwarda; The Dead Man*. New York: Marion Boyars.

———. 1991. *The Impossible*. San Francisco: City Light Books.

———. 1988. *Guilty*. San Francisco: Lapis Press.

———. 1987. *Story of the Eye*. San Francisco: City Light Books.

———. 1986. *Erotism: Death and Sensuality*. San Francisco: City Lights Books.

Beckett, Samuel. 1996. *Nohow On*. New York: Grove Press.

———. 1976. *I Can't Go On, I'll Go On: A Samuel Beckett Reader*. New York: Grove Press.

Benavides, O. Hugo. 2006. *The Politics of Sentiment: Imagining and Remembering Guayaquil*. Austin: University of Texas Press.

———. 2004. *Making Ecuadorian Histories: Four Centuries of Defining Power*. Austin: University of Texas Press.

———. 2002. "The Representation of Guayaquil's Sexual Past: Historicizing the Enchaquirados." *Journal of Latin American Anthropology* 7(1): 68–103.

Berumen, Humberto Félix. 2003. *Tijuana la horrible: Entre la historia y el mito*. Tijuana, Mex.: Colegio de la Frontera Norte.

Borges, Jorge Luis. 2003. *Ficciones*. Madrid: Alianza Editorial.

Boswell, John. 1980. *Christianity, Social Tolerance, and Homosexuality: Gay People in Western Europe from the Beginning of the Christian Era to the Fourteenth Century*. Chicago: University of Chicago Press.

Bowden, Mark. 2001. *Killing Pablo: The Hunt for the World's Greatest Outlaw*. New York: Atlantic Monthly Press.

Brontë, Charlotte. 2003 [1847]. *Jane Eyre*. New York: Barnes and Noble Books.

Brooks, Peter. 2005 [1976]. *The Melodramatic Imagination: Balzac, Henry James, Melodrama and the Mode of Excess*. New Haven, Conn.: Yale University Press.

Butler, Judith. 1997. *The Psychic Life of Power: Theories in Subjection*. Stanford, Calif.: Stanford University Press.

Butler, Judith, Ernesto Laclau, and Slavoj Žižek (editors). 2000. *Contingency, Hegemony, Universality: Contemporary Dialogues on the Left*. New York: Verso.

Cabral, Amilcar. 1974a. *Unity and Struggle: Speeches and Writing*. New York: Monthly Review Press.

———. 1974b. *Return to the Source*. New York: Monthly Review Press.

Cajas, Juan. 2004. *El truquito y la maroma, cocaína, traquetos y pistolocos en Nueva York: Una antropología de la incertidumbre y lo prohibido*. Mexico City: M.A. Porrúa.

Calvino, Italo. 1986. *The Uses of Literature.* New York City: Harcourt Brace and Co.

Castillo, Ana. 1996. *Loverboys.* New York: Plume.

———. 1994. *Massacre of the Dreamers: Essays of Xicanisma.* Albuquerque: University of New Mexico Press.

———. 1992. *The Mixquiahuala Letters.* New York: Anchor Books.

Césaire, Aimé. 1969. *Return to My Native Land.* New York: Penguin Books.

———. 1966. *State of the Union.* Cleveland, Oh.: Asphodel Books.

"Channel This." 2000. *Vanity Fair* (August).

Cortez, Jaime. 1999. *Virgins, Guerrillas, and Locas: Gay Latinos Write about Love.* New York: Cleis Press.

Cueva, Agustín. 1988. *Las democracias restringidas de América Latina: Elementos para una reflexión crítica.* Quito, Ecu.: Editorial Planeta.

"David Scott by Stuart Hall." *Bomb,* no. 90 (Winter 2004): 54–59.

Dávila, Arlene M. 2001. *Latinos, Inc.: The Marketing and Making of a People.* Berkeley and Los Angeles: University of California Press.

Dávila Vásquez, Jorge. 1985. *Las criaturas de la noche.* Quito, Ecu.: Colección Letraviva.

Dawson, Alexander. 2004. *Indian and Nation in Revolutionary Mexico.* Tucson: University of Arizona Press.

de la Cadena, Marisol. 2000. *Indigenous Mestizos: The Politics of Race and Culture in Cuzco, Peru, 1919–1991.* Durham, N.C.: Duke University Press.

de la Cuadra, José. 1985. *Horno y repisas.* Quito, Ecu.: Ed. El Conejo.

de la Peza, Carmen. 1998. *Cine, melodrama y cultura de masas: Estética de la antiestética.* Mexico City: Consejo Nacional para la Cultura y las Artes.

"Los dominicanos desfilaron con orgullo en Nueva York." 2000. *El Diario* (August 14).

Duras, Marguerite. 1985. *The Lover.* New York: Harper and Row.

———. 1967. *The Ravishing of Lol Stein.* New York: Grove Press.

Escobar, Arturo. 1995. *Encountering Development: The Making and Unmaking of the Third World.* Princeton, N.J.: Princeton University Press.

Escobar, Arturo, and Sonia Álvarez (editors). 1987. *The Making of Social Movements in Latin America: Identity, Strategy and Democracy.* Boulder, Colo.: Westview Press.

Fanon, Frantz. 1967. *A Dying Colonialism.* New York: Grove Press.

———. 1966. *Black Skin, White Masks.* New York: Grove Press.

———. 1965. *The Wretched of the Earth.* New York: Grove Press.

Fein, Seth. 2002. "Myths of Cultural Imperialism and Nationalism in Golden Age Mexico Cinema." In *Fragments of a Golden Age: The Politics of Culture in Mexico 1940–2000.* G. Joseph, A. Rubenstein, and E. Zolov, eds. Durham, N.C.: Duke University Press.

Ferguson, James. 1990. *The Anti-Politics Machine: "Development," Depoliticization, and Bureaucratic Power in Lesotho.* Cambridge: Cambridge University Press.

Foucault, Michel. 1998. "A Preface to Transgression." In *Aesthetics, Method and Epistemology.* J. Faubion, ed.; R. Hurley et al., trans. New York: New Press.
———. 1991. *Remarks on Marx.* New York: Semiotext(e).
———. 1990. *The History of Sexuality: An Introduction.* New York: Vintage Books.
———. 1980. *Power and Knowledge: Selected Interviews and Other Writings 1972–1977.* New York: Pantheon Books.
Franco, Jean. 2002. *The Decline and Fall of the Lettered City.* Cambridge, Mass.: Harvard University Press.
———. 1989. *Plotting Women: Gender and Representation in Mexico.* New York: Columbia University Press.
Freire, Paulo. 1992. *Pedagogy of the Oppressed.* New York: Continuum.
Freyre, Gilberto. 1963. *Brazil.* Washington, D.C.: Pan American Union.
———. 1946. *The Masters and the Slaves: A Study in the Development of Brazilian Civilization.* New York: Alfred A. Knopf.
Fuentes, Carlos 2003. *Inquieta compañía.* Mexico City: Alfaguara.
———. 2002. *Los años con Laura Díaz.* Madrid: Punto de Lectura.
———. 1991. *La campaña.* Mexico City: Fondo de Cultura Económica.
———. 1981. *La muerte de Artemio Cruz.* Mexico City: Fondo de Cultura Económica.
Fusco, Coco. 1995. *English Is Broken Here: Notes on Cultural Fusion in the Americas.* New York: New Press.
———. 1994. "The Other History of Intercultural Performance." *The Drama Review: The Journal of Performance Studies* 38(1): 143–67.
Galeano, Eduardo. 1973. *Open Veins of Latin America: Five Centuries of the Pillage of a Continent.* New York: Monthly Review Press.
García, Gustavo. 1997. *Pedro Armendáriz: México en el alma.* 3 vols. Mexico City: Ed. Clío.
García Canclini, Néstor. 1999. *La globalización imaginada.* Buenos Aires: Paidós.
———. 1994. *Los nuevos espectadores: Cine, televisión y video en México.* Mexico City: IMACINE.
———. 1992. "Cultural Reconversion." In *On Edge: The Crisis of Contemporary Latin American Culture,* G. Yudice, J. Flores, and J. Franco, eds. Minneapolis: University of Minnesota Press.
———. 1989. *Tijuana: La casa de toda la gente.* Mexico City: Instituto Nacional de Antropología e Historia—Escuela Nacional de Antropología e Historia and Programa Cultural de la Frontera.
———. 1968. *Cortázar, una antropología poética.* Buenos Aires: Editorial Nova.
Genet, Jean. 1974. *Querelle.* New York: Grove Press.
Giddings, Paula. 1984. *When and Where I Enter: The Impact of Black Women on Race and Sex in America.* New York: Morrow.

Gilroy, Paul. 2000. *Against Race: Imagining Political Culture Beyond the Color Line.* Cambridge, Mass.: Harvard University Press.

———. 1987. *"There Ain't No Black in the Union Jack": The Cultural Politics of Race and Nation.* Chicago: University of Chicago Press.

Gledhill, Christine. 2003. *Reframing British Cinema, 1918–1928: Between Restraint and Passion.* London: British Film Institute Publishing.

——— (editor). 1991. *Stardom: Industry of Desire.* New York: Routledge.

——— (editor). 1987. *Home Is Where the Heart Is: Studies in Melodrama and the Woman's Film.* London: British Film Institute Publishing.

Gómez-Peña, Guillermo. 1996. *The New World Border.* San Francisco: City Lights.

———. 1994. "The Multicultural Paradigm: An Open Letter to the National Arts Community." In *Negotiating Performance: Gender, Sexuality, and Theatricality in Latin/o America.* D. Taylor and J. Villegas, eds. Durham, N.C.: Duke University Press.

———. 1993. *Warrior for Gringostroika: Essays, Performance Text, and Poetry.* St. Paul, Minn.: Graywolf Press.

———. 1991. "Border Brujo." In *Being America: Essays on Art, Literature, and Identity From Latin America.* R. Weiss and A. West, eds. New York: White Pine Press.

Gonzales, Rodolfo "Corky." 2001. *Message to Aztlán.* Houston: Arte Público Press.

González, Anita. 2004. *Jarocho's Soul: Cultural Identity and Afro-Mexican Dance.* Lanham, Md.: University Press of America.

González, Ray (editor). 1996. *Muy Macho: Latino Men Confront Their Manhood.* New York: Anchor Books, Doubleday.

Griffith, James S. 2003. *Folk Saints of the Borderlands: Victims, Bandits and Healers.* Tucson, Az.: Rio Nuevo Publishers.

Gruzinski, Serge. 2002. *The Mestizo Mind: The Intellectual Dynamics of Colonization and Globalization.* New York: Routledge.

Guerra, Erasmo. 1999. *Latin Lovers: True Stories of Latin Men in Love.* New York: Painted Leaf Press.

Guillermoprieto, Alma. 2004. *Dancing with Cuba: A Memoir of the Revolution.* New York: Pantheon Books.

———. 2001. *Looking for History: Dispatches from Latin America.* New York: Vintage Books.

———. 1995. *The Heart That Bleeds: Latin America Now.* New York: Vintage Books.

Gupta, Akhil, and James Ferguson. 1997. "Beyond 'Culture': Space, Identity and the Politics of Difference." In *Culture, Power, Place: Explorations in Critical Anthropology.* A. Gupta and J. Ferguson, eds. Durham, N.C.: Duke University Press.

Hall, Stuart. 1997a. "The Local and the Global: Globalization and Ethnicity." In *Culture, Globalization and the World-System: Contemporary Conditions for the Representation of Identity*. A. King, ed. Minneapolis: University of Minnesota Press.

——. 1997b. "Old and New Identities, Old and New Ethnicities." In *Culture, Globalization and the World-System: Contemporary Conditions for the Representation of Identity*, A. King, ed. Minneapolis: University of Minnesota Press.

——. 1993. *Stuart Hall: Critical Dialogues in Cultural Studies*. New York: Routledge.

Hellman, Lillian. 1980. *Maybe*. Boston: Little, Brown and Co.

Horswell, Michael. 2005. *Decolonizing the Sodomite: Queer Tropes of Sexuality in Colonial Andean Culture*. Austin: University of Texas Press, 2005.

Huntington, Samuel. 2004. *Who Are We? The Challenges of America's Identity*. New York: Simon and Schuster.

Johnson, Randal. 1987. *The Film Industry in Brazil: Culture and the State*. Pittsburgh: University of Pittsburgh Press.

——, and Robert Stam. 1982. *Brazilian Cinema*. London: Associated University Press.

Kaminsky, Amy. 2001. "The Queering of Latin American Literary Studies." *Journal of Latin American Research* 36(2): 201–219.

Kincaid, Jamaica. 1997. *My Brother*. New York: Farrar, Straus and Giroux.

——. 1996. *The Autobiography of My Mother*. New York: Farrar, Straus and Giroux.

——. 1989. *A Small Place*. New York: Plume Books.

Kristeva, Julia. 1991. *Strangers to Ourselves*. New York: Columbia University Press.

Krauze, Enrique. 1997. *Mexico: Biography of Power (A History of Modern Mexico, 1810–1996)*. New York: HarperCollins.

Kuhn, Annette. 1987. "Melodrama, Soap Opera and Theory." In *Home Is Where the Heart Is: Studies in Melodrama and the Woman's Film*. C. Gledhill, ed. London: British Film Institute Publishing.

Kundera, Milan. 2000. *Life Is Elsewhere*. New York: Perennial.

Kureishi, Hanif. 2001. *Intimacy (a Novel) and Midnight All Day (Stories)*. New York: Simon and Schuster.

——. 1990. *The Buddha of Suburbia*. London: Faber and Faber.

——. 1985. "Dirty Washing." *Time Out* (November 14–20).

Lacan, Jacques. 1977. *Écrits: A Selection*. New York: W. W. Norton.

Lancaster, Roger. 1996. *Life Is Hard: Machismo, Danger, and the Intimacy of Power in Nicaragua*. Berkeley and Los Angeles: University of California Press.

Lévi-Strauss, Claude. 1973. *Tristes Tropiques*. New York: Atheneum.

Limón, José Eduardo. 1998. *American Encounters: Greater Mexico, the United States, and the Erotics of Culture*. Boston: Beacon Press.

————. 1994. *Dancing with the Devil: Society and Cultural Poetics in Mexican-American South Texas.* Madison: University of Wisconsin Press.

Lorde, Audre. 1977. "Age, Race, Class, and Sex: Women Redefining Difference." In *Dangerous Liaisons: Gender, Nation, and Postcolonial Perspectives,* A. McClintock, A. Mufti, and E. Shohat, eds. Minneapolis: University of Minnesota Press.

Malatesta, Parisina, and James P. Kiernan. 1999. "The Glitter of Brazil's Baroque Boom (Gold Rush of Late 1690–1700s)." *Americas* 51(1)(February 4).

Mallon, Florencia. 1996. "Constructing Mestizaje in Latin America: Authenticity, Marginality, and Gender in the Claiming of Ethnic Identities." *Journal of Latin American Anthropology* 2(1): 170–181.

Mariátegui, José Carlos. 1955. *Siete ensayos interpretativos de la realidad peruana.* Santiago de Chile: Editorial Universitaria.

Martín-Barbero, Jesús. 1987. *De los medios a las mediaciones: Comunicación, cultura y hegemonía.* Barcelona: Ed. Gustavo Gili.

Martínez, Rubén. 2001. *Crossing Over: A Mexican Family on the Migrant Trail.* New York: Picador.

————. 1998. "Technicolor." In *Half and Half: Writers on Growing Up Biracial and Bicultural.* C. O'Hearn, ed. New York: Pantheon Books.

————. 1992. *The Other Side: Notes from the New L.A., Mexico City and Beyond.* New York: Vintage Books.

McClintock, Anne, Aamir Mufti, and Ella Shohat. 1997. *Dangerous Liaisons: Gender, Nation and Postcolonial Perspectives.* Minneapolis: University of Minnesota Press.

Medrano Platas, Alejandro. 1999. *Quince directores del cine mexicano: Entrevistas.* Mexico City: Plaza y Valdés.

Memmi, Albert. 1991. *The Colonizer and the Colonized.* Boston: Beacon Press.

Menchú, Rigoberta. 1998. *Crossing Borders.* New York: Verso.

————. 1985. *Me llamo Rigoberta Menchú y así me nació la conciencia.* E. Burgos, ed. Mexico City: Siglo Veintiuno.

Mignolo, Walter. 2000. *Local Histories/Global Designs: Coloniality, Subaltern Knowledges, and Border Thinking.* Princeton, N.J.: Princeton University Press.

Miller, Daniel. 1990. "The Young and the Restless in Trinidad: A Case of the Local and the Global in Mass Consumption." In *Consuming Technologies: Media and Information in Domestic Spaces.* R. Silverstone and E. Hirsch, eds. New York: Routledge.

Monsiváis, Carlos. 2000. *Salvador Novo: Lo marginal en el centro.* Mexico City: Ediciones Era.

————. 1997. *Mexican Postcards.* New York: Verso.

Moraga, Cherríe. 1994. "Art in América con Acento." In *Negotiating Performance: Gender, Sexuality and Theatricality in Latin/o America.* D. Taylor and J. Villegas, eds. Durham, N.C.: Duke University Press.

————. 1986. "From a Long Line of Vendidas: Chicanas and Feminism." In *Feminist Studies/Critical Studies.* T. de Lauretis, ed. Bloomington: Indiana University Press.

Morrison, Toni. 1993. *Playing in the Dark: Whiteness in the Literary Imagination.* New York: Vintage Books.

Navia, Patricio, and Marc Zimmerman (editors). 2004. *Las ciudades latinoamericanas en el nuevo (des)orden mundial.* Mexico City: Siglo Veintiuno.

Otero Garabís, Juan. 2000. *Nación y ritmo: "Descargas" desde el Caribe.* San Juan, P.R.: Ediciones Callejón.

Paredes, Américo. 1958. *"With His Pistol in His Hand": A Border Ballad and Its Hero.* Austin: University of Texas Press.

Parker, Richard. 1991. *Bodies, Pleasure, and Passions: Sexual Culture in Contemporary Brazil.* Boston: Beacon Press.

Paz, Octavio. 1997. *El laberinto de la soledad y otras obras.* New York: Penguin Books.

————. 1972. *The Other Mexico: Critique of the Pyramid.* New York: Grove Press.

Pérez Firmat, Gustavo. 1995. *Bilingual Blues.* Tempe, Az.: Bilingual Press/Editorial Bilingüe.

Pérez-Reverte, Arturo. 2002a. *The Queen of the South.* Andrew Hurley, trans. New York: G. P. Putnam's Sons.

————. 2002b. *La reina del sur.* Madrid: Alfaguara.

Poniatowska, Elena. 2001. *Here's to You, Jesusa.* New York: Farrar, Straus and Giroux.

Poole, Deborah (editor). 1994. *Unruly Order: Violence, Power, and Cultural Identity in the High Provinces of Southern Peru.* Boulder, Colo.: Westview.

Puig, Manuel. 1986. *Pubis Angelical.* New York: Vintage Books.

Quijano, Aníbal. 1993. "América Latina en la economía mundial." *Problemas del Desarrollo* 24: 5–18.

Ramón, David. 1997. *Dolores del Río: Volver al origen.* 3 vols. Mexico City: Ed. Clío.

Renan, Ernest. 1990 [1982]. "What Is a Nation?" In *Nation and Narration.* Homi K. Bhabha, ed. London: Routledge.

Restrepo, Laura. 2004. Interview. *Tratos y retratos* (Mexican television program) (February).

Rhys, Jean. 1982a. *Wide Sargasso Sea.* New York: W. W. Norton.

————. 1982b. *Voyage in the Dark.* New York: W. W. Norton.

Ribeiro, Darcy. 1988. *El dilema de América Latina: Estructuras de poder y fuerzas insurgentes.* Mexico City: Siglo Veintiuno.

————. 1972. *The Americas and Civilization.* New York: E. P. Dutton.

Rodriguez, Richard. 2002. *Brown: The Last Discovery of America.* New York: Penguin Books.

————. 1992. *Days of Obligation: An Argument with My Mexican Father.* New York: Penguin Books.

————. 1982. *Hunger of Memory*. New York: Penguin Books.

Rodríguez Cruz, Olga. 2000. *El 68 en el cine mexicano*. Puebla, Mex.: Universidad Iberoamericana, Centro de Difusión Universitaria.

Rosaldo, Renato. 1989. *Culture and Truth: The Remaking of Social Analysis*. Boston: Beacon Press.

Roseberry, William. 1994. "Hegemony and the Language of Contention." In *Everyday Forms of State Formation: Revolution and the Negotiation of Rule in Modern Mexico*. G. Joseph and D. Nugent, eds. Durham, N.C.: Duke University Press.

Rowe, William, and Vivian Schelling. 1992. *Memory and Modernity: Popular Culture in Latin America*. London: Verso.

Rubenstein, Anne. 2002. "Bodies, Cities, Cinema: Pedro Infante's Death as Political Spectacle." In *Fragments of a Golden Age: The Politics of Culture in Mexico 1940–2000*. G. Joseph, A. Rubenstein, and E. Zolov, eds. Durham, N.C.: Duke University Press.

Ruiz, Vicki. 1998. *From Out of the Shadows: Mexican Women in Twentieth-century America*. New York: Oxford University Press.

————, and Virginia Sánchez Korrol. 2005. *Latina Legacies: Identity, Biography, and Community*. New York: Oxford University Press.

Rulfo, Juan. 2003 [1955]. *Pedro Páramo, y El llano en llamas*. Madrid: Ed. Planeta.

Sábato, Ernesto. 1998. *Antes del fin (memorias)*. Buenos Aires: Seix Barral.

Said, Edward. 2000. *Reflections on Exile and Other Essays*. Cambridge, Mass.: Harvard University Press.

————. 1989. "Representing the Colonized: Anthropology's Interlocuters." *Critical Inquiry* 15: 205–225.

————. 1978. *Orientalism*. New York: Pantheon Books.

Salinger, J. D. 1978. *The Catcher in the Rye*. New York: Bantam Books.

Sandoval, Chela. 2000. *Methodology of the Oppressed*. Minneapolis: University of Minnesota Press.

————. 1991. *Feminist Theory under Postmodern Conditions: Towards a Theory of Oppositional Consciousness*. Santa Cruz: University of California at Santa Cruz.

Santiago, Esmeralda, and Joie Davidow (editors). 2000. *Las Mamis: Favorite Latino Authors Remember Their Mothers*. New York: Alfred A. Knopf.

Santos, Lidia. 2001. *Kitsch tropical: Los medios en la literatura y el arte de América Latina*. Madrid: Iberoamericana.

Sayer, Derek. 1994. "Everyday Forms of State Formation: Some Dissident Remarks on 'Hegemony.'" In *Everyday Forms of State Formation: Revolution and the Negotiation of Rule in Modern Mexico*. G. Joseph and D. Nugent, eds. Durham, N.C.: Duke University Press.

Schmidt-Camacho, Alicia. 2004. "Body Counts on the Mexico–US Border: Feminicidio, Reification, and the Mexican Subjectivity." *Chicana/Latina Studies: The Journal of Mujeres Activas en Letras y Cambio Social* 4: 22–61.

Scott, David. 2004. *Conscripts of Modernity: The Tragedy of Colonial Enlightenment.* Durham, N.C.: Duke University Press.

———. 1999. *Refashioning Futures: Criticism after Postcoloniality.* Princeton, N.J.: Princeton University Press.

Scott, James C. 1998. *Seeing Like a State: How Certain Schemes to Improve the Human Condition Have Failed.* New Haven, Conn.: Yale University Press.

Serna, Enrique. 1993. *Jorge el bueno: La vida de Jorge Negrete.* Mexico City: Espejo de Obsidiana.

Spivak, Gayatri Chrakravorty. 1999. *A Critique of Postcolonial Reason: Toward a History of the Vanishing Present.* Cambridge, Mass.: Harvard University Press.

Stam, Robert. 1997. *Tropical Multiculturalism: A Comparative History of Race in Brazilian Cinema and Culture.* Durham, N.C.: Duke University Press.

Stavans, Ilán. 1998. *The Riddle of Cantinflas: Essays on Hispanic Popular Culture.* Albuquerque: University of New Mexico Press.

———. 1995. *The Hispanic Condition: Reflection on Culture and Identity in the Americas.* New York: HarperCollins.

Stevens, Maurice. 2003. *Troubling Beginnings: Trans(per)forming African American History and Identity.* New York: Routledge.

Stoler, Anne. 2002. *Carnal Knowledge and Imperial Power: Race and the Intimate in Colonial Rule.* Berkeley and Los Angeles: University of California Press.

———. 1996. *Race and the Education of Desire: Foucault's History of Sexuality and the Colonial Order of Things.* Durham, N.C.: Duke University Press.

Stutzman, Ronald. 1981. "El Mestizaje: An All-inclusive Ideology of Exclusion." In *Cultural Transformations and Ethnicity in Modern Ecuador.* N. Whitten, ed. Urbana: University of Illinois Press.

"Tais Araújo." 2000. *Latin Style* 6(6) (April).

Taussig, Michael. 1992. *The Nervous System.* New York: Routledge.

Theroux, Paul. 2005. *Blinding Light.* New York: Houghton Mifflin.

Thorsen, Karen (director). 1991. *James Baldwin: The Price of the Ticket.* Videorecording. San Francisco: California Newsreel.

Trelles Plazaola, Luis. 1991. *Cine y mujer en América Latina: Directoras de largometrajes de ficción.* San Juan, P.R.: Editorial de la Universidad de Puerto Rico.

Trexler, Richard. 1995. *Sex and Conquest: Gendered Violence, Political Order, and the European Conquest of the Americas.* Ithaca, N.Y.: Cornell University Press.

Vallejo, Fernando. 1994. *La virgen de los sicarios.* Santafé de Bogotá, Colombia: Editorial Santillana.

Vanderwood, Paul. 2004. *Juan Soldado: Rapist, Murderer, Martyr, Saint.* Durham, N.C.: Duke University Press.

Vasconcelos, José. 1997. *The Cosmic Race: A Bilingual Edition.* D. Jaén, trans. and annot. Baltimore, Md.: Johns Hopkins University Press.

Vélez-Ibáñez, Carlos. 1996. *Border Visions: Mexican Cultures of the Southwest United States.* Tucson: University of Arizona Press.

West, Cornel. 1994. *Race Matters.* New York: Vintage Books.

White, Edmund. 1993. *Genet: A Biography*. New York: Alfred A. Knopf.

Wilde, Oscar. 1964. *De Profundis*. New York: Avon Books.

Williams, Linda. 2004. "Skin Flicks on the Racial Border: Pornography, Exploitation, and Interracial Lust." In *Porn Studies*. L. Williams, ed. Durham, N.C.: Duke University Press.

————. 2001. *Playing the Race Card: Melodramas of Black and White from Uncle Tom to O. J. Simpson*. Princeton, N.J.: Princeton University Press.

Williams, Raymond. 1977. *Marxism and Literature*. Oxford: Oxford University Press.

Wylie, Alison. 1995. "Alternative Histories: Epistemic Disunity and Political Integrity." In *Making Alternative Histories: The Practice of Archaeology and History in Non-western Settings,* T. Patterson and P. Schmidt, eds. Santa Fe, N.M.: School of American Research Press.

Yudice, George, Jean Franco, and Juan Flores (editors). 1992. *On Edge: The Crisis of Contemporary Latin American Culture*. Minneapolis: University of Minnesota Press.

"Xica, su final es inesperado." 2000. *TeleRevista* (May).

Žižek, Slavoj. 2002. *Welcome to the Desert of the Real*. London: Verso

INDEX

ABC. *See* American Broadcasting
Company (ABC)
Adrián está de visita, 6, 21, 67–87
African Americans, 8–10, 31, 34, 47, 51,
59–60, 69, 71, 73, 81, 82, 86, 168,
212
Algeria, 46, 54
American Broadcasting Company
(ABC), 211
Amigos Invisibles, Los, 18
Anaya, Rudolfo, 171
Andersen, Hans Christian, 56
Anderson, Benedict, 20
Andes, 18, 67–69, 75–76, 80, 84–87,
101, 102, 130
Antonioni, Michelangelo, 103
Anzaldúa, Gloria, 54–55, 118, 169, 171
Arabs, 47
Argentina, 6, 19, 56, 68, 98, 113–114,
210
Armendáriz, Pedro, 14, 115
Astorga, Luis, 21, 135
As You Like It, 192
Aterciopelados, 18

Bacilos, 18
Baldwin, James, 9, 21, 33, 49–53, 64,
66, 75, 122, 156, 208; and *Notes of a
Native Son*, 49–53
Banderas, Antonio, 176
Bárbara, Ana, 81

Bartra, Roger, 21
Beckett, Samuel, 87
Betty la fea, 5–6, 21, 55–59, 62, 64–66,
67. See also *Ugly Betty*
Black Skin, White Masks, 46
Bogotá, 89
boleros, x, 18, 90, 183
Bolivar soy yo, 205–210
border culture, 3, 18, 53, 90, 124, 134,
136, 149, 179, 199
Borges, Jorge Luis, 113
Brazil, 4, 6, 19–21, 25–26, 28–29, 56, 59,
62, 68, 126
British Empire, 122, 199
buenas costumbres (normative decency),
39, 43–44, 69, 70, 86, 94, 99, 105,
173, 178

Café Tacuba, 18
Cali, 89
Camacho, Olga, 136–137
Cantinflas, 14
Caribbean, 16, 65, 199
Castañeda, Jorge, 189
Castillo, Ana, 171
Castro, Fidel, 198
Catholic Church, 28, 30, 132–136,
143–151, 194
Cervantes, Miguel de, 159, 163
Chávez, César, 118
Chiapas, 118, 165, 185

Chicanos, 116–118; and La Raza, 118

Chihuahua, 17, 119, 188

City of God, 126

class, social, 29, 82, 86, 92–97, 101, 115, 163–170

Clave siete, 112

Colombia, 6, 15–16, 18, 20, 88–95, 105–107, 204–210; and Afro-Colombians, 21, 68, 94

colonialism, 6, 7, 29, 31–33, 36–37, 43–44, 53, 59, 68, 79–83, 135, 199; and desire, 7; legacies of, 7, 8; and the past, 7, 79–83

crimen del Padre Amaro, El, 14

Cuba, 198, 200

cueva de los alacranes, La, 112

Culiacán, 153–157, 188

culture, 6, 9–11, 15, 17, 28, 51, 85, 89, 96, 101, 105, 113, 121, 128, 135, 145–146, 151, 171, 182–186, 193

cumbias, 16, 18, 22, 88–92, 105–107, 171–190

Dallas, 211

del Río, Dolores, 13

democracy, ix, 6, 12, 19, 89, 130, 157

desire, 32–35, 76, 78, 80, 90, 114, 136

Desperado, 162

Diegues, Carlos, 27

Don Quijote, 158–167

drugs, 3, 15, 17, 21, 91, 93, 127, 130, 134, 160; and cartels, 16, 17, 106, 126, 130

Duras, Marguerite, 54, 158

Dynasty, 211

Ecuador, ix, 19, 117, 208

Escalona, 6, 67–68

esclava Isaura, La, 28

Escobar, Pablo, 130

Esquivel, Laura, 18

Fabulosos Cadillacs, 18

Falcon Crest, 211

family, 36–42, 69, 72–73, 77, 88, 101–105

Fanon, Frantz, 21, 31, 36, 46–49, 66

Félix, María, 14

Ferrera, America, 211–213

folletines, 1, 2

Foucault, Michel, 5, 35, 78, 85, 144, 187, 196

Fox, Vicente, 189

Fuentes, Carlos, 18, 118

Fusco, Coco, 54

García Bernal, Gael, 198

García Canclini, Nestor, 1, 105, 120, 185, 211

García Márquez, Gabriel, 10

Genet, Jean, 85

globalization, 5, 47, 51, 64, 106

Globo, El, 6

Godfather, The, 127

Gómez Peña, Guillermo, 54

Greece, ancient, 76

Guess Who's Coming to Dinner, 21, 69

Guevara, Che, 150

Guillermoprieto, Alma, 198, 200

Hall, Stuart, 8–9, 47, 63, 105, 131

Hayek, Salma, 212–213

Hayworth, Rita, 13

hegemony, 1, 33, 51, 53, 55–56, 105–107, 115, 143, 146, 160, 196

Hermano Gregorio, 133, 198

hijo de Lamberto Quintana, El, 111

hip-hop, 127

Hollywood, 114

identity, 49, 53, 59, 61, 66, 84, 112, 147, 151, 201; and history, 209; and race, 71–75, 163–167; transnational, 167–170; Western, 49–53, 63–66

india María, La, 14

Indians. *See* Native Americans

Infante, Pedro, 14, 115

Japan, 43
Jay-Z, 127
Jesús Malverde. *See* Malverde, Jesús
Jewish ancestry, 25
José I of Portugal, 29
Juan Soldado. *See* Soldado, Juan
Juárez, 17, 97, 119, 188

Kincaid, Jamaica, 37, 55
Kundera, Milan, 177
Kureishi, Hanif, 8, 9, 53

Latin America, ix, 1–2, 4–5, 7–8, 10–15,
    19–22, 25–26, 29, 32, 41, 43, 45, 48–
    49, 52, 55, 57, 59, 65–66, 68, 72, 77,
    87, 90, 92–94, 96–97, 101, 103–105,
    107, 112–118, 121, 123, 128–133,
    138–142, 156, 171–183, 186–187, 192,
    198–205, 209–215
Latinos, 54–55, 58–59, 63–66, 76, 88,
    90, 105, 107, 119, 122, 176, 211–215
Lévi-Strauss, Claude, 125, 194
Lorde, Audre, 52
Lucía, Lucía, 14

Macbeth, 80, 123
machismo, 40
Madres de la Plaza de Mayo, Las, 97
Mafia, 15, 154
Maldita Vecindad, 18
Malverde, Jesús, 21, 132–136, 140–143,
    166
Mandingo, 44
mariachi, El, 126, 162, 172, 175–179
Martín-Barbero, Jesús, 2, 8, 10–12, 36,
    41–42, 44, 56, 71, 105, 194
Marx, Karl, 5
Medellín, 89
Meillassoux, Claude, 125
melodrama, 8, 12, 14–15, 22, 25, 43–44,
    67, 76, 79, 82, 101, 104, 107, 113, 121,
    126–127, 129–131, 135–136, 143, 159,
    161–162, 172, 191–210, 211–215

mestizaje, 117–120, 168
methodology, 3–4
Mexico, x, 1–4, 6, 17, 21, 56, 80–81,
    90–92, 97, 106–107, 111–113, 176,
    178, 183, 186–187, 190, 199, 211;
    and cinema, 13–14, 114–116; and
    exile, 154–158
Mexico City, x, 17, 115–116, 129–
    130
Misterio Estudio Q, 191–197
Molotov, 18
Monsiváis, Carlos, 21
Moraga, Cherríe, 169
Morrison, Shelley, 213
motherhood, 97–101
Motorcycle Diaries, The, 198
Motta, Zezé, 27
My Brother, 37

NAFTA. *See* North American Free-
    Trade Agreement (NAFTA)
narco-*corridos,* 15–16, 18, 131, 135, 141,
    152, 168, 170, 181, 185
narco-dramas, 1–3, 9, 13, 15, 21–22,
    121–131, 156, 168–169, 172, 179, 181,
    183, 186, 188, 190, 196–197; and
    border narratives, 111–116, 132–151,
    175–179; and Colombia, 16–18, 21,
    88–92; and culture, 111–113, 147,
    182–185; and illegality, 116–120;
    and migration, 132–136; and parody,
    179–182
Native Americans, 72, 82–87, 113, 116,
    168
Negrete, Jorge, 115
New York City, x, 26, 119
norteño culture, x, 81, 90, 119, 120,
    124, 127–128, 151, 172, 174, 181,
    184–189, 198, 201
North American Free-Trade Agree-
    ment (NAFTA), 120, 189
Nosotros los pobres, 14
Nuevo Laredo, 188

Oedipus complex, 36
Ontiveros, Lupe, 213
Orquídea sangrienta, 111

pachucos, 118, 119
PAN. *See* Partido de Acción Nacional (PAN)
Panama, 19
Paredes, Américo, 171
Paris, 129
parody, 179–182
Partido de Acción Nacional (PAN), 189
Partido Revolucionario Institucional (PRI), 13, 17, 113, 117, 189
Pasión de gavilanes, 6, 16, 21, 88–107
patriarchy, 15, 126, 188
Paz, Octavio, 18, 118
Pedro Páramo, 139, 155
Pérez-Reverte, Arturo, 21, 152, 155, 157, 160–161, 164, 172
Perón, Eva, 132–133
Peru, 16, 113
Piero, 210
Pobre diablo, 67
politics, ix, 3, 59, 79, 86, 147, 149–150, 164, 195, 200, 203
Poniatowska, Elena, 18
Portugal, 29, 40, 60
post-colonialism, 6–8, 17–20, 52; and cultural icons, 147–151; and desire, 29–36, 59–63, 79–83; and family, 36–42, 97–105; and melodrama, 197–202; and the other, 121–128
postmodernism, 1, 191–197. *See also* post-colonialism
power effects, 5, 78
PRI. *See* Partido Revolucionario Institucional (PRI)
Puerto Rico, 19, 114

Quijano, Aníbal, 7, 53
Quinn, Anthony, 13

race, 9, 21, 25–27, 30, 66, 71–75, 80–83, 86, 95, 113, 118, 152, 158, 167–170. *See also under* identity
rancheras, 16, 18, 183, 185. See also *cumbias*
rape, 29, 91
Ravishing of Lol Stein, The, 54
Raza, La, 117
Real, The, 103–104, 193
Real Women have Curves, 213–214
reina del sur, La, 1, 21, 91, 126–127, 152–170, 172
Restrepo, Laura, 15
Rhys, Jean, 37, 63, 65, 66
Rodrigo D. no futuro, 89
Rodriguez, Richard, 118
Rodriguez, Robert, 172, 175
Rulfo, Juan, 155, 161
Rushdie, Salman, 9

salsa, 18
Sandoval, Chela, 169
Santo, El, 14
Scott, David, 199
Scott, James, ix
Seven Brides for Seven Brothers, 96, 101
sexuality, 9, 15, 22, 27–31, 34, 39, 65, 80, 82, 84, 172–174; heterosexual, 31, 73–75, 91, 96, 101–105; homosexual, 19, 28, 34, 57, 68, 73, 75–79, 85, 151; and womanhood, 31–33, 38, 82, 100, 158–163, 165
Shakespeare, William, 163, 192
Shining Path, 16
Sinaloa, 21–22, 133, 141
slavery, 9, 26, 35, 51, 81
Soldado, Juan, 21, 132–140
Solís, Javier, 115
Spain, 21, 72, 117, 158, 162, 199

telenovelas, 1–2, 10, 37, 56–57, 75, 79, 85–87, 92, 98, 101, 105–107, 127; history of, 4–6

Tellado, Corín, 10
Tempest, The, 163
Tigres del Norte, Los, x, 15, 22, 152
Tijuana, 119, 134, 139, 140, 188
transgression, 35, 85–86
Tucanes, Los, 15
Tupac Amaru, 16

Ugly Betty, 5, 56, 211–215. See also *Betty la fea*
United States, 6, 8, 16–19, 22, 26, 43, 48, 50–51, 54–55, 64, 76, 88, 101–105, 112–114, 119, 120, 122–124, 129, 130, 138, 148, 149, 162, 168–169, 189, 210–211

vallenato, 67
Vargas, Chavela, 115
Vargas Llosa, Mario, 10
Vasconcelos, José, 113–114, 168
Venezuela, 6, 19, 56, 208

venganza del rojo, La, 112
Villa, Lucha, 115
Virgen de los sicarios, La, 89
Vives, Carlos, 67
Voyage in the Dark, 65

West, the, 12, 52, 54. *See also under* identity
Wide Sargasso Sea, 37, 63
Wilde, Oscar, 33, 192
Williams, Linda, 8, 12, 44
Williams, Vanessa L., 212
Wright, Richard, 50

Xica, 6, 8–9, 20–21, 25–45, 55, 59–63, 71, 105
Xica da Silva, 20, 27

Y tu mamá también, 14

Zavala, Julio, 81

Lightning Source UK Ltd.
Milton Keynes UK
UKHW010653070820
367845UK00001B/10